After Silence

AFTER SILENCE

Rape and My Journey Back

Nancy Venable Raine

A *Virago* Book

Published by Virago Press 1999

This edition published by arrangement with
Crown Publishers, Inc., New York

Copyright © Nancy Venable Raine 1999

The moral right of the author has been asserted

A CIP catalogue record for this book
is available from the British Library

ISBN 1 86049 644 X

Printed and bound in Great Britain by
Clays Ltd, St Ives plc

Virago Press
A Division of
Little, Brown and Company (UK)
Brettenham House
Lancaster Place
London WC2E 7EN

For Steve, with love
And in tribute to Deborah S. Rose

Contents

I came to explore the wreck.
The words are purposes.
The words are maps.
I came to see the damage that was done
and the treasures that prevail.

ADRIENNE RICH,
"Diving into the Wreck"

Throw away the lights, the definitions
And say of what you see in the dark

WALLACE STEVENS,
"The Man with the Blue Guitar"

To My Reader

Speech is civilization itself. The word...
preserves contact—it is silence which isolates.

THOMAS MANN, *The Magic Mountain*

On an October afternoon in 1985 I was raped by a stranger who crept through the open back door of my apartment while I was taking out the trash. My back was turned to that door for less than a minute as I shoved the slippery green bags down into the garbage cans. Seven years to the day and hour, I carried trash out of another home thousands of miles away from that place, and as I bent over the barrels with my back to the street, the fear of that day returned to me as if no time had passed. I spun around and scanned the driveway, my heart pounding. No one was there. Just dry leaves, caught up in the wind, rattling along on brittle edges in light filtering through the trees.

This day was very like that day seven years before—warm, the sun bright in a flawless sky. I was single then, living in Boston, Massachusetts. Now I was married, living in Sausalito, California. But my husband, Steve, was at work. I was alone. Taking out the trash. Seven years—and this daily chore was still charged. I lived with sudden fear the way others live with cancer. The fear was always there, in warrens just below the surface of my skin, waiting. Through associations that were a language only I knew, the fear could spring suddenly into the light with its squinting brood of memories tumbling after it.

Back inside the house, the door locked behind me, I thought how odd it was that this date—October 11, 1992, the seventh anniversary of my rape—was more significant than my own birthday, and yet there was only silence. It was more significant because it marked again the death of the person I had been for thirty-nine years. This woman had a history—she had worked her way through a master's degree and a brief, unhappy marriage, more or less at the same time. She had held responsible positions in government, written articles, published poems, produced independent documentary films, run several nonprofit arts organizations, and started her own consulting business. She had frustrations, straw hats, boyfriends, unreturned phone calls, cellulite, debts. The usual stuff. But on October 11, 1985, she died. Another person was born that day.

Yet no one remembered. No one pinned a medal on my lapel. Not that I was any sort of heroine, but I had survived. And yet no one celebrated. The police said I was lucky not to have been murdered. I knew they were right. A year and a half after the rape I had married a man who brought a son and daughter into my life; I moved across the country to be with them. We had renovated a dilapidated house in a lush ravine with a creek that tumbled over stones year round, filling our home with its voice. Steve and I had turned a blackberry bramble into a woodland garden with crooked paths and a happy riot of ferns, Meidiland shrub roses, sweet woodruff, and calla lilies. I had made new friends and colleagues. Bought new hats. What I now called my life was extra time.

But that day, when the police told me I was lucky, I didn't feel grateful. Their observation only reminded me of my powerlessness, that even my survival had been out of my hands. There is no explanation for why I was raped, no explanation for why the rapist didn't kill me, as he threatened over and over. It is hard to live without explanations. It hurls you into a whirlwind of dangerous forces you have lost the power to name and the rituals to appease. After seven years I was only beginning to abandon the search for reasons, only beginning to know the flesh-and-blood person I had become, the one who marked her anniversaries in silence. But after seven years I wanted more than silence and isolation. I wanted to celebrate the life of the woman who was born on October 11.

But could I celebrate my survival in silence and alone? Not according to Webster's, which defines the verb "to celebrate" this way: "to perform (a sacrament or solemn ceremony) publicly and with appropriate rites." There were no appropriate rites, no public ceremony. It pained my family and friends to remember. To acknowledge my experience might bring up what they hoped I had forgotten—that terrible day, those hours of horror. They hoped to spare me that. For me to remind them that I had not forgotten seemed unkind, even cruel, because I knew they needed to believe I had. Our rite was, therefore, silence.

I thought about the numbers: the conservative statistics from the FBI's Uniform Crime Reports of 1.5 million women in America being victims of rape or rape attempts in the twenty-year period between 1972 and 1991; the Census Bureau's larger number of 2.3 million rapes in the fifteen-year period between 1973 and 1987. Taking into account the fact that rape is notoriously underreported—a 1992 study (conducted by the National Victim Center and the Crime Victims Research and Treatment Center) found that only about one out of six rapes was reported to the police—the number of rapes between 1972 and 1991 may be closer to 9 million.

As I sat at my kitchen table on my seventh anniversary, I tried to put the numbers together with the nearly seamless silence that shrouds being raped and living with its memory—for rape does not end when you find yourself "lucky." That is only the beginning. Despite the numbers, there were merely a handful of personal accounts that bore witness to this experience. I thought about Wittgenstein's observation that the limits of language are the limits of reality. Was rape off limits to our most distinctly human attribute—language? I had been a writer, yet since the rape I had written very little, and finished nothing. The poems and essays I published before the rape seemed to have been written by a stranger. Words, which I had always thought of as living things, had turned as brittle as the leaves that minutes before had called the memory of rape out of the wind. Why had I lost faith in the redemptive power of language? I had written nothing at all about what was, in fact, the most profound experience of my life. It seemed I would plod through the years writing around this experience, writing out of a phantom world, a world that ended on October 11, 1985.

I could no longer consent to silence. I began to write about the seventh anniversary of my rape and the six that came before it, and when I wasn't sure how to end what I was writing, something happened. Flowers arrived from the flower shop at the foot of the hill: "Happy 7th. You are not alone. Love always, Kate."

Kate was the daughter of a close friend and we had always had a special bond. I'd watched her struggle to come into the world when I had coached her mother through a long and difficult labor, and I'd been present for every passage in her life since. The summer after Kate graduated from high school, I felt she was old enough for me finally to tell her that I had been raped several years earlier. Her loving response brought us closer. Then over spring break in her freshman year of college, Kate was attacked by a pack of young men in a nightclub in Miami. The clinical term for what these men did to her is "digital penetration," an act of rape according to most, but not all, state rape statutes. Somehow she was able to fight her way out of that place of horror to the street and safety. By the time she did, her dress was in tatters. She had razor cuts on her legs, bruises on her breasts. And the seeds of memories—of fingers and hands and words—that would grow over time, just as mine had done, into a tangle of invasive exotics in her spirit.

Five years after her attack, she asked me, "How do I tell people who don't know, people who might become close friends? If I don't tell them, it makes it a secret, like something to be ashamed of. When I do tell them, they make it worse. They never ask me about it. It's a part of me, part of who I am now, but they don't want to know about it. It's no-win. Just no-win." I didn't have an answer.

But the flowers Kate sent that day had power. For the first time in seven years I had the sense of connection and community. I was celebrating my anniversary in the only way I knew how, and Kate was there. This anniversary, unlike all the others, was shared. I suddenly knew how to finish what I was writing—with an image of women, marching, openly and together, celebrating their anniversaries, speaking their names, carrying flowers.

The essay I wrote that day was published in *The New York Times Magazine* in early October 1994. In the weeks and months that followed the publication of "Returns of the Day," I received many deeply inspiring letters from both women and men. Without exception, all of the letters from survivors described the isolation of the aftermath of rape, its life-altering transformations. One woman wrote, "Every time we tell our story it helps take away the power this experience, and its subsequent shame, have over us." I agree. But telling our stories is complicated, as Kate had discovered. Several months after my article appeared, a woman I met at a luncheon remarked, after a few kind words about my article, "Let's face it, people don't want to read about such terrible things." What was the source of the resistance to rape survivors becoming witnesses to their own experience? Was there nothing universal in our struggles to make meaning from our ruptured histories, as others had done with terrible experiences? Had we no treasures to salvage from the wreck?

The silence of survivors is, I believe, supported by a profound collective anxiety about rape that borders on cultural psychosis. We—all of us—deny. We wrestle with the definition of rape. We make distinctions between "aggravated rape," "date rape," and other kinds of rape, dissecting issues of consent. We struggle with questions about the meaning of rape—what the alarming numbers tell us about our society. We struggle with issues of punishment and rehabilitation. We do not know if rape is part of the human condition, and therefore "normal" in some sense, or whether it is a grotesque deviance.

But silence has the rusty taste of shame. The words *shut up* are the most terrible words I know. I cannot hear them without feeling cold to the bone. The man who raped me spat these words out over and over during the hours of my attack—when I screamed, when I tried to talk him out of what he was doing, when I protested. It seemed to me that for seven years—until at last I spoke—these words had sunk into my soul and become prophecy. And it seems to me now that these words, the brutish message of tyrants, preserve the darkness that still covers this pervasive crime. The real shame, as I have learned, is to consent to them.

I have written this book to renew my faith in the alchemy of language to transmute a patch of darkness into a memory that I may claim as my own. I have tried to record as faithfully as I can not only what I experienced and felt on the day I was raped and in the years since, but also what I understand about my experience based on what experts have observed about rape's impact on the mind, body, and spirit. I have noted what has come into my view as I go about my life, seeing the world through the eyes of a woman who remembers rape.

Rape has long been considered a crime so unspeakable, so shameful to its victims, that they are rendered mute and cloaked in protective anonymity. In giving language to my own experience, I hope I can make rape less "unspeakable." I hope to dispel at least some part of the fear and shame that has made victims mute. If I can expand the possibility for other survivors to speak, if they so choose, in an environment of informed tolerance and, ultimately, of acceptance, I will feel blessed by the darkness I have known. The victims of rape must carry their memories with them for the rest of their lives. They must not also carry the burden of silence and shame.

O N E

The Bird

A gold-feathered bird
Sings in the palm, without human meaning,
Without human feeling, a foreign song.

WALLACE STEVENS, "Of Mere Being"

Some people believe that a bird appears when someone dies to carry
the soul away. Perhaps it is true. A few minutes before I was raped, a
bird I had never heard before flew into the branches of the cherry tree
outside my kitchen window and began to sing. I couldn't see it through
the small window over the sink and the filament of buttery leaves. I saw
only jigsaw puzzle–shaped quiverings of lapis sky. It was autumn, a season I thought of as a time of beginnings. I still moved to the rhythms
of my school years, the year beginning with my walk in new saddle
shoes through the showy woods to catch the school bus, collecting but-
ternut hickory, oak, and maple leaves to press in my books.

The city trees were at their peak of color when I moved back to
Boston after a year in Maine, where I had taken an extended consulting contract. I felt I was beginning again in Boston, although I'd lived
there before for nearly a decade. The day I was raped I was settling into
a new apartment in a familiar neighborhood, and enjoying the feeling

7

of putting my world in order, leafing through books before placing them on the shelves, polishing candlesticks and washing dishes.

The bird that sang from the cherry tree felt welcoming. I wanted to identify it, but my field guide was hopelessly inaccessible, still packed up in the jumble of boxes stacked in the living room. So I closed my eyes and listened. I remember still that the notes were tumbling down one after the other. They seemed to carry a singular joy, as if the light of the Indian summer day were becoming sound.

I remember, too, that the song brought to mind something I had read a few days before in Henry Beston's *The Outermost House* and made note of in my journal, about animals having senses we have lost or never had, about them "living by voices we shall never hear." I had grown up in the country, and understood exactly what Beston meant. The creature that miraculously produced this sweetness was beyond my measure, a mysterious gift. Listening to the song was a prayer, a sudden and effortless motion of my being outward. Even in the city, nature went about her own affairs—birds sang, the leaves on the city trees blazed, and the weeds in vacant lots turned their flowers into stiff wombs full of seeds. In those last minutes before my terror began, I felt blessed.

As suddenly as it had appeared, the bird—a migrant, perhaps, on its way south—flew away and the mutterings of the city returned—traffic on the busy avenue a block away, a distant siren, the shouts of children playing baseball. I returned with renewed concentration to my tasks. I unpacked my kitchen utensils and put them in a drawer. I sharpened my kitchen knives and laid them on the counter. Then I filled a plastic bag with packing paper and dragged it out of the back door to the metal garbage cans at the side of the house. The air was a summery dream, sweeter still because a New England winter paced impatiently in the wings. As I stuffed the trash bag into a can, my back to the kitchen door, I listened for the bird, but it was gone. When I returned to the kitchen, I locked the back door behind me.

There is nothing more reassuring than a locked door—unless you've locked the devil in with you.

8

I am standing at the sink, washing a pan. I see my kitchen knives on the counter. I am always seeing my kitchen knives. I am still standing at the sink, washing a pan.

A storm from behind, and impact. It sucks away the air around me in a great rush. I cannot breathe. Rage is turning the air to pumice. I cannot hear. Something in my eyes. The pain is in my eyes. I am closing my eyelids but they do not meet. Something is in my eyes, something is coiling around my neck, something alive. Something furious and terrible. Words, but I cannot hear them. I am thrashing in the air. There is a foul odor. My body is on fire from inside. My blood is rushing as if trying to escape. I hear only it. There is no air. It is all going out of me. Who is screaming? I do not know who is screaming. I cannot breathe.

Now I hear the words. These are the words I hear: Shut up shut the fuck up you bitch you dirty bitch you fucking cunt shut up do you hear me you fucking dirty bitch I'm going to kill you if you don't shut up you bitch I'm going to kill you.

Now I am sucking air into my lungs. I am prey, grasping for air.

Now I have a thought: So this is Death.

Now I have a feeling: Anything to live.

Now I feel something hard pressing against my back. I know what it is. It is a penis.

Later I wondered, Did the man who raped me hear the bird's song? And if so, what did the notes sound like in his ear? How could he have heard what I heard and still be what he was? Was the bird a warning that I should have heeded? How could I have felt so alive and not have sensed his shambling darkness drawing near? Had I not been awake at all, but asleep? I could not trust even my most fundamental perceptions. The feelings of wholeness evoked by my connection with nature, feelings that had been a glimpse of heaven since my childhood, were transformed in an instant into feelings of foreboding.

In a single moment, I was robbed of what had always soothed me. A bird's song became a harbinger of evil, the prelude to a season in the underworld.

∎ ∎ ∎

The rapist was wearing slippers. This, the police said, suggested he had planned his attack. The slippers were enormous and my description of them was all the police had to go on. It wasn't enough. He attacked from behind and from the first instant had the advantage—stealth and surprise. His right arm held my neck in a stranglehold and I could not extricate myself. The fingers of his other hand dug into my eyes. After he had me immobilized, only my feet kicking out wildly, he hesitated for an instant. It came to me then that my mouth was still free. Words. I still had words. I spoke words as he began to push me toward the bedroom. Words that tried to reason where there was no reason. I was struggling against the movement forward with all my strength and speaking the words. His fingers slipped from my eyes briefly and I saw his foot, a dirty, worn slipper. To this day the sight of a dirty slipper makes me gag.

He threw me on the bed facedown, his knee in the middle of my back. He pressed down with his full and great weight so that I thought he might snap my spine in two, like a twig. At this point I became intensely focused on him and a strange calmness suddenly displaced my terror. He grabbed my arms and bound them together behind me with duct tape. Then he jerked my head up by grabbing a handful of hair and spun the tape around my head, over my eyes. "Don't do this," I said. "Shut up, you bitch, or I'll break your arms." He pulled my bound hands upward toward my head to demonstrate, but I felt no pain. Then he threw me over on my back, and sitting on my hips, tore open my shirt, jerked my bra up around my neck, unzipped my jeans, and pulled them down as far as he could without shifting his position. He then had to stand beside the bed to get them all the way off, fighting against my shoes, flats that fit snugly. Then he yanked off my underpants. At that moment, time disappeared into a continuous present.

Over the next three hours he raped me and tormented me with descriptions of how he would kill me with a knife, telling me exactly where he would cut me. Or maybe, he said, he would smother me with my pillow. He seemed undecided about the method. Many times he did cover my face with the pillow and press it down so that I could not draw a breath. Each time I expected to die, but he always relented just before I lost consciousness. He slapped my head with open palms after these episodes, the way you swat a fly.

In the scheme of things, his penis, although employed as a bludgeon, did not make much of an impression. What he did with it was the least of my worries. Those parts of my body that hitherto had been reserved and private were no longer mine, but in this they were indistinguishable from the rest of my body, also no longer mine. It was his rage, a fierce, unearthly tempest, that cast me into an immensity of dread.

Sometimes he left me and vented his fury on my possessions. He hurled a wooden jewelry box that my father had made for me against the wall, shattering it. He broke lamps, kicked chairs, threw glasses. His frenzy increased when he couldn't find any cigarettes in the house. I had finally quit smoking just a week earlier. As he demanded them over and over I contemplated the irony that I would be murdered because for the first time in twenty years I didn't have a cigarette handy.

Twice before he finally left, he pretended to leave. By then, hours had passed and I had acquired another sense. Although I was blindfolded, I could "see" everything clearly. I could see around corners. I could see my entire apartment as if it were a hologram I could walk around. I had no attachment at all to my body, although I wanted only one thing: to preserve it. It seemed this was something my body wanted and I had become nothing but body. Whatever part of me was "watching" did not feel alive because it no longer seemed to possess a body. When he pretended to leave, I didn't move because I knew he was hiding in the small pantry off the kitchen. I could "see" him standing there. I knew he was playing cat to my mouse. I lay there, exposed and bound, waiting, bracing as best I could for the next attack.

The first time he did this, he waited a long time before rushing from his hiding place and leaping upon me. The knife, he said, was at my throat. But instead of cutting, he held the pillow over my face and then vanished again, back into his lair. While he was gone, I turned over on my face, so that my back was exposed. I calculated that I might survive a knife thrust in my back and began to rehearse the move I would make when he returned with the knife—how I would thrust up my left shoulder at the precisely right moment so that the knife would strike my shoulder blade rather than plunge into my heart. I waited, gathering strength, "watching" him tiptoe across the kitchen and hover at the door to the bedroom. He seemed to hesitate. Then he sprang onto the bed and began slapping the top of my head, as if he were putting out a raging fire. And then, for reasons I shall never know, he ran to the back door, unlocked it, and disappeared into the sunlight.

■ ■ ■

The explorer David Livingstone was once attacked by an African lion, and his description of that moment had so impressed me when I first read it—many years before the rape—that I'd recorded it in the first of many commonplace books that I have kept beside me over the years when I read. My own experience of shock is remarkably similar.

Livingstone reported that the lion sprang on him as he stood on a small hill, catching him by the shoulder. They both fell to the ground below. "Growling horribly close to my ear," Livingstone wrote, "he shook me as a terrier dog does a rat. The shock produces a stupor similar to that which seems to be felt by a mouse after the first shake of the cat. It caused a sort of dreaminess, in which there was no sense of pain nor feeling of terror, [al]though [I was] quite conscious of all that was happening.... This singular condition was not the result of any mental process. The shake annihilated fear, and allowed no sense of horror in looking round at the beast. This peculiar state is probably produced in all animals killed by the carnivora; and if so, is a merciful provision by our benevolent Creator for lessening the pain of death."

During the attack my terror seemed to implode and compress until it was like a hard dry seed. Once I was free of this devouring fear, a cold, even calculating awareness took its place, illuminating everything all at once and destroying all capacity for emotion. I agree with Livingstone that this anesthesia is merciful, although I do not share his teleological explanation. God aside, this "singular" insensibility has survival value, because feeling nothing liberates some aspect of mind that under normal conditions is crowded with bodily sensations and the constant ebb and flow of emotions—a mob of small wishes and desires generated by the body and an odd assortment of thoughts that are both nagging and petty. All this was chaff torn from the grain and cast into the whirlwind.

I was focused only on him, focused microscopically. He was my world. He defined the parameters of the world, shrunken and hateful as it was. He was the creator of this world, occupied now by both of us. He decided what was and wasn't possible. His world was, by my former measures, insane. A universe of ferocity that was sustained by fear and pain. I had no emotional reaction to this universe and observed it with the detachment of a yogi.

In this detachment, a state I reached the moment I knew I could not physically escape, I experienced his rage as if it were a separate entity, a shadow self to his physical being. I understood that this entity was hungry and that it was feasting on something from me—my terror, my physical and psychic pain. It got energy from me and in the initial moments of the attack, when my terror was uncontrollable, it had gained strength. I sensed the rapist wanted me to beg and plead, humiliate myself so he could feed this furious entity that was tormenting him in its hunger. I withdrew all reaction, although this act was involuntary.

I understood that this might increase his brutality, but my emotional detachment was so great, and my physical senses so dulled, that it no longer mattered. I was fully conscious, but I had no emotions at all. I believe now that his cat-and-mouse game and his destruction of my possessions were attempts to re-create the energy exchange of the initial attack. I greeted these replays with indifference, as I did all the other demands he made. I went through the motions, but nothing more.

The awareness that accompanied what Livingstone called a sort of dreaminess was perfectly faceted and unclouded. The experience of this awareness was itself a kind of death. My life did not flash before me. I did not see my mother's face. I knew the words to prayers, but they meant nothing and I did not use them. Words had no referents and no beauty of their own. Memories were drained of meaning, because the person who had them no longer existed. Faith was a distraction. Nothing I had known or felt before he attacked seemed the least bit useful.

It has been difficult over the years to rid myself of the experience of this irrelevancy—concepts, emotions, prayers, faith, love, words. All illusions. There was, in the end, only a focus on living one more second within the logic of each moment that was all moments. There was nothing enlightening about this reduction. It seemed I was far less than I had ever imagined—no more than flesh that would do anything to preserve itself in the form to which it had become accustomed.

What was left behind, and what still remains, is the memory of this encounter with my reduction. It sits in the center of my being like a glacier. Pieces may break off and fall into the sea, but the glacier with its yawning crevasses is bound to the shore. What I know is the shape of that shore, a cold and wordless place that is forever strange and inhospitable. A part of me is bound to it for the rest of my life.

■ ■ ■

Just before he left, he demanded that I tell him where his knife was. He kept slapping me on the head, making this absurd demand. I knew there were four excellent knives sitting on my kitchen counter, the ones I had cleaned and sharpened just before I took out the trash. What he really meant was that his rage, this hungry beast that drove him, was satisfied—for the moment. He'd lost, as it were, his edge.

"How am I supposed to know where you put the knife?" I said, sounding bored and not responding to his blows. "I can't even see you."

He seemed to consider this. Then he said, "Don't you move. I'll be watching you. Don't you move for an hour, you stupid cunt." He had said these words before, but there was something different this time. I knew that he meant to leave. He was now afraid. I knew he was too afraid to kill me.

"Why would I move?" I replied in a ho-hum tone of voice, as if I were perfectly content to be wrapped up like a UPS package. He hovered for an instant and then fled. I lay still for no more than a minute.

Getting the tape off my wrists was difficult because they were taped together behind my back. I pulled one hand down, the other up, until I could work the thumb of my right hand over an edge. My efforts seemed to be in slow motion. Finally my hands were free. I tore the tape off my head, pulling out hair in clumps. I was beginning to feel pain, a distant dull pain that was like hearing a train in the distance.

The instant I was free, the seed of terror that had been planted in those hours burst open, spitting out an uncharted island where I was now stranded. Its peaks and valleys, its shores and streams would take a lifetime to explore, but I didn't know that. I stood on its shore bewildered. Terror overwhelmed me. My body shook uncontrollably. My thoughts were flawed in structure, like cups without bottoms. Words fell through them. Words no longer referred to anything, even themselves. My shock was so great that I could not walk. I crawled to the back door, expecting it to burst open again, expecting him to be there. If his rage fed on terror, now there was terror in abundance. All I could focus on was locking the door. This I did with great effort. Then I crawled back through the bramble of overturned chairs toward the bedroom for my clothes. It was now as unbearable to be naked as it had been moments before to be in an unlocked apartment. My shirt was torn, but I was still wearing it. My bra was dangling under my armpits. I secured it and crawled around in the debris of my bedroom looking for my underpants and jeans. The air on my naked flesh seemed to burn, like dry ice. I found my jeans under the bed, but could not find my underpants—this thin membrane of cloth, the margin of safety, the ledge that if regained might keep me from plunging into the abyss. I thought that if I put my underpants back on, I could undo the thing I could not yet name. But my underpants were gone, sucked down into the vortex of violence. I did not remember that other underpants were in a suitcase, the contents of which were dumped on my dresser. Defeated, I pulled on my jeans, sitting on the floor. My hands shook so violently I could not zip them, but somehow I managed to secure the snap at the waist.

The phone was in the living room, a continent away. I crawled to it. I could not remember the three-digit emergency number, 911. Later, I recalled this lapse with shame, as if it were a measure of my inadequacy. I dialed the operator because there were letters on the "0" button—OPER—and I could still read them. The part of me that had detached continued to drift. She did not seem to know the trembling person who was using the telephone.

As I waited for someone to answer, it seemed to me that the air itself had been split open. The image came unbidden of a rent in visual space, which was merely a thin piece of fabric stretched over another darker world. Any moment another tear might appear, suddenly and without warning. Inside that other universe were fierce and unholy demons who sprang from it and vanished into it again at will. I felt then that the demons were pushing from the other side of the fabric, and if I looked closely I could see the imprint of their palms pressing against it as they hunted for a slit through which they could squeeze, like weasels poking paws through a hole in a tent. The waking world as I had known it became nothing more than a thin permeable membrane that could not hold back this other world occupied by horrors.

I knew I was not insane because I remembered that a few hours before I had been sane. Yet I experienced the world as a place that included real demons from a real hell, just as some insane people do. They do not know that the voices they hear or the monsters they see are not real. Perhaps the fact that I never saw my rapist, that his human form was never revealed, combined with the suddenness of his assault, increased my impression that I had been attacked by a demon. I knew demons weren't real in the physical sense—I had banished this belief in my early childhood. Yet my experience was physical and my belief that the real world was nothing more than a frail tent full of holes was as firm as the opposite belief had been only hours before. Although the intensity of this belief has since diminished, I cannot shake it altogether. Sometimes, when I'm working in my garden, I look around at its beauty and feel for a moment that it is no more than a beautiful egg out of which a predatory, reptilian creature, a crocodile perhaps, will emerge, head first and slimy. It feels like something I know, not something I imagine.

■ ■ ■

I suffered from vivid and powerful nightmares as a child, dreaming of monsters and horrors that were perhaps projections of feelings too frightening and powerful to be claimed in my waking life. But I always woke up. And the waking state was always different enough from the dreaming one so that no confusion between them was possible.

In this post-Freudian era, we have embraced the idea that dreams are part of ourselves, creations of our unconscious that we can analyze for clues to our hidden feelings or, following Jung's approach, that can be understood in terms of archetypes, primordial images, the *a priori* forms of myth common to the human species. But the English word for *nightmare* once referred, not to a part of the psyche, but to fleshly beings thought to be real. The first definition, for example, of *nightmare* in the *Oxford English Dictionary* is "a female spirit or monster supposed to beset people and animals by night, settling upon them when they are asleep and producing a feeling of suffocation by its weight." More precisely, the female monsters were called succubi and attacked men in their sleep. The male versions, incubi, preyed on women. Rape was a favorite brand of torment. Webster's also defines the word *nightmare* as referring to (1) "an evil spirit formerly thought to oppress people in their sleep." The second definition is more familiar: (2) "a frightening dream that usually awakens the sleeper." You know it is a nightmare because you wake up and discover it to be one. But for me, the experience of my rape was a contradiction, a waking nightmare. My mind was no longer modern, but medieval. No longer adult, but childish. The rapist was a real monster, an incubus who attacked in the light of day. The experience of having this confusion cast on the world I inhabited as an adult was as full of terror as the actual physical experience of that day. Suddenly, all the sorting out of real and unreal I had done as a child had to be done over.

I have never forgotten a nightmare I had when I was seven. In the dream, the floor beneath the grand piano in our living room fell away into a green slope studded with granite boulders that formed one side of a valley cut by a river. There were mountains in the distance, and in the foreground, next to the river, a sagging, weathered cabin with an open door. In front of the cabin sat a woman with a sewing basket on her lap. Sitting on its haunches next to her, held by a leash of the thinnest of threads, was a panther. Its eyes were a greenish yellow and merciless and its ebony coat shimmered in the sunlight. As I walk past the piano I happen to glance down into this landscape, which at first I think is beautiful. How odd I never noticed it before. I could play there and no one would know. Suddenly the woman looks up and sees me gazing down from my perch at the piano. I know I am in mortal danger. Smiling wickedly, she reaches into her sewing basket and removes a pair of scissors. She cuts the thread that holds the beast and it lunges forward, up the slope toward me, growing in size as it runs and growling fiercely. I race toward my bedroom, but the panther is swift and covers the ground in arching leaps. Claws rake my back and its huge mouth closes on my throat. I wake up screaming, too terrified to move, to cry out. Too terrified to run to my mother's room because I know the panther is hiding in the hallway.

For weeks after this dream I ran through the living room in fear, day and night. I knew that the woman and the panther were not really there, but I felt they were. Finally my mother noticed that a casual stroll through the kitchen and dining room turned into the fifty-yard dash when I got anywhere near the piano. One night she asked me about it. Reluctantly, I told her about the dream. I must have sensed that I was revealing something about myself, not only my fierce emotions, but also a confusion about the nature of reality that I felt I was too old to have.

She took me by the hand and walked me over to the piano. She got down on her hands and knees and crawled under it. "See?" she said. "It's just ol' boards under here." She sat on the panther's threshold, hunched over so she could fit, patting the boards and collecting little tufts of dust on the hem of her skirt.

I stopped running through the living room after that, but never forgot how the valley looked or how the panther sat, next to the woman, constrained by a single frail thread.

■ ■ ■

I held the telephone and pressed the button that had the letters OPER on them and actually wondered if this nightmare was something I had done to myself. That was the explanation I had always given to nightmares. Nightmares and dreams were "material" from my unconscious. I wrote them down. Talked about them. There was a habit of explanation that limited the world of horrors to myself alone. The other explanation was one I had dispensed with in childhood. At some point, I stopped believing that the monster who lived under my bed would grab me if my foot slipped out of the covers. I stopped believing there was a hag with a panther living under the piano. I had claimed the shapes of terrors as my own. Even come to admire their loathsome qualities and the tenebrous landscapes they inhabited.

Monsters, the kind that lived in nightmares, were now suddenly real again. The being that had been in my home for three hours was not "just ol' boards." It was painful to discover this belief in myself, and impossible for me to describe my state of mind to anyone. Yet I had no other way to explain what had happened, not in those early hours and days after the attack.

Perhaps part of the self-blame that is such a common reaction of people who have been raped begins in these deep waters of the unconscious. The fact that a dream I had when I was seven contained the emotions of an experience I had thirty-two years later may be relevant to how I experienced the rape. Perhaps because the experience is a waking nightmare, victims feel they have brought forth the rapist out of their unconscious mind, that they have created him. Although we know the rapist is external—a fact in the world that is as dangerous as a hurricane, a flood, an earthquake, or a terrorist's bomb—he resembles internal childhood terrors. For me at least, this likeness seemed to compress within me the sensation of becoming the object of another human being's inexplicable hatred. And the fact that I was the sole victim and only witness seemed to compound the feeling of awful lonesomeness. Solitary sailors who misstep and find themselves bobbing in the sea must feel something similar as they watch their boat sail on without them, grow small in that cold immensity, and finally vanish over the horizon.

I do not remember what I said to the operator who responded when I pressed the OPER button on the telephone. The sound of a human voice, even one trained to be inhuman, was a shock. I felt myself falling inward. I must have asked for the number of the local police station because the operator gave me a seven-digit phone number. I hung up. The only thought in my mind was the phone number. I'm notoriously bad at remembering numbers. But if I forgot the number, I was sure the rapist would return. I dialed the number. Then there was another voice on the line, a male voice. The voice said, "Good afternoon."

To say that I had been raped, to use the word, required that I sort out the incubi from the saber tooths from whatever it was that had just destroyed my apartment. I was choking on the word.

"Who are you?"
"Shut up, you shut up, you bitch, or I'll kill you."
"There's something I have to tell you."
"What?"

"I have a disease. It's very contagious. I'm really sick. That's why I'm home."

"What is it?"

"It's called hepatitis B. It's very contagious. Rare. Deadly."

"Shut up, you fucking bitch. Shut up. I'm going to kill you. I'm going to break your fucking arms and then I'm going to cut you up, you fucking cunt."

So much for words.

■   ■   ■

Through the living room window I see the squad car pull up, but I cannot move. I am holding the phone. Someone is telling me to open the door, but the voice is dead and unreal. Someone is pounding on the back door. Someone is opening the back door. It is me, backing away from the door, holding my torn shirt together with one hand. A tall, overweight man in his fifties is standing in the doorway. He is wearing black shoes the size of fish poachers, a dark uniform. He stares at me and I recoil. He is afraid of me. I can feel his fear. I can see he doesn't know what to say. Silence. He doesn't speak. I am terrified of him.

A woman appears behind him and he steps aside, relieved. She is carrying a medical kit. I see more policemen behind her. They follow her into the kitchen. I think if I do not speak to any of these people I will wake up. Police come and go while the woman talks to me. I am in a bubble of air and all these people are in the water around me. I am like the pond spider that builds a nest of bubbles on the stems of reeds underwater. The spider grabs air and takes it down, one bubble at a time until the nest is done. Then the spider crawls inside. Inside is safe.

The woman is gently urging me to go with her to the hospital. She helps me find a jacket and a change of clothes, including another bra and pair of underpants I pull from the heap of clothes on my dresser. She suggests that I zip my jeans. I am humiliated because I am not wearing underpants.

"I can't find my underpants," I tell her. "He stole my underpants."
I'm down on my hands and knees looking for them. What a terrible
thing to do, to steal someone's underpants, I am thinking.

The woman wants them, too. "What color are they?"

"White and blue. Little flowers." We both hunt for them.

"We have to go," the woman finally says.

■ ■ ■

I want water. My thirst is vicious. I am in the kitchen now. I turn on
the faucet at the kitchen sink. My mouth is full of dirt. "Was there oral
penetration?" the woman asks.

"Yes," I say.

"No water," the woman replies. "You might wash away evidence."

Her words are terrible. I want to wash my mouth out with fire.
What is in my mouth? Dirt is in my mouth. In my body. His dirt.

Everything is upside down. Words are backwards. The floors are littered with debris everyone is stepping over. My jewelry box is in pieces.
"My father made that for me," I say to everyone, gathering up the
pieces. I hold two together, but when I let go, they fall apart again. The
policemen stare at me. I don't want to go to the hospital. I say I have
to clean up the apartment. I can't leave it like this. I have to find my
underpants. The woman helps me gather together the contents of my
purse because I am going to the hospital. My wallet is empty and on
the floor. My purse is under the bed.

When I finally get in the ambulance it is dusk. The sky is lavender
and gray. The first thing I do is ask the woman for a cigarette. Miraculously, she has one. A Salem. The menthol is cleaning my mouth, burning my throat. Smoke is water. All the birds are dead.

> *Open your legs. Go on, you dirty bitch. Groan. That's not
> good enough. I'll cut you. Groan good. Now suck it. You bite me
> and you die, you fucking bitch. You gag and I'll kill you. Tell
> me how good it was. Now you die.*

22

Shadow Dance

I am alone
my shadow runs back into me to hide
and there is not room for both of us
and the dread

W. S. MERWIN, "Second Psalm: The Signals"

The only time in the past I'd gone to a hospital emergency room was when I cut my thumb with a straight-edge razor while trying to pry the lid off a can of paint. I was bleeding so badly I didn't have to wait. After eighteen stitches and a lecture about why we have screwdrivers, I was as good as new. This time I was not bleeding. I had soft-tissue damage in my back and arms, but nothing was broken. I had not been beaten into unconsciousness. I was bruised and in emotional shock, but on my feet. I felt like a fraud being whisked past the formalities and a waiting room crowded with sick and injured people.

Yet because a hospital is a place that cares for people, I hoped for comfort and I sensed that the hospital staff wanted to provide it. But for a rape victim the hospital emergency room functions as an extension of the police department, and the medicine being practiced there is primarily forensic.

After satisfying themselves that I was not seriously injured, the

taff began performing the work of criminologists,
  that might be used in a court of law. My body was
. It was evidence. I was not a patient whose wounds
. I was the scene of a crime.

I was   d over to a nurse who guided me to a small examining
room and told me not to urinate, defecate, wash myself, smoke, or
drink anything. She asked me to undress standing over brown paper.
Then, handing me a hospital gown, she wrapped my clothes up in the
paper. She inquired about my underpants. I told her the rapist had
stolen them. Then she left me alone.

The room was cold and I had nowhere to sit except on the examining table. I stared at the metal stirrups with disgust, and then at
the faucet over the small stainless-steel sink. My thirst was gnawing at
me. It was as if fear had desiccated me. Dust devils swirled inside my
body. My mouth was full of sand and spiders. I was alone in the room
for a long time with my thirst. Somewhere nearby a man was wailing.
More time passed. The man began to scream. My thirst became an
agony. I knew the nurses and doctors were busy with an emergency.
The man who was screaming was a real emergency. Maybe he was
dying.

The part of me that had split off during the attack was still
detached, a shadow self that perched above me like a sparrow, waiting
for her dead mate on the sidewalk below to wake up from a high-speed
encounter with a plate-glass window. This shadow self followed the
ambulance and was hovering just outside my body, observing me and
my surroundings with indifference. The continued presence of this
"observer," the one that had emerged during the rape, was a misery
now. The longer I waited in the examining room, the more frightened
I became of this separation. Nothing was predictable. Nothing had
sequence. I was a language without punctuation or structure. Verbs
dangled at the end of sentences, tenseless. Subjects began to drop out
altogether. The observer could read the text, but she seemed to
be drifting off, like someone at a party who is pretending to listen,

but whose eyes are across the room on the person she really wants to talk to.

Suddenly, I didn't know the person who was sitting on the examining table. I was waiting for something to happen that felt different from what had just happened, but I was still alone, caught up in another upside-down logic, the logic of the hospital that was trying to treat me like an injured human being while re-injuring me, minute by minute, simply by tending to a real emergency—doing the job they were there to do. I did not feel angry at their priorities. I did not resent the logic of the screaming man in the next room. I recognized that I was the one who was out of place.

I felt that the scent of the rapist's rage and hatred was on me somehow, and that the nurses sensed it. I did not resent the fact that with all of their training, skill, and good manners, no one in that place of healing could hug me, even in passing. No one could perform the simplest of human gestures, an embrace that is a welcoming reassurance, a staying-close, a soothing and cherishing that reaffirms a shared humanity. Looking back, I realize that had I been in their place, I, too, might have hesitated, might have sensed the rawness of the spirit that inhabited the violated flesh that trembled before me. What would a hug mean to someone whose body no longer felt as if it belonged to her? In my strange disunity that night, I might not have been able to bear it. I will never know. A three-hour rape exam was anything but reassuring.

In the hospital I felt as I imagine an animal might feel—without words, and therefore without understanding or a sense of sequence. Every emotion was singular and unmixed. I wanted "real" wounds then, the kind that bleed. The kind the doctors could stitch up. The kind I imagined the man screaming in the next room had. I had done everything I could to avoid them, but waiting alone, feeling as I did, I realized "real" wounds could be tended. I wanted them. I wondered who it was that was thinking like this because I felt at the same time that I was dying.

• • •

The rapist had stolen something at the center of what I had known as myself. It was gone with the cash, credit cards, jewelry, underpants, and whatever else he took. All these things that meant nothing to me might be recovered by the police, but how could this missing self be retrieved? The rapist himself might be caught, but he could never produce the woman who had not been raped.

Waiting for care that could not be provided was my first encounter with the world outside the nightmare. I sensed that this experience was a foretelling of all that would unfold in the future. I was cut off, not only from myself, but from other human beings. I thought then that I had made a mistake in calling the police, coming to the hospital. If I kept the nightmare to myself, it would begin and end with me. I could confine it to those hours. If no one knew, no one else could hurt me. Now the nightmare was changing wavelengths, but it was still going on.

I resisted the thought that I had made a mistake in calling the police. I reminded myself that rape was a crime. Rape and robbery and murder were all crimes. Crimes were bad. The rapist was bad. I was good and he was bad. No one can do something like this and get away with it. But I felt as if being raped were the crime because any moment now a doctor was going to come in and ask me to lie down and put my heels in the stirrups. If I had not been so afraid of what was outside the room, I would have run off into the night. But the night was the long hallway where a panther waited. I was trapped in a room with a faucet and all of Boston's water supply within reach, dying of thirst. Alone.

The "observer" was getting bored with my confusions. She was leaving me. There was no place for her inside me. I no longer saw myself from the ceiling, or from just over my right shoulder. I was lost inside with no escape from my inner world, more alone than the ancient hermits who were sealed up in mud cells, never to emerge.

I still had to function. From that moment forward I seemed to become a human water beetle with enormously long legs, miles of legs that held me on the surface of "normal life" in wondrous tension. I could not dive or fly. I stayed out of white water, living on the edges in stagnant pools. I had to move beyond the universe I inhabited with the rapist into an inhospitable outside world. No one noticed I was a water bug. I still looked like a person.

The life I had saved was not, after all, *my* life. I was living moment to moment, slapping down cards as they were dealt. For the first time, I understood my mistake. I had made a deal with the rapist and now I regretted it. From now on, everyone would assess that deal, starting with the police and the doctors and, moving further out, family and friends. What if he never intended to kill me? Why did I believe his threats? Why didn't I have the physical strength to break his hold in those first few minutes? Was there something about me that allowed me to cave in to his demands? Was I a despicable coward? Why had I given in to his hateful needs to spare a life I no longer recognized as my own? The wisdom of my deal vanished the moment other human beings encountered it. I understood it perfectly when it was just the rapist and me in the nightmare in which I was fragmenting and reassembling in new ways that seemed to have meaning. But now that recomposition of being made no sense. Yet it could not be reversed. It had changed me cell by cell. It was my fault that I was alive. If I had fought harder, I would either be dead or be as I was before. Now I was neither. I was evidence.

I could wait no longer. I turned on the faucet and let the water pour into my mouth without swallowing. I washed away his dirt. Then I drank.

■ ■ ■

I beg the nurse to stand outside the bathroom. While I collect a urine sample, I keep asking her through the locked door if she is still there. "Don't leave," I say. When I'm done, I follow her back to the examining room.

The nurse is taking pictures of my body with a Polaroid camera. She photographs my wrists where the bruises are finger-shaped and the color of dried mustard. She photographs my face. My breasts. My neck. My thighs. She records her findings on a form and puts the photographs in an envelope. My fingernails are scraped, my hair combed over a piece of paper. Then strands are plucked. More envelopes. The nurse then draws two vials of blood.

A female doctor comes in for the pelvic exam. I am not sure I can go through with it. There is evidence inside me. They need it. The pain of the instrument inside me will be worth it, I tell myself. If I hurt some more, they will catch him. When the speculum enters me, I bite my lip. When it opens inside me, I do not think it is worth it.

■ ■ ■

The room is dark. The doctor cuts off the overhead lights and holds an ultraviolet lamp between my legs. She names parts where she has found semen, which glows from its bacteria in the eerie light. I am stunned that she has found semen in my vagina. At first I can't believe it. I had not felt his penis in my body, although I "saw" him pumping frantically on top of me as I hovered on the ceiling. I see the sperm in my mind, the size of maggots. I shudder and feel I am curling up, like a worm that has been cut in half by a trowel. The doctor swabs my anus with a large Q-Tip, although I have told her there was no anal penetration. I feel she does not believe me. Then she combs my pubic hair, cuts and plucks hair. Finally she removes the speculum.

Now she comes toward my mouth with the blue light. I confess. I've destroyed the evidence. I am ashamed of my weakness. She says that's too bad, but swabs my mouth anyway with another giant Q-Tip. She turns on the lights. My skin is purple from the cold.

Then she administers penicillin—two shots in the buttocks and a pill. Venereal disease. Gonorrhea, syphilis, chlamydia, trichomoniasis. I tell myself again that the pain is worth it. Then I think of genital herpes, warts. Then I think of AIDS.

The doctor asks me when I had my last period. I cannot remember. She explains that I should return to the hospital in six weeks—for a pregnancy test—if I have not had my period by then. She gives me estrogen in a high dose: two tablets now, two in twelve hours that should induce it. The doctor tells me the pills may make me sick, so she gives me another pill. If I vomit, I must call her.

I hadn't considered venereal disease and pregnancy when I was bargaining for my life.

I ask the doctor about HIV. She seems surprised at my concern.

"Very unlikely," she says. But she writes down the phone number I should call to make an appointment for the test. She tells me that the virus cannot be detected immediately—I could start getting tested in six weeks. Maybe I'm still going to die, slowly and expensively. I put the number in my purse. The doctor writes a prescription for a muscle relaxant.

"You're going to be very sore and stiff for a while," she says.

"I can't stand to think of all the other victims out there."

"You're not a victim," the doctor says. "You're a survivor. You did something right or you'd be in the morgue."

■ ■ ■

In 1985 I didn't know that the risk of contracting HIV from a one-time, unprotected encounter with someone of unknown HIV status was low—less than one in 5 million. Less than 0.2 percent. The doctor's observation that it was unlikely that the rapist had infected me with HIV was fair, and her surprise at my anxiety understandable. But even if I had known the odds, they would not have brought much comfort. I would have been more comforted if she had said, "Totally impossible." Even that one "unlikely" chance in 5 million made me feel as if I was walking around with broken glass in my shoes. Five years later, in 1990, a medical reporter speculated that the risk of contracting HIV infection as a result of rape by someone of unknown status was 6 percent. The odds are not, I suspect, getting any better.

■ ■ ■

It is time for me to get dressed in the change of clothes the emergency medical technician helped me collect back at my apartment. The doctor tells me two detectives are waiting to interview me. She asks me if I'm comfortable seeing them.

"I want to get this bastard," I say.

"After you've spoken to the detectives, we'll be releasing you. We'll give you a coupon for a cab."

I realize I have nowhere to go. I try then to remember my friends, who they are. I had not thought about my friends before. My closest friend is out of town, visiting her mother in Florida. I ask the doctor what time it is. It is close to eleven P.M. I ask if I can make a phone call from the wall phone in the examining room. The doctor leaves me alone for a few minutes. I get dressed and call my friend Sara, who is getting ready for bed. I don't know how to tell her what has happened. I try to ease into it. Nothing to worry about. I'm at the hospital. No, nothing serious. Well, it is serious, but I'm okay. Wonder if I could spend the night. The couch is fine. Sorry it's so late. What?

I can't say the word. The word is too terrible to say. If I tell someone who is not a professional stranger, the fact will spin out of control, like a car hitting ice. But I need to tell Sara.

"I was raped this afternoon. In my new apartment." For the first time, I feel unable to hold back my tears, but the detectives are waiting. I can't break down.

"Oh, my God," Sara says.

"God wasn't around this afternoon," I say.

"I'll come get you."

"It's okay. The hospital is getting me a cab. He stole my money...." I pause. For some reason it is important to tell Sara something else. "He stole my underpants."

Sara is silent for a moment. "You're going to be okay. I'll wait for you at the front door."

"Promise you'll be at the front door," I say.

■ ■ ■

I am dressed, sitting on the examining table, clutching my purse. I have tried to be precise with the detectives. I think of Joe Friday. Just the facts. Time. Location. I report the words—mine, his. They have heard them before. I report where he put the tape, his penis, his hands. When I tell them I did not see the rapist, they exchange a look. The woman detective has big hair, dyed blond. Perfectly manicured hands, long fingernails with red polish. I keep staring at her hands while she takes notes on what I am saying. The man is older. Thin. He stands against the door, behind the woman. The woman hands me a card. I am to call them, come to the station to give a formal report. I notice the woman's gun, strapped to her body. I think how lucky she is, to have a gun and such beautiful fingernails.

■ ■ ■

A week later I filed my report at the police station. Andrew, the husband of my friend Pamela, went with me because I was too frightened to go back to the neighborhood alone. For many years, Andrew would be the only friend or family member who knew the details of my rape. No one ever asked me. He sat through the report, trying, as I was, to sever the pain of facts from the facts themselves. How Andrew or I felt about the facts was irrelevant. The details, which were otherwise unspeakable, were of great interest to the detective.

The effort of holding the pain away from the cause of it—the facts that were both memory and immediate experience (there seemed to be no distinction between them)—heightened my sense of fragmentation. What the rapist did to my body was not in the past, as I had no past—because the memory of what happened did not feel like a memory. It felt here and now, in the present tense. Yet I needed to speak of this present as if it were the past. I needed to do this so the rapist (who might, for all I knew, be having a cup of coffee at the coffee shop next to the police station) could not do this to me or any other woman again.

The result of this peculiar predicament was an inner stupor. I began to feel either that everything that had happened was happening now, or I felt nothing at all. It was like being on a fast-moving train in the mountains where the view of rivers and forests, blurred by the train's speed, but bright in noon light, suddenly and without warning goes black as the train hurtles into unlit passages through the rock. Feeling nothing at all was tunnel life. Although unpredictable, the tunnels were a relief from the blurred corridors of searing light that intruded from the past that was present.

In this stupor, I submitted to the interview with the detective. Only one remark she made fixed itself in my memory, although, like toxic waste, it was many years before I could get near it.

"The worst part would have been to be trussed up like a chicken about to go in the oven," she said.

It's an odd thing to think of yourself as a splayed naked chicken. An inert piece of flesh. Odder still that this image took on the quality of a dirty secret. It became the image of myself, raped. It became more painful for me to encounter this image, produced by a careless remark, than for me to recall the hours I spent with the rapist. Why this was the case, I do not know. Maybe because it was, after all, a damn good metaphor.

■ ■ ■

I ask the nurse to wait outside with me for the cab, and when it comes, she goes around to the driver's window and hands him a coupon while I slide into the backseat. I leave the door open. "Do you know him?" I whisper to the nurse when she goes to close the door. "Yes," she says. "Are you sure he's okay?" I say. She is sure, but I don't believe her. Still, I let her close the door. I can't think of the name of Sara's street, can't picture how to get to it. I start to get out of the cab, then I remember. I tell the driver to head for Harvard Square. My shadow is not in the car.

■ ■ ■

I have no recollection of what the taxi driver looked like. When I think back to this ride, I see only a shadow in the front seat. Featureless, the driver was all male strangers, each and every one of whom might be a rapist. The postman. The man walking behind me on the sidewalk. The man sitting in his car at the grocery store. They might all be rapists.

I stared at the back of his head, thinking he might be my rapist. Driving a cab would be a perfect occupation for a rapist. Prey coming to you, rather than the other way around. The rapist could have followed me to the hospital in his taxi, waited all these hours. I thought he could get away with anything. Fear slapped me back into the seat, where I became smaller and smaller. I kept my hand on the door handle so I could throw myself out into the puddles of light left by the street lamps. I was like a coastal island submerged by a storm surge. I had no shore, no definition, no borders.

I said nothing until we got to Harvard Square. Then I told him to head up Massachusetts Avenue.

"Here, turn here!" We sped past the little market on Sara's corner.

"Turn around," I said, weeping at last. The driver pulled over.

"Are you okay, lady?" he said.

This moment is preserved whole in my mind, and still holds a mysterious significance. It was as if I were tuned to a frequency that transmitted nothing but static—the sound of thousands of fingernails scraping blackboards, thousands of metal brushes scrubbing copper pots, millions of bees locked in a metal box—and suddenly, but just for an instant, the static stopped and I heard a single, clear word. For an instant, the woman who had not been raped existed.

■ ■ ■

My cat, Larry, has earned a nickname at the vet's. They call him Satan, although at home he is called Sweetie and Luscious and Darling. When Larry was young, his previous owners told me, he was hit by a car and his treatments at the vets were prolonged and painful. They warned me, but I didn't believe them. The first time I witnessed the metamorphosis from house cat to monster, I beheld a creature so vicious he could only be approached by three people wearing fireman's gloves. I was stunned at what fear could do. In the midst of the struggle to shake Larry from the cardboard carrying case, which was being held upside down over the steel table with no effect whatsoever, I bestowed an endearment in the tone of voice I used at home. For an instant, the spell of fear was broken. Larry stopped howling, released his claws from the corners of the case, and hit the table on all fours. He was still for the briefest of moments, but he had heard me.

The cabdriver's question had much the same effect on me. It was the question of a human being. I could not answer him, but I heard him speaking from the other side of my fear.

He handed me a Kleenex, then made a U-turn, and a right onto Sara's street. Her porch light was on, but I did not see her waiting. Her driveway was dark, and the dimly lit space between the curb and her porch seemed to crawl with hidden threats.

"Is this the place?" he asked because I had not moved.

"Yes," I said.

"It's going to be okay," he said.

Sobbing into the Kleenex, I scanned the street from inside the cab. I could not trust the darkness in her driveway. "Will you wait? Until I'm inside?"

Although this was an infinitesimally small leap of faith, it was the second one I had taken alone in my new state, the first being to get into the cab in the first place. I cannot remember the first time I hurled myself into uncertainty—crawling across the room, perhaps. All the way to my father's easy chair. Alone in the unformed vastness of a world without concepts, and hence without words. Perhaps I am wrong to imagine that it felt like opening the door to the taxi, running up the steps to Sara's front door. But I often think so.

I pounded on her door, and after what seemed an eternity, the pounding finally produced her. I was furious she had not kept her promise.

"Why weren't you waiting?" I screamed. Then I slammed the door behind me, hard, as the taxi pulled away.

Boxes

Time goes from present to past.

DOGEN ZENJI

Sausalito, California, January 1993

More rain. The creek is the color of butterscotch with frothy cream on top.

The rain has brought more disasters—floods and mud slides on top of the fires and earthquakes—in this land of not doing something for a long time and then doing a lot of it. All those people on the Russian River, clutching their picture albums, their homes buried under mud.

I try not to think that the San Andreas Fault runs less than a mile from our house, just over the headlands—the Pacific Plate grinding against the North American Plate, moving to the northwest at the rate of six centimeters per year unless it gets stuck on something. I have this dumb idea that the rain will grease the skids and the whole thing will

snap—"The Big One" will hit. The rain makes me nervous.
I don't want all those feelings to come back—nothing to
trust, not the earth, not a locked door.

I try not to think about the picture on television last
night, the little white dog swimming in rising water round
and round inside a chain-link fence. I couldn't sleep because
of that little white dog, and thinking how the owner felt,
dangling from a rescue helicopter and watching the dog get
smaller and smaller.

Life must be lived forward. This is the way the thread unravels. This is
our biology, our physical destiny. But Kierkegaard said somewhere that
life can only be *understood* backwards. Perhaps he should have said life
can only be *lived* backwards. It seems to me we live backwards because
we remember. But remembering is not a return to a fixed point.
Remembering is a re-creation that gives meaning to the present, itself
a moving point.

There is a chronology of loss, but it is not linear. The stages of grief
we read about in psychology books—shock, anger, denial, sorrow,
acceptance—do not occur in a tidy sequence. We experience them not
as a progression, but as an orbit. The losses in catastrophes are like the
birth of a universe, matter exploding violently outward into an infinity
of consciousness, moving outward in all directions at once from the
moment of creation. Memory, unreliable and inventive, returns again
and again to this center, because it is the beginning of changes that
encompass both the past and the future. But always from a point that
is moving away. A catastrophe, an overturning of normal living, moves
forward in this way along with everything else.

"Snap out of it," "put it behind you," "forget about it"—words of
advice I heard many times from those closest to me—hardly seem reasonable requests. Indeed, these pleas are especially painful because they
come with love. To a rape survivor, nothing is more desired or more
impossible than forgetting.

■ ■ ■

Twelve days after my rape I went home to my family—"the place,"
Robert Frost said, "where, when you have to go there, they have to
take you in." I'd been living like a refugee, moving every three days or
so from one friend's home to another, pushing myself like a wheelbar-
row of wet cement through days consumed with practical necessities
dictated by a list of things to do I carried around like a sacred text. At
night I crawled into the cement; in the morning I chipped myself out
with a toothpick. The notes I made during these twelve days are as
devoid of content as white noise.

My only recollection of the trip from Boston to Virginia was sitting
in the United terminal at Logan waiting for my flight to be called.
There were two men in gray business suits sitting across from me.
They were as innocuous as glasses of milk, but their proximity was searing, just as the cabdriver's had been. It seemed the air around them was
agitated with red bolts of menace. It was unbearable to be near them,
but I was afraid to move. Afraid they would notice me. I tried to
remember how I used to act sitting across from strange men. I
couldn't. I felt like prey. Millions of years of evolution to get out of the
food chain and here I was, somebody's dinner. So this is madness, I
thought.

When the plane finally took off, I was certain it would crash.
The thought brought relief. Somewhere over New York I pulled
out my list, wondering who had drawn a line through each and
every item.

MASTER LIST

D AY 1 : Saturday, October 12

Meet detective at apt.
Pack suitcase/get papers
Make appt. clinic for follow-up urine test
Move to Chris's
Report stolen credit cards

DAY 2: Sunday, October 13

Follow up Chris's lead on new apartment (Concord)
Make appt. to see apartment
Make arrangements for place to sleep (w/ Simone)
Call Rape Crisis Center—gen. info.

DAY 3: Monday, October 14, Columbus Day

Move to Simone's
Organize papers
Make arrangements to stay with Linda

DAY 4: Tuesday, October 15

Move to Linda's
Make appointment Rape Crisis Center
Make appointment w/ police for report
Call Andrew—will he go with?
DMV—replace license
Call landlord—notify leaving/want security deposit back
Make appt. for AIDS test & follow-up—6 weeks
Cancel phone; gas & electric

DAY 5: Wednesday, October 16

Interview landlord, Concord
Call S.J.—explain can't do article
Call Victim Witness Program—gen. info.

DAY 6: Thursday, October 17

Appt. police station: 10:30 A.M.
Call health insurance re: paying for counseling

DAY 7: Friday, October 18

Call movers—arrange "moving crew" to pack
Call phone company re: connecting phone, Concord

Call locksmith—additional locks Concord
Money to new landlord—deliver

D A Y 8 : Saturday, October 19

Pay bills
Arrange place to stay (w/ Sara)
Call landlord re: when movers will arrive

D A Y 1 0 : Monday, October 21

Move to Sara's
Clinic, urine test
Counseling appt.—Rape Crisis Center: 9:30 A.M.
Change of address form at P.O.—forward mail to Sara's
Make airline reservations, Virginia
Call "moving crew"—instructions
Pick up boxes & deliver to G. w/key

D A Y 1 1 : Tuesday, October 22

Moving Day: confirm time of delivery w/ landlord
Pick up new contact lenses
Make arrangements for place to sleep (w/ Neva)
Call "moving crew" to thank

D A Y 1 2 : Wednesday, October 23

Pack for Virginia
Call clinic, results of urine test
Call police re: progress on investigation
Move to Neva's

D A Y 1 3 : Thursday, October 24

Pick up antibiotics on way to airport
United Airlines Flight, 11:00 shuttle

The practical problems that kept me in Boston gave my body time to heal. I was glad because I didn't want my parents to see the bruises on my wrists and arms or the way I walked, my old-lady shuffle. Looking back, I don't know how I functioned. I could not sleep; I forced myself to eat. I had no recognizable identity, nothing inside at all, and no sense of a future, although I was somehow performing actions that seemed to suggest I would have one. I knew that I was imposing on my friends, but my friends were no longer real to me. I was observing them from another dimension. They lived in the Great Before, a place I could never return to.

I alternated between periods of shattering anxiety and a crushing exhaustion that made getting dressed in the morning almost impossible. Fear knit the anxiety and exhaustion together in an agitation that was a substitute for energy. My friends helped in hundreds of practical ways. The word spread quickly. People called. What did I say to them? I cannot remember. I did not exist.

■ ■ ■

My parents' house looks as if it belongs in California, in the Sierra Nevada or the Santa Cruz Mountains, rather than in a remote corner of Fairfax County, Virginia. The house was not the house I had grown up in. That house had been taken by the state of Virginia so the land could be used for a mental institution, a case of eminent domain that my brothers and I thought had a certain poetic justice. In their typical fashion, my parents found a silver lining in the affair and built another house only a few miles away. Constructed entirely of cedar logs, the house is perched on a wooded hill overlooking a stream. From the deck, which runs the entire length of the house on the west, you look into the forest at belly-button level. They had found the only remaining dirt road that was not on a flight pattern into Dulles.

They met me at the airport and the recollection of the sight of them, standing side by side in the crowd, their faces brave, my mother's grief, my father's rage pushed down like a suppressed cough, is one of the most painful memories of those first days. The rapist had hurt them, too. The violence kept spreading out across the void, touching everyone I loved.

I, too, put on a brave face, smiled and waved to my parents. My mother embraced me. I could smell the shampoo in her hair. It smelled like lilacs. My father hung back awkwardly, so I reached for him. Passengers flowed around us. If the men in gray business suits walked past, I didn't notice them.

■ ■ ■

Anchors slipped down into the water: the dusty perfume of oak leaves when they are raked into piles, the delicate aromas from my mother's kitchen, the smell of pine shavings and shellac in my father's workshop, the rank sweetness of leaves decaying in the quiet pools under roots along the creek. These were safe harbors, familiar. I could stop cleaning up the practical mess of my life, stop intruding on my friends with needs that frightened them and humiliated me. My younger brother, Ed, who was in his mid-thirties, was renting the apartment on the ground floor of my parents' house, saving me the admission that I was still too terrified to stay there alone. If there were a hell, I was sure it was on the ground floor. I moved into my father's office upstairs; it had a love seat that folded out into a single bed, and access to a tiny bathroom. But I never slept there. I slept with my mother.

Being physically alone was torment. I had once treasured solitude. Now being alone was a continuation of the physical state of terror, which, unlike pleasure, unfolds in slow motion. So for six weeks I followed my mother around all day, as I must have done when I was two. Perhaps it seemed strange to her; perhaps she felt suffocated by my need for her presence. But she never resisted. I followed her outside to rake leaves, followed her to the kitchen to make lunch, followed her to the mailbox to get the mail, followed her back to the kitchen to start dinner, followed her to the living room in the late afternoon when she liked to curl up under an afghan and read.

A few days after I settled in we were sitting side by side on the couch with our books. "What are you reading?" she asked.

"The Tibetan Book of the Dead," I said. It was Evans-Wentz's third edition with commentary by Carl Jung. She was reading a paperback

novel that had a picture of a woman in a red silk dressing gown leaning against a man who held her arm from behind. They were about to turn toward each other. Behind them a red pagoda and sharp jagged mountains, and another figure: a handsome Chinese man in a yellow robe, his arms crossed, his look defiant.

My mother got a worried look on her face. "It's sort of a Buddhist prayer for the dead," I said, knowing she would find it an odd choice. I'd started the book a few days before the rape—I had studied Western philosophy in college and had been reading Eastern literature in a leisurely sort of way for years. I thought that if I could pick up where I'd left off, I could bridge the rupture in time that had just occurred, and get back to the woman who had not been raped—so I'd packed the book. The rape and this particular book were connected only by propinquity. But the need to find an explanation for what had happened to me was overwhelming—any explanation, no matter how illogical or magical, seemed better than nothing at all. I was incapable of sustained concentration, but I opened the book anyway.

I began to worry that perhaps reading a book about the death of the ego had caused the rape. Maybe I was dead but didn't know it. Maybe I was traveling in the Sidpa Bardo, the third stage of death. "Thick awesome darkness will appear in front of thee continually, from the midst of which there will come such terror-producing utterances as 'Strike! Slay!' and similar threats." Maybe the rapist had a buffalo head like the Gelugpa's Spirit of Death or was one of the horde of the tormenting Eumenides. I put the book down and began to cry.

"It would have been better if he'd killed me," I blurted out.

"Not for your father and me," my mother said, holding my hand.

"I didn't really mean that," I lied.

"I know what you meant. I've felt the same way—when your brother died. You don't think you can go on—but you do."

"What did I do to deserve this?"

"Nothing, sweetheart," my mother said.

■ ■ ■

42

In the evening, after my mother and I cleaned up the dinner dishes, we got ready for bed. Then we propped ourselves up on pillows to read or watch television programs she liked—*Golden Girls, Murder She Wrote,* and *Sixty Minutes.* Her room looked as it always had. The rocking chair where she had rocked her babies occupied the corner next to her desk, a reproduction of Longfellow's writing desk with mysterious compartments I'd found fascinating as a child. Over her desk hung a reproduction of an unsigned painting, a gray cottage on a wide creek that reflected overcast March light and bare trees. The scene was serene, silent. When I was little I used to imagine the inside of the cottage and invent lives for the people who lived there. On her dresser, the same white porcelain angels playing instruments, their backs reflected in the mirror, stood side by side near her Austrian jewelry box with the ballerina that twirled to the tune of "The Blue Danube."

Sometimes my father, whose bedroom was on the other side of the master bath, joined us for the ten o'clock news. Then there were three of us in her bed watching television. Mama and Papa in their seventies. Baby almost forty.

■ ■ ■

Six years after the rape I told a close friend about these weeks, proud of myself for taking them, proud of my parents for giving them to me. Something in her reaction put me on guard. Talking about rape, as my young friend Kate had discovered, was dangerous. No one, except the police detectives and my therapists, had ever asked me the details of what happened that day. At first, I was stunned by this. After the Loma Prieta earthquake of 1989, I was frequently asked to describe what it was like to experience a major earthquake. Telling my story, and hearing my friends tell theirs, was soothing, especially in the early weeks when we all still had the jitters. Even years later, pieces of our stories, now part of our collective folklore, work their way into conversations. We don't talk about the earthquake much anymore, but we haven't forgotten. But no one wanted to know about the rape.

I was sympathetic to people's reluctance to press me for the facts that had been of such interest to the detective. I knew part of the reason was that they felt it was too private, too personal. Because rape is, among other things, an assault on sexual organs, it carries traces of a dark, dirty kind of sex that other assaults do not. But how could anyone think that it was a sexual experience?

Still, people's resistance to hearing about the aftermath of the rape—the new patterns of thought and feeling that turned, year after year, like the bright shards of glass in a kaleidoscope—pained me. It seemed to me that even close friends either withdrew or judged me.

When I told my friend I'd slept in my mother's bed for six weeks, she looked incredulous.

"You slept with your mother?" When anyone turns what you have stated as a fact into a question, you know something is up.

"Yes."

"Have you ever discussed that with a therapist?"

"No."

"Don't you think you should?"

"Not really," I said. "Under the circumstances."

"I think there are some unresolved issues there," she concluded.

Even after six years, it hurt to have someone I decided to confide in suggest that what I remembered as a healing act might be something sick. Self-doubt, a cousin to the self-blame that so often plagues rape survivors, lingers for years like a dormant virus waiting for a moment of compromise. I felt exposed and defenseless sitting there with my friend, staring into my coffee and knowing that "the circumstances" would never make any sense to her.

But I can appreciate good intentions even when they sting. My friend's inability to understand was an indication not of her unkindness, but of her ignorance. Anyone who thought it odd that a thirty-nine-year-old woman followed her mother around like a puppy for six weeks was one of the lucky ones—a woman who had not been raped.

I was fortunate that my mother understood instinctively the physical residue of terror. She had the wisdom to accept that I was stuck, like a phonograph needle in a scratch, in the fight-or-flight response. It was like river rafting without stretches of calm water. I was paddling desperately to stay upright, living second to second without a sense of sequence. In these rapids I had to sleep, eat, and conduct all the ordinary business of daily life. I had to carry a cup of tea across the raft and not mention to anyone that the water, my new medium, was a ribbon of white fury. To find my mother sitting beside me on the raft, unafraid and uncritical, even somehow serene in her faith that love conquers all, was a blessing that continues to heal to this day.

October 21, 1985

My first journal entry since the rape. Words seem dead.

Last night a heavy-breather called. I think it is him, tracking me. Mom tries to calm me, but I am shaking all over and can't breathe. Dad shows me his gun and takes me around to show me all the doors are locked, fixes me a Scotch, but I can't stop crying. Finally I do because I see I am upsetting them. I couldn't sleep, but was too scared to get up and leave Mom. I do seem to sleep, but then wake up because something is shuffling on the deck. I wake Mom, hysterical. It was just an animal. "That ol' raccoon," Mom says, like she knows him. I can't get back to sleep. My heart is pounding so hard I think I'm having a heart attack. I feel so vulnerable. I don't know who I am anymore.

This morning my body felt like lead. Went with Mom to the drugstore. A man walked by me in the aisle and stopped. I wanted to scream for Mom, but thank God I didn't. I was sweating so hard I changed shirts when I got home.

This afternoon I made myself go help Mom rake leaves and clip weeds. Felt better getting exercise. Mom said, "Did you know you cut down a dogwood sapling?" I felt devastated and started to cry. I was an idiot. It seemed the thing I was doing to help myself, working outside, just proved my bad judgment, carelessness, inattention. That's why I got raped. Mom said the dogwood didn't matter, that she wanted it cut down, that there were plenty more. She cut down another one to prove it.

Last night the oddest thing—before I fell asleep I remembered a dream I had when I was six or seven—the Big Bad Wolf was chasing us. He was wearing red overalls and a top hat. Tom was running out in front because he was the oldest and fastest. Dad was carrying Eddie and Mom was carrying Johnny. I knew it was because they were babies. I was running as hard as I could, but I was falling behind. Mom kept pleading with me to go faster, turning around and reaching out her hand. I could feel the wolf's hot breath on my neck.

I think I am having a nervous breakdown.

The second week I was in Virginia, my brother injured his back in a motorcycle accident. The doctor ordered five days of bed rest, and I spent hours every day looking after him. I drove him to the doctor's, fixed his breakfast, cleaned his kitchen, and did his laundry. I felt needed, even useful. But my helpfulness was fueled by a secret guilt that I had brought bad luck home. I felt powerless, yet I was filled with delusions of possessing power, like a child who believes there's a monster in the closet and that she can make it go away by hiding under the covers. I was a jinx. I should be cast out alone in a dingy to appease the storm and save the crew. I couldn't confide these feelings to anyone because I didn't want anyone to tell me they were crazy.

My father always hoped Ed would go into the priesthood because he was the only one of the four children who was even-tempered. In a household of finicky eaters, Ed ate everything. While the rest of us fussed, resisted, and complained, Ed was cheerful, cooperative, and easygoing. My brothers and I had scattered out across the country once we left home and I had not spent time alone with Ed since we were teenagers. Now we were both home—my brother because he'd left

Richmond to take a new job in Washington and was waiting for an apartment in town, and me because I was a two-year-old again.

Ed and I had always gotten along. Once, when we were children, we had a disagreement that we decided to settle by duking it out behind the woodshed. Since my father strictly forbade my brothers to lay a hand on me, Ed and I agreed that the fight must remain our little secret, no matter what the outcome, which we expected to be bloody. We solemnly shook hands on it. Then we marched to the shed, drew a line in the dirt, double-dog-dared each other to step over, hurled insults at each other, put up our fists—and burst into tears. That was the first and last disagreement we ever had.

Ed and I crawled into a parenthesis in the narrative of the rape, digressing into the reconstruction of scenes from our childhood— amusing set pieces we enjoyed embellishing for comic effect. Sometimes, too, I talked about the aftermath of the rape. Ed listened without judgment. Nothing I said about the way I felt seemed to bother him. He listened while I described in excruciating detail the practical problems I had solved before coming home. He listened to my description of each and every kindness my friends had shown. Every decision I had made was the right one. I was smart, strong, and funny. Nothing had changed. I was his big sister. I had to believe she still existed.

November 14, 1985

So difficult to write in this journal. It used to be a comfort.

I am sitting on the deck in my bathrobe, moved to write by the scene: four or five squirrels busy in the leaves that lie thick and brown on the ground. The air is sultry, like early summer with just an edge of coolness. The leaves are falling from the trees, making a sound like rain, so many falling in the still air. I have watched the trees go from orange and red to brown. Now many are bare. I am glad the bright colors are gone. I've delayed my trip back to Boston because I don't feel ready. I felt terrible anxiety even thinking about the tangle of associations that await me, being alone again and knowing it will feel like the wolf is licking the window. It is depressing to know these feelings are going to stay with me. For how long? They seem crippling, but there is no way out.

I must not cry when I leave. Mom and Dad urge me to stay longer, but I know I have to go. I'm afraid. If I cry, I'll make them afraid.

The squirrels are chasing each other. They look so happy. The sun has broken through the clouds, but rain is in the air. I will sweep the leaves off the deck before the rain comes.

I wish I were dead.

When I was a child, my father's workshop, a large room between the garage and the house, was a kingdom unto itself—and strictly off limits. What happened in my father's workshop was serious business; it was no place for kids. Working at night and on weekends, my parents designed and built our first house themselves, starting with a three-room cottage covered in tar paper that I remember only from pictures. By the time I was nine, we all had our own rooms. My father laid and hand-pegged the floors, lined the closets with cedar he cut down from the property, and made the French doors for the living room and the cabinets for four bathrooms. He hung Sheetrock, plastered, painted, mixed cement. My mother, who cooked meals for a year without kitchen counters or cabinets while my father built them out of knotty pine, handed him nails, fetched tools, patched holes, sanded, painted, cleaned brushes—and took care of four children.

The smell of turpentine, WD-40, wood shavings, and sawdust still emanated from my father's workshop, but it was a more modest affair now, a twelve-by-fourteen room off the laundry room that had lost its air of urgency. My father was making ship models and boxes instead of houses. The boxes were made of exotic woods—ebony, cocobolo, padouk—and had elaborate hinges. He made sewing boxes that folded out into tiers when opened, trunk-sized boxes of mahogany and walnut, tiny boxes with little trays inside and hinges so small they fit on the end of his finger.

My father and I spent the mornings together in his workshop after Ed went back to work. In the morning, boxes in various stages of completion—some still in sections held together by rubber bands while the glue dried, some ready for their second coat of varnish—greeted us as the sun poured in through the window facing the creek. Sipping our coffee, we'd discuss the day's work. Then my father would turn on the radio and we'd work companionably until lunch.

We made them in an order that only I understood. The first was for Sara, who had taken me in after I left the hospital. She'd forgiven me for yelling at her because she wasn't waiting at the door. She'd left her post for a moment to check on the meal she was preparing—pasta with fresh vegetables—and to run me a bath. She brought me honeysuckle-scented bath oil from a blue bottle and a gin and tonic with a wedge of lime as I scrubbed and wept, feeling I would never be clean again. She laid a flannel nightgown and a pair of slippers on the chair in the bathroom, coaxing me out of the bath to the table, set with her best china and a silver candlestick with an ivory-colored candle. Sitting next to my plate was a tattered teddy bear that had once belonged to her son. I slept with it for weeks afterward. After I'd eaten, she tucked me in— fresh sheets on the couch, two blankets, a night-light and Bach's *Goldberg Variations* in the background, a fire crackling in the fireplace.

There was a box for Linda, the strategist, who figured out how I could move out of the apartment where I was raped into a new apartment out of the city. It was she who assessed which friends could do what to help me, she who firmed up assignments and schedules, she who designed the master list of tasks that I carried around in a special notebook she'd provided. Linda held me when I broke down and rejoiced when I crossed something off my list.

There was a box for Simone, who put me up and took time off from her job to help me run errands, and a box for Chris, who found me the new apartment, the attic of a Victorian house in Concord, Massachusetts, the heart of Thoreau country. There was one for Andrew, who had endured my police report, one for Neva, who thought to lend me money without my having to ask, and four boxes for the friends who had supervised the movers while I was in Virginia.

I worked with care, sanding the wood until it felt like velvet, cleaning it with a tack cloth, then sanding it again. My father made the holes for the hinges using a miniature power drill and I screwed in the brass screws so that they were perfectly straight, their heads flat against the hinges. The wood sucked in the varnish, making small bubbles that disappeared into the grain. I measured for the lining and cut the suede with a mat knife and a ruler.

The days passed in these meditations. When I was working on the boxes, I wasn't asking myself why or worrying about getting "back on my feet." I was only sanding or varnishing or gluing. I was with my father in a way I had never been as a child. The time I spent with him in his workshop was time that had lost all forward motion, time that was caught and stilled, like an insect in amber. It was a gift and a lesson. When the boxes were all done, I brought them upstairs, proudly showed them to my mother, and together we wrapped each one up in a gift box with lavender tissue paper inside, to match the suede linings. I wrapped the gift boxes in purple paper and tied them with satin ribbon.

One morning, while he was making a wooden latch for one of the boxes, my father said out of the blue, "If I ever got my hands on that sick bastard, I'd kill him, slowly. First, I'll castrate him." The taste of my father's rage was bitter and unwelcome. My rage, too, was monstrous. But when its back broke the surface, its hidden vastness terrified me; the wake it left swamped me, sent me tumbling into frigid water with nothing to cling to. I could not bear to look upon its barnacled head, fearing it would swallow me whole. It would surface much later and in disguised forms that did not seem to resemble it but were its spawn nonetheless. It had gone down to the bottom with the blind fish—to metamorphose. I knew my father needed to torment his invis-ible enemy, needed the words. But I already knew they would not bring release. They would snare him and make him feel more helpless.

"Maybe they'll catch him," I said. We both knew it would be diffi-cult. Because the rapist had grabbed from behind and blindfolded me before I saw him, I'd never be able to identify him in a police lineup. The police had nothing to go on except the most detailed description of slippers they had ever heard. If a lineup included closing your eyes and sniffing each suspect, I could have picked him out in an instant.

"Even if they do catch him," my father replied, "he'll be out in a year or two." I didn't know the statistics, but my father was right. Ninety-eight percent of rapists are never caught, according to a 1993 report prepared by Senator Joseph Biden's Senate Judiciary Committee staff. The 2 percent that are caught and convicted, the report noted, "can expect to serve an average of a year or less behind bars."

If I had been aware of these statistics then, they would have extin-guished the small flicker of hope I still had that my rapist might be caught. I entertained fantasies that he would brag to someone who would snitch, the best-case scenario offered by the police a few days before I left for Virginia. No one ever did.

I did not know then the effect this crime would have on me—that it would be I, not the rapist, who would be given the life sentence. If I had known most rapists get off with a slap on the wrist, I might have felt my isolation even more intensely than I did. The punishment, or lack of it, would have suggested that I was overreacting. Rape was bad, but not that bad—it was only a-year-in-the-slammer bad. Right up there with dastardly deeds like passing bad checks.

My father's rage that day as he stood at the workbench, his fists clenched, filled me with pity. The rapist was subhuman, worse than an animal, my father said. He should be castrated, burned alive. He wanted to be the one with the knife, the one pouring the gasoline. He wanted to hire a private detective to find this monster. Then he would kill him. It was terrible to hear him and to sense that the only thing that would comfort him was for me to stop hurting. He was full of rage because he loved me and I was suffering. My suffering was the problem.

"Killing him won't change what happened," I said.

"Maybe you shouldn't go back," my father said. "He's still out there somewhere."

"Dad, there are rapists in Virginia, too."

He thought about this for a minute. "You're sure you want to go back?" he asked. I knew he wanted to protect me, that he would defend me with his life. That was why he wanted me to stay.

"I have a life in Boston—my work, friends. I'm not going to let this bastard take it away from me. I promise, Daddy, I'm going to be fine."

■   ■   ■

In 1995 I visited Sara. The box my father and I made for her was sitting on her dressing table, next to the silver mirror and hairbrush that were engraved with her mother's initials. I picked it up, looked at the hinges, ran my finger along the top. Seeing the box again reminded me of how fortunate I had been to have those mornings with my father in his workshop, to have my memories of him at his workbench in a pool of morning light with his tools and brushes and cans of varnish. My promises to my father are all coming true, but not in the way I'd imagined. I did not go back to the life I had left, and it had taken me a decade to accept the textures of the life that had replaced it.

Adrift

Who, in the dark, has cast the harbor-chain?
This is no journey to a land we know.

LOUISE BOGEN, "Putting to Sea"

It is late February 1993. I have locked myself out of the house in the rain. No coat. No purse. Only my car keys. I was ahead of myself. Steve and I have disagreed for years about hiding a key for just such a mishap. I know what can happen if someone finds it, even though the kind of someone I have in mind doesn't need a key. We compromise by leaving a key at a neighbor's. Of course, she is not home.

In the eight years since the rape, I have never misplaced my keys. Keys are triggers, and so I am careful with them. The morning before I was raped I lost the keys to my car. It was parked at a friend's house where I'd been staying for a week—until I could unpack. I believed for years that the reason I was raped was because I lost my keys. If I hadn't lost my keys, I reasoned, I would not have been at my new apartment. I would have been interviewing an artist for a profile I was writing for a local newspaper.

Problems with keys, losing them or not having them when you need them, upset even people who tolerate inconvenience well. Problems with keys are usually a sign that you have too much to do. I did the day I was raped, and losing the keys seemed, at first, to be a blessing. May Sarton said that open-ended time is the only real luxury, the luxury that made her feel "stupendously rich." That day, sitting on the front steps of my friend's house waiting for the locksmith, I suddenly had nothing to do. I had rescheduled the interview with the artist and canceled a lunch date. I was rich. The sprite who steals socks, keys, and nail files had left unscheduled time behind as compensation for her mischief—time to myself. Time to unpack.

■ ■ ■

I am standing in a phone booth, calling my husband's office in downtown San Francisco, worrying that he may have forgotten his keys, too. He often does. I stand a long time because he is on a conference call. The rain thickens around the phone booth, runs down the sides in torrents so that I can't see out. I joke with him when he finally gets on the line because this is a little victory for his side of our key debate, but I am tense.

In the car now, crossing the Golden Gate Bridge, I am listening to the radio traffic report. The cars in front of me are barely visible. Things are rough out there, the announcer says, sounding happy. He rattles off the accidents—an overturned garbage truck, a tree down, a major road to the north closed because of a mud slide. I realize that I am holding the steering wheel so hard my knuckles are white.

After the earthquake in Kobe, Japan, while the images of toppled freeways and prone twelve-story buildings were consuming the news broadcast, a local television station aired a computer simulation of what would happen to the Golden Gate Bridge if a quake of the same size and duration struck the Bay Area. Fortunately, the simulation was abstract, the kind of image engineers like. Cars, trucks, buses, and pedestrians were tastefully left out of the picture, which was a series of lines resembling a spiderweb built on the principle of the square. According to the experts, the south span—between the tower and Fort Point—would snap from its moorings and fall into San Francisco Bay. The rest of the bridge would thrash back and forth like a snake with its head under a boot.

The radio announcer informs me that in the last week there have been fifty small earthquakes in the Bay Area, mostly 1.0s, but a few stronger, especially along the Calaveras Fault. The experts say this is an unusual amount of activity. I am now mid-span on the Golden Gate Bridge. I have the sensation that I am splitting apart. One part is driving the car, following at a safe distance two red specks, the taillights of a BMW; the other part is observing what the first part is doing. The part that is driving is thinking too much. The part that is watching is numb. I try to get them back together, but the effort makes it worse. My concentration is fragmenting. True concentration requires relaxation.

I am on the last span now. The south span. The one the experts have said will collapse. A Golden Gate transit bus is behind me, pressing me. Suddenly I feel I am falling. The bus plunges past me. I look out my window and see all the passengers tumbling around, their mouths little ovals. The driver is clinging to the wheel. Everything is happening in slow motion. The part of me that is driving screams, but no sound comes out. The other part observes, remote. And it is all my fault—because I locked myself out of the house. But I am still on the road and the road is still connected to the spans. Perhaps a second, maybe two has passed.

When I get to the tollbooth, I am elated. Fishing around in my purse for three dollars, I thank the nice lady with the black fingernail polish, then shoot out of the booth, back into the rain.

Keys have nothing to do with rape. Rape has nothing to do with earthquakes. But these associations have a life of their own. Everyone who survives a disaster has them. They are time warps, curves in emotional space, as unpredictable as the shock that created them.

"Soul, or psychic, murder," Dr. Leonard Shengold explains in his book *Soul Murder,* "involves trauma imposed from the world outside the mind that is so overwhelming that the mental apparatus is flooded with feeling." What Shengold calls "the terrifying too-muchness" of feeling is the world spawned from trauma, and like an island formed from undersea volcanoes, it is cut off from inhabited continents. Castaways who are carried to these shores by storms adapt—or die. To write about this too-muchness, the inundation of feeling that covers the landscape of the mind and physical brain after terror, raises a question: Can language resurrect the murdered soul, reroute the brain's signals? I must believe it can.

• • •

The human response to overwhelming life experience is viewed by modern medicine as an anxiety disorder, an illness of the mind. Because I do not like to think that the man who raped me infected me with a mental illness, I resist calling the effects of overwhelming terror an illness. I claim my sanity, and view my response as human, even appropriate and dignified.

In the 1980 third edition of the American Psychiatric Association's DSM-III *(Diagnostic and Statistical Manual of Mental Disorders)* the response to terrifying too-muchness finally got a name: post-traumatic stress disorder, or PTSD—a bundle of symptoms that collectively might be thought of as the experience of the past undermining the present. Living with PTSD is like standing on the edge of an ocean churned by fierce winds—the present moment—as the past curls, breaks, and surges forward onto the land. It erodes the ground, dragging those who stand on it away. But this is a limited metaphor because the action of the past on the present is more complex—it erodes the ground on which you stand from all directions at once.

In 1990, five years after my rape, a friend sent me a newspaper article that delineated the symptoms of this disorder: flashbacks, nightmares, depression, denial, a sense of estrangement and isolation, guilt, rage, emotional numbness and constriction, insomnia, being fearful and easily startled, loss of capacity to symbolize, fantasize, or sublimate, difficulty concentrating. Although I had been depressed and anxious for several months, I made no conscious connection between my feelings and the rape. I had convinced myself I was "over it." This assumption, combined with my longing for it to be true, had a narcotic effect on my cognitive ability to entertain the idea that three hours of over-whelming terror had had any long-term effects.

I read down the list of symptoms in a state akin to intoxication. I was aware of meaningful content in what I had read, but my emotional and intellectual grasp of the information was suppressed. Although the thought did cross my mind that perhaps I was suffering from something very much like post-traumatic stress, it was only a fleeting thought, the kind someone with a headache might entertain, for just an instant, when she wonders if the throbbing pain in her temples is a brain tumor.

The focus of research cited in the article was on Vietnam veterans. Rape wasn't mentioned as a cause of PTSD. Because the tide of my emotions worked against a cognitive grasp of my condition, I blamed my unhappiness on external circumstances. I understand now that the rape had changed form, evolved into a new kind of feeling. It was no longer an event in the past. It was my present emotional landscape, the jungles of the island upon which many survivors of even a single instance of overwhelming terror find themselves stranded, sometimes forever. The dense undergrowth cuts off the view of the sea, where, with luck, a sail might eventually be spotted. The impenetrable tangle of emotion itself works against not only escape, but the idea of escape.

Looking back, I wonder at my inability to engage in any kind of research on the topic. When I was told I needed surgery for fibroid tumors, for example, I read everything I could get my hands on about the subject. I have one shelf in my bookcase devoted to the intricacies of stepparenting. When my mother was diagnosed with breast cancer, I spent a week in the medical library before flying to Virginia to consult her doctors. But this instinct was atrophied when it came to the rape or anything connected with it.

In 1995 Steven Rose reviewed two books on the subject of repressed and false memory for *The New York Times Book Review*. He began by noting that a new disease was sweeping America. "I call it," Rose explained, "syndromitis—the invention of quasi-medical categories to suit almost any deviation from what is perceived as the norm: the ideal state of middle-performing, middlingly happy Americans in their 30's." He goes on to list some of these fashionable labels: ADD (attention deficit disorder), DID (dissociative identity disorder), Munchausen syndrome by proxy, and post-traumatic stress disorder, among others. "Once the labels have been created," he wrote, "the tendency for therapists to search them out in their clients snowballs, for there are careers to be made in defining as well as in treating these conditions." This fashion, he concludes as he spurs on his hobby horse, is helped along by "middle America's rewriting of the Declaration of Independence. It is no longer merely the pursuit but the possession of happiness that has become an inalienable right."

Rose was being fashionably cynical, but that isn't why I clipped the article. I had spent two and a half years in treatment for post-traumatic stress disorder. Because it was in the DSM-III, my insurance company should have footed the bill. Because the rape specialist who treated me was not a preferred provider, they didn't. The treatment was expensive, and it was I, not the rapist, who wrote out the checks every month. Perhaps I was still feeling resentful about this when I read Rose's piece. What bothered me about his complaint was the suggestion that post-traumatic stress disorder was a hyphenated, frivolous glitch of fashion, like those rhinestone-eyed poodles girls wore on felt skirts to sock hops in the fifties. It wasn't a real problem, he seemed to imply. It was a psychiatric Hula-Hoop, merely an excuse that middling unhappy people used to explain their middling unhappiness.

But what is now called PTSD is not some new fashionable acronym for middling unhappiness, since for centuries physicians recognized a mysterious human condition they understood in a general way as hysteria. It was long associated with women (from the Greek, *hystera,* womb) and thought to originate in the uterus. No doubt people were aware that soldiers subjected to the horrors of battle also exhibited hysterical symptoms, but a term for the male version of hysteria—"shell shock"—did not enter the language until 1916 when military physicians began to document cases of the condition in men returning from World War I.

In his 1995 book, *Emotional Intelligence,* Daniel Goleman, who covers the behavioral and brain sciences for the *New York Times,* describes experiences like the one I had on the Golden Gate Bridge as "emotional hijackings." He writes that these "hijackings" occur because, as scientists are beginning to discover, the brain has a "neural back alley"—a shortcut for feeling that bypasses the main avenues of the neocortex, the last part of the brain to evolve (about 100 million years ago) and the seat of all that is, as Goleman puts it, "distinctly human." One of the leading researchers in the field, Joseph LeDoux, a neuroscientist at the Center for Neural Science at New York University, discovered in the late 1980s that there is an anatomical basis for the capacity of feelings to overwhelm the thinking mind. As he told Goleman, "Anatomically the emotional system can act independently of the neocortex. Some emotional reactions and emotional memories can be formed without any conscious, cognitive participation at all." To extend Goleman's metaphor, people with PTSD become back-alley rats, living in a maze of emotions that folks ambling along on sunlit avenues don't know exists. But for the alley rats, the maze is the only way to get around.

Goleman's hijacking metaphor is especially apt. When I was attacked by sudden, incoherent fear, I felt as if I had a shadow rapist living inside me that struck from behind when I least expected it, just as the flesh-and-blood rapist had done. The shadow rapist was not an image of the real rapist or his actions—the images of the rape seemed to be fossilized Technicolor holograms that were stored in an abandoned mine shaft inside my brain. The shadow was imageless, wordless, formless. It was a terrorist inside my brain, a part of me. What I didn't know in the period when these attacks were most severe was that the terrorist in my head was probably biological. Research conducted at the National Center for Post-Traumatic Stress Disorder over the last fifteen years indicates that the key to PTSD may lie in the chemistry of the brain. Overwhelming terror, even a single instance of it, can physically alter the brain forever.

Goleman points out that some of the main changes are in the locus ceruleus, a structure located in the brain stem that regulates the secretion of the hormones adrenaline and noradrenaline (called catecholamines), which mobilize the body for an emergency. These substances also make memories stronger and more vivid. The physiological changes that accompany rising to these occasions are temporary infusions of energy, although the memories of these occasions remain powerful even years later. For people with PTSD, however, the rush never stops. After overwhelming and uncontrollable stress, the locus ceruleus becomes hyperactive, secreting an overabundance of these hormones, even in situations that hold no actual threat but somehow "resemble" the original event, although this "resemblance" is often peculiar.

For example, sitting with my back to a door "resembles" the rape because I had my back to a door that October afternoon. For years I arranged the furniture in my office so that I never had my back to the door, even though the contortions often offended my aesthetics and were impractical. I didn't think about it. I just couldn't concentrate that way.

But I'm writing this now with my back to the door. Although I can still trace the text of my former discomfort, it is like reading an inscription on an ancient grave marker—words were once there, but the action of wind and rain has all but erased them. The view from my window is more important to me now than protecting my back. Although there is still a faint discomfort, I have learned how to short-circuit the physical memory before it has a chance to trigger fear. I have learned to do this with more complex "resemblances," including the act of concentration itself. For some years concentrating on any task produced a feeling of intense foreboding because I had been concentrating—on unpacking—when I was attacked.

Increases in the levels of CRF, the main stress hormone the brain releases for the fight-or-flight response, also occur in people suffering from PTSD. Too much CRF floods the body with chemicals that produce the same emotions as those produced by the original trauma. Surges of CRF make people "overreact." The classic example is the combat veteran who gets the shakes when he hears a car backfire. The backfire is not "like" the battlefield. It *is* the battlefield, and he is there now.

The movie *Apocalypse Now,* Francis Ford Coppola's masterful rendering of Joseph Conrad's *Heart of Darkness* in the modern context of the war in Vietnam, opens with Martin Sheen's character, Lieutenant Willard, "overreacting" to the spinning of a ceiling fan as he lies in a hotel bed in Saigon. Images of battle—rotating helicopter blades and the billowing infernos of napalm—are associated with the fan overhead as Willard tumbles into the emotions of an overwhelming past-that-is-present. In a 1993 *New York Times Magazine* article about PTSD in nurses who served in Vietnam, Laura Palmer describes PTSD as "hand-to-hand combat with yourself." Sheen's portrayal of this combat with the self and the collapsing structure of time that is its arena brilliantly captures the agonizing intensity of living with PTSD.

Goleman also details how overwhelming terror can bring about changes in the opioid system of the brain, which secretes endorphins to dull the feeling of pain. It, too, becomes hyperactive, constricting feeling. The numbness associated with PTSD seems to spread out over the entire emotional landscape, like fog. Not only is pain blunted, but pleasure as well. Of all the consequences of the rape, this was the hardest to perceive and the hardest to endure. It was living with novocaine in the heart, condemned to life on the glassy surface of the emotional horse latitudes. I felt cut off from everything and, as the years passed, even from the memory of emotional life as I had once experienced it. My capacity to feel deep concern about my feelings or the feelings of others seemed to have been freeze-dried, like instant coffee. The problem was, I didn't remember what brewed coffee tasted like.

New studies into the destructive path that overwhelming experience cuts through the neural pathways of the brain suggest that "getting over it" is nothing short of miraculous. A study published in the *American Journal of Psychiatry* in July 1995, for example, reports that the hormones that flood the brain to mobilize it in the face of terror may even be "toxic to cells in the hippocampus," a brain structure vital to learning and memory, actually shrinking it. The neurological circuits involved in these alterations of the brain are just beginning to be mapped by scientists, but we are learning that the experience of living can never be the same after an overwhelming experience because the brain that experiences that life may not be the same brain.

Although a five-volume study on the legacies of Vietnam that delineated the syndrome of post-traumatic stress had been published in 1981 by the Veterans' Administration—four years before my rape—there was still some debate about whether there was such a disorder even five years after I was attacked, when my symptoms finally began to surface. The recent scientific evidence of a biological basis for PTSD is another chapter in the history of the study of the human response to overwhelming stress, a history that has its own ironies and an odd pattern of denial.

In 1992 Dr. Judith Herman, an associate clinical professor of psychiatry at the Harvard Medical School, published a sophisticated and original work, *Trauma and Recovery,* that the psychologist Phyllis Chesler described as "one of the most important psychiatric works to be published since Freud." I do not think Chesler is exaggerating. In my case at least, Herman's book, which I read in the summer of 1992, was the beginning of hope. Perhaps I could do more than endure the unrelenting aftershocks of my rape. I began to believe that I had a chance not only to live my life after the rape, but to understand it. Perhaps my rape was not unspeakable. Perhaps, I began to think, the rite of silence—all that is unspoken—only made it seem so.

Herman's review of what she calls the "forgotten history" of the study of trauma was particularly healing for me. By the time I finished reading it, I felt less ashamed. I discovered that the rite of silence that plagues victims also seems to plague those who study them.

"The study of psychological trauma," she writes, "has a curious history—one of episodic amnesia." Herman eloquently states the reason:

Adrift

To study psychological trauma means bearing witness to
horrible events. When the events are natural disasters or
"acts of God," those who bear witness sympathize readily
with the victim. But when the traumatic events are of human
design, those who bear witness are caught in the conflict
between victim and perpetrator....It is very tempting to take
the side of the perpetrator. All the perpetrator asks is that the
bystander do nothing....The victim, on the contrary, asks
the bystander to share the burden of pain. The victim
demands action, engagement, and remembering.

Herman observes that although the response to uncontrollable,
terrifying life events had been a central focus of psychiatric interest in
Freud's time, his shift toward the belief that female hysteria was more
related to childhood *fantasies* of sexual seduction than to *actual* sexual
abuse postponed the serious study of the psychological and neurological consequences of women's response to trauma for decades. I
admired her fairness to Freud, whom I had been bashing since college,
when I first encountered the idea of penis envy. She reminded me that
Freud, whose *Aetiology of Hysteria* appeared in 1896, did not have a
political or social context that could support his findings that childhood
sexual assault, abuse, and incest were the cause of his female patients'
hysterical symptoms. Even today, with the support of a feminist movement and a worldwide human rights movement, I believe Herman is
right when she says that "to speak publicly about one's knowledge of
atrocities is to invite the stigma that attaches to victims." Freud's retreat
from this view (which has come to be seen as a matter of scandal) and
from the study of psychological trauma in women had costly consequences. Sadly, it would take nearly a century of horrific wars and their
effects on men for women's reactions to rape, incest, and domestic
abuse to begin to be taken seriously.

Herman explains that although the psychiatric casualties during
World War I were high—according to one estimate she quotes, mental

breakdowns represented 40 percent of British battle casualties—military authorities were reluctant to release information that might demoralize the public. Men subjected to the horrors of trench warfare were behaving like Freud's hysterical female patients, but the explanation for their behavior could not be attributed to "sexual fantasies." Yet even with so obvious an external explanation for their behavior, the hysteria of soldiers tended to be attributed not to trauma imposed from the outside world, but to internal weaknesses. Most medical authorities believed that soldiers with shell shock were "moral invalids," inferior human beings, and treatments reflected this view. Men were shamed and punished.

It is impossible for me to imagine the agony of men gone mute from terror being told they were shameful cowards, then being subjected to hours of electric shock. I remember a gentler accusation that came in a letter from a cousin two months after the rape. That was painful enough. She didn't like saying it, but someone had to: I was feeling sorry for myself and was throwing money down a rat hole by going to a therapist who would only lock me into my self-pity by encouraging me to remember what I should be forgetting. She wanted silence, cover-up, denial. I felt at the time she was on the rapist's side.

Eventually, as the psychiatric casualties mounted, soldiers were given more humane treatment and combat neurosis came to be viewed as a psychiatric, not a moral, condition. But soon after the war, Herman writes, "medical interest in the subject of psychological trauma faded once again. Though numerous men with long-lasting psychiatric disabilities crowded the back wards of veterans' hospitals, their presence had become an embarrassment to civilian societies eager to forget."

In 1941 Abram Kardiner published *The Traumatic Neuroses of War*, the first comprehensive clinical and theoretical study of war trauma. In this study, updated in 1947 in collaboration with a psychiatrist who had treated men at the front, Kardiner complained about the intermittent amnesia that had plagued the study of combat neurosis and society's tendency to discredit men who exhibited the classic symptoms of hysteria. Armed with his study, World War II military psychiatrists focused on how to prevent and treat combat neurosis, now understood to be an inevitable consequence of battle. Once again medical interest intensified. The stigma was fading—so much so that General Patton nearly lost his command in 1943 after he slapped two "shell-shocked" soldiers. Although new treatment methods, such as hypnosis and the use of sodium amytal (a hypnotic sedative popularly thought to be a "truth serum"), were considered effective in getting men back to the business of war as quickly as possible, it is now clear that until the traumatic memories are integrated into consciousness—what Goleman calls "emotional relearning," which involves intervention by the brain's prefrontal cortex—they still have the power to drag the present into the past. In recent years there has been an increase in the number of elderly World War II veterans seeking treatment for post-traumatic stress symptoms that have been dormant for fifty years. They have a better chance now for treatment than they would have had fifty years ago. Just as it had after World War I, medical interest in the fate of these men waned once they returned home. "The lasting effects of war trauma," Herman writes, "were once again forgotten."

■ ■ ■

Perhaps we had to have a "bad war" to see that overwhelming terror cannot simply be forgotten. Herman writes that it was not until the Vietnam war that "systematic, large-scale investigation of the long-term psychological effects of combat" was undertaken, and then only because of the organized efforts of the soldiers themselves, who, unlike their fathers and grandfathers, refused to be silent. "Someday this war's going to end," Lieutenant Willard says in *Apocalypse Now.* "That would be just fine with the boys on the boat. They weren't looking for anything more than a way home. Trouble is, I'd been back there, and I knew that it just didn't exist anymore." The Lieutenant Willards of the Vietnam war could not go home. Their pasts, as well as their futures, tumbled into the pain that is the present for survivors of terrifying too-muchness. The television images of Vietnam veterans standing before the wall where the names of their fallen comrades are recorded, weeping and remembering with dignity, have become etched in public consciousness.

Because these men refused to stand behind the screen of heroic myth with their fathers and grandfathers, the lasting impact of psychological trauma could no longer be denied. And it was only after 1980 (when the syndrome of psychological trauma ended up in the DMS-III), Herman writes, that it became "clear that the psychological syndrome seen in survivors of rape, domestic battery, and incest was essentially the same as the syndrome seen in survivors of war." And not until the "women's liberation movement of the 1970s was it recognized that the most common post-traumatic disorders are those not of men in war but of women in civilian life."

Although the neurological and psychological response to war and rape may be the same, the fact that rape is the most intimate crime, usually a solitary and secret horror, that it is the only violent crime that tarnishes the victim as well as the perpetrator, and that it is primarily men who can and do rape may affect our willingness to acknowledge rape's inevitable long-term effects. By denying them, we deny survivors their voice and dignity. And, like my cousin, we can end up on the side of the rapists. But we may also be denying the implications for society that the presence of these survivors makes clear. Herman makes the point with astonishing simplicity: If the psychological disorder seen in survivors of rape, domestic battery, and incest is "essentially the same as the syndrome seen in survivors of war," we can only conclude that "the subordinate condition of women is maintained and enforced by the hidden violence of men. There is war between the sexes. Rape victims, battered women, and sexually abused children are its casualties. Hysteria is the combat neurosis of the sex war."

And how big is this "sex war"? Statistics on rape are tricky. Experts agree that rape is notoriously underreported and that we may never get a full picture of the incidence of rape in America—or anywhere else in the world, for that matter. In *Transforming a Rape Culture*, a collection of essays published in 1993 that explores visions for a future without rape, the editors—Emilie Buchwald, Pamela Fletcher, and Martha

Roth—provide an excellent summary of the available data. One source
of information is the FBI's Uniform Crime Report (UCR), compiled
from more than sixteen thousand law-enforcement agencies covering
96 percent of the nation's population. In 1991 the UCR recorded
106,593 rapes: 292 each day, twelve every hour, one every five minutes.
During the twenty-year period of 1972–1991, the UCR reported that
1.5 million women were victims of sexual assault—forcible rape or rape
attempts. And during this twenty-year period there was a 128 percent
increase in the number of reported rapes. The editors note that the
UCR figures are "the most conservative numbers available and should
be considered *the baseline or minimum rape figure.*"

The National Crime Victimization Survey (NCVS), the largest
household-interview crime survey in the country (administered by the
Bureau of the Census for the Bureau of Justice Statistics), reported
64,827 more rapes in 1991 than the UCR number: 171,420 rapes, or
469 rapes each day, nineteen each hour, or one every 3.5 minutes.
Between 1973 and 1987 the NCVS recorded 2.3 million rapes. "Thus,
in a fifteen-year period, the NCVS recorded almost 1 million more
cases of rape than the twenty-year UCR numbers."

The difference between the UCR and NCVS numbers suggests
that women may have been more willing to report rape in a Census
Bureau household-interview survey than they were to report to the
police, for obvious reasons. Reporting rape to the police sets in motion
an inexorable legal process that, despite some recent adjustments, all
too often puts the victim on trial.

These numbers are large enough. But the 1992 study *Rape in
America: A Report to the Nation,* conducted by the National Victim
Center and the Crime Victims Research and Treatment Center, noted
that only 16 percent of rapes were reported to the police. Buchwald et
al. point out that if "the Uniform Crime Report numbers represent only
one of about six rapes actually committed, the true number of rapes in
the United States each year is likely to be in the range of 639,500. *At
that rate over a twenty-year period, there would be more than 12 million
American women rape survivors.*" (Twenty-nine percent of all rapes

occur when the victim is less than eleven years old, and 32 percent occur when the victim is between the ages of eleven and seventeen.)

Twelve million women—61 percent of them under the age of seventeen? I find numbers this big carry little emotional punch. I know that each number from one to 12 million represents an individual woman or girl who has a face, a name, a family, a favorite book, a certain way of smiling. But I can't see the image of a single human face from a number. So I play games with other numbers to try to imagine the twenty-year accumulation of human beings like myself who live with rape. Twelve million women raped in twenty years is almost eleven times the number of U.S. military casualties (killed and wounded) in World War II. It is roughly thirty-four times the number of people in the United States who died of AIDS by 1995. It is approximately 21 percent of the 1994 population of the United States. Not really much help because I'm still looking at numbers, not at names or faces.

When I first visited the Vietnam War Memorial in Washington, D.C., I wept, although not a single name on that dark slab was one I knew. I realized as I followed the solemn line of visitors in front of me that we needed this gathering place, one that could translate our collective shame and guilt into a shared grief. In grieving we honored those who died and redeemed a part of ourselves. There are numbers here, but they are not abstract. They are real names engraved on dark stone, each one a human being without a life. In the descent, year by year, name by name, the shape and color of the wall itself brought me to mourning, to a loss I could finally embrace.

Perhaps it is unfair of me to evoke these deaths and this sacred place in an attempt to make the statistics on rape mean something. Still, the image of the wall comes to me. Taking the most conservative UCR figure for 1991 of 106,593 rapes, 48,458 more women were raped in this one year than American military personnel killed—58,135—during the entire Vietnam war. Picture the Vietnam War Memorial almost twice as long, and that's one year's record of reported rapes. If I combine the number of reported rapes in the UCR figures and the findings from the 1992 study by the National Victim Center and the Crime Victims

Research and Treatment Center that only one out of six rapes are reported to the police, the wall would need to be eleven times longer just to accommodate the names of women raped in 1991.

Wars end and memorials in stone are fitting. But rape goes on. Perhaps a memorial for rape needs to look more like the ever-escalating electronic tally of the national debt displayed on the side of a building on 42nd Street in Manhattan—digits changing every 3.5 minutes. And next to each number, a name.

■ ■ ■

I had no knowledge of these staggering numbers and no understanding of my hysteria while I was with my parents in Virginia, nor was I aware that my hysterical symptoms would evolve and change over time, filling every emotional niche in the world I inhabited. Articles like the one a friend sent me in 1990, Herman's excellent book, and studies that point to a biological basis of PTSD were still years off when I finally made the decision to return to Boston, six weeks after the rape.

Making that decision was peculiarly convoluted. I had no desire to leave. Although I did not feel safe, even with my father's loaded gun in plain view, my parents' love was soothing. I acted on the basis of how I thought I *would have acted* if I were still the woman who had been delighted by a bird's song that she'd never heard before. I felt that woman had been snuffed out like the wick of a candle, although I still hoped the candle could, in time, burn again. It was bewildering to decide anything now because the woman who had always made decisions seemed to be little more than a puff of smoke.

I thought of her—of myself before that terrible instant at the sink— as a character from a film. Her story—my life up until that moment— had a sequence, and I was caught up in the action. Then the film stopped. I remembered her story up until that moment, and I decided to imagine how it might go on. Acting *as if* I were she—although I didn't feel like her in the slightest—was the only available alternative to never leaving Mommy and Daddy again. What, then, would she do?

She would go on with her own life. She would be restless after six weeks of helping her mother rake leaves, six weeks of watching *Golden Girls* on television. Even as a child, she'd felt restless in November. The frogs that vaulted into the creek like acrobats through the summer and early fall had crawled into stiffening mud, and the patch of tiger lilies where she read on warm afternoons was a withered bog, good for nothing but getting chilled feet. Brittle and barren, the huckleberry patches and blackberry brambles were reminders of the season's stinginess. In November she wished she lived in town where she could play with her friends or hang out at the library. Back then, she could only imagine escape.

She was a grown-up now. Thirty-nine. She would be making plane reservations.

■ ■ ■

As the day of my flight approached, I found myself fantasizing about living with my parents permanently: making myself useful around the house, working as a secretary in town to cover expenses. I'd be there to take care of them in their old age. I pictured myself fixing them dinner, building fires in the fireplace on winter days, driving them to Florida for vacations. We'd be happy, the three of us. Then I would wonder: Who wanted to do these things, who wanted to stay with her parents forever?

I didn't know.

I began to feel in those last days with my parents that I had suffered a profound loss. It was like losing a sense that I had not known I possessed—a hidden sense—but one I'd used every waking moment of my life, like sight, only more important than sight. I was beginning to feel what was missing—the woman who had not been raped. I was acting as if I were that woman, but only out of habit, when I packed my bags for Boston and kissed my parents good-bye at the airport. I was not ready to accept her loss or mourn her passing.

She stowed her bags in the overhead compartment. She buckled her seat belt. She pulled out the copy of The New Yorker

*she'd bought in the airport terminal. She thumbed through it
for the cartoons, then started reading it cover to cover. She read
until she was thirty-five thousand feet up and an hour from
Boston. Then she looked out of the window. She could see the
brown earth below. All the trees down there are bare, she
thought. Then she thought, What movie am I in?*

It is humiliating to cry in public. I shoved on dark glasses, turned my
back to the aisle, and swallowed sounds. I wasn't her. She was a fiction.

The fear was unbearable, and soon modulated into a feeling of
intense sorrow. I longed for my mother and father until the longing
turned to bone-warping grief. Somewhere over Pennsylvania, I felt they
were dead. I was certain that they had been killed in a car crash on the
way home from the airport. I had lost them forever.

A frantic telephone call to Virginia from a phone booth in the
United terminal at Logan should have reassured me that my parents
were fine. Still, I felt I would never see them again. When I tearfully
confided this to the friend who picked me up at the airport, she got that
uncomfortable look on her face people get when they think they might
be dealing with someone who is insane.

■ ■ ■

I am sitting at Sara's kitchen table, going through my mail. I've been
back in Boston two hours. I cannot shake off the idea that I have lost
my parents, so I call them again. When I hear their voices, I want to go
home. I have nothing to say: Sara, I tell them, is fixing dinner. It's cold,
but Sara has built a fire in her sitting room fireplace. Very cozy. I tell
them I am glad to be back to my own life because I don't want to
worry them.

My parents are fine, I tell Sara, as if they are recovering from a serious illness. Sara fixes me a gin and tonic with a wedge of lime. My car
has been parked in her driveway for a month and a half. Tomorrow I
will drive thirty miles, alone, to a new apartment in Concord.

I sip my drink, open bills I cannot pay—the moving companies, the hospital emergency room, the phone company, Visa, American Express. A letter from the travel book publisher informing me, with deep regret, that she has hired another freelance writer to edit the book I was working on before the rape. A notice that I am to report for jury duty in two days and that failure to do so may result in a two-thousand-dollar fine. The rental agent writes that he is unable to return my security deposit. It must be applied to damages to the Boston apartment, as per paragraph 16 of the lease.

I open my bank statement—see hemorrhages of rent.

I come to an envelope from the clinic at the hospital. I assume it is a bill. "Here's another one," I say to Sara.

Trichomonas. The word crouches on the page. I say it out loud. Sara hurries to her bookshelf, returns with a *Merck Manual.* I understand what she is doing. She is trying to gain some small measure of control over this thing that keeps spinning out of control. She reads: "A flagellate protozoan, pear-shaped with four flagella anteriorly and a fifth embedded in an undulating membrane." I imagine swarms of these creatures inside me. The indignity—his filth alive and still inside my body. I remember the odor of his unwashed flesh, the taste of semen. I fish the wedge of lime out of my drink and chew it.

"Sounds worse than it is," Sara says, getting to the section on treatment. "Metronidazole, two grams orally once," Sara reads out loud, "will cure ninety-five percent of women submitting to initial treatment if sexual partners are treated simultaneously."

I feel the strangeness of the thought that the rapist was a "sexual partner."

I will get a prescription, stand in line at the drugstore, meet the eye of the pharmacist, swallow a pill, give another urine sample at the clinic. But will I ever forget the smell and taste of hate? Will I ever feel clean again?

I get up and walk over to the window. The contours of Sara's garden are lost in the dusky air of evening. The ornamental cherry trees that in summer screen her garden from her neighbor to the east are bare. I can see lights on in the neighbor's kitchen. "I have to stop by the clinic tomorrow morning anyway," I say. "For an AIDS test."

Sara stands beside me, puts her arm around my shoulder. I am grateful for her silence.

I wonder who I am, now that I am a grown-up woman with a life of her own.

FIVE

Under the Eaves

A presence of departed acts
at window and at door

EMILY DICKINSON

My new apartment consisted of three rooms in the attic of a sprawling Victorian house on a country lane near Concord, Massachusetts, only a few miles from Walden Pond and the site of Thoreau's drafty temple. Unlike the other houses on the quiet lane, which were white or weathered shingles, the house was painted pale yellow—with white trim—and had a graceful front porch that made me think of houses I'd seen in Charleston, South Carolina. All it needed was a swing.

The house was set close to the road, but three ancient oaks and a stone wall that ran along the lane gave a feeling of privacy. I felt the trees and the wall had once protected another, simpler dwelling, one that Thoreau might have passed on one of his solitary walks. Behind the house was a pond with a small sagging dock, and at least an acre of weeds and four of woods.

My apartment had been servants' quarters in the days when people didn't need to be rich to have them. It could be reached only by a stair-

74

way that coiled up through the interior of the house in that invisible way things connected with servants have a tendency to do. The narrow stairs began behind what seemed to be a closet door in the back hallway, two floors below, and ended a foot from my stove.

The rooms below mine—my landlords' domain—were generous and airy, with high ceilings and cherry wainscot that looked as if it had been polished faithfully for more than a hundred years. Lenore and Gary were in their mid-thirties and had a son in elementary school. They had bought the property several years earlier, when, as Lenore told me on my first visit, five days after the rape, their "ship had come in"—although from where I never knew. They had just completed remodeling the kitchen, constructing a solarium for their hot tub and a playroom for their son, Jason.

On the day Lenore showed me the attic, the thought did cross my mind that perhaps they could have bestowed some of the bounty from that ship on their rental unit. Under normal circumstances, I wouldn't have considered renting it, even if Lenore and Gary were asking a fair price and did not want both a security deposit and the first and last month's rent up front. The attic was barely insulated, the bathroom was little more than a closet, and the wooden floors had gaps between the boards where dirt had collected for decades. Even if the apartment had been splendid, the fact that it did not have its own private entrance would have eliminated it from serious consideration. Under normal circumstances, walking through someone else's home to get to my own would have fallen somewhere between awkward and unacceptable.

But the circumstances were anything but normal.

What I saw when I inspected these rooms for the first time, five days after my worst nightmare had come true, was not the bare lightbulbs dangling from the ceiling or the potential for confusions about the landlord-tenant relationship. I saw an aerie in the crown of a thorn tree. I saw everything with the eyes of a woman who had just been raped. As Lenore was apologizing for the dirty shower stall and the chips in the kitchen sink, I wasn't listening. I was thinking about the rapist—and what he would have to go through to get me.

He would have to drive more than thirty-five miles into the country and find this house on an unmarked road. He would have to contend with Lenore's three pet ducks, who had waddled up to my car the minute I turned the engine off and then followed me up the front walk, quacking. He would have to get inside the house without disturbing the dogs, two yippy Pekingese who had gone into fits of barking and growling when my foot hit the threshold. "Oh, I keep forgetting to feed those damned ducks," Lenore had said when she opened the door. Then, to the dogs, "Bad girls!" and to me, "I wouldn't try to pet them. Sometimes they bite."

Then he would have to extricate himself from Lenore's mother-in-law, Olivia, who had swooped in from somewhere and started talking a mile a minute while I was still shaking hands with Lenore. Lenore talked over her, as if she were not there, and then explained to me as I followed her to the back hall and up the stairs to see "the quarters," as she called them, that her mother-in-law was "nutty as a fruitcake."

"We never listen to her," Lenore had said.

Then there was the housekeeper (whose name I never did know), whom I'd seen thumping about in the living room with a vacuum cleaner. Lenore informed me that she came four days a week "to keep up with this enormous house," although it seemed to me the house was winning the race. I thought the place was a mess—even the grand staircase, fit for a descending Scarlett O'Hara, was littered with Jason's toys, stacks of newspapers, and piles of clothes. Lenore had apologized for the disorder. "We build this expensive playroom and he still throws things all over the place." She threw up her hands. "Kids. What can you do?"

Lenore, I'd learned, didn't work anymore. "I'm a lady of leisure now," she'd told me, "and loving it." Gary was "in the investment business" and usually got home around six P.M. for dinner. "If there's one thing I believe in, it's family time," Lenore had said.

If the rapist could, somehow, slip unnoticed into the back hall, he would have to know which one of the three doors led to the attic. He would probably open the closet door first because it was bigger. Or the door to the cellar. He would have to pick two dead-bolt locks, which Lenore agreed I could install on the door, at my own expense, if I decided to take the place. Then he would have to climb two flights of squeaky stairs.

"What do you think?" Lenore was saying after she'd finished apologizing for not having time to clean the apartment before my appointment. Olivia had crept upstairs from the kitchen below and was babbling away at my back. What do I think? I was thinking that the rapist would face a challenge. I was thinking about all the thorns on my tree.

"I'll take it," I said, never thinking that some of those thorns might prick me.

■ ■ ■

The day after I returned from Virginia I spent half the day in Boston—at the clinic where I waited two hours for an AIDS test. Then I drove alone to Concord, telling myself how unlikely it was that the rapist was killing me slowly with a virus. As it turned out, I was right. The results of that test and the two additional tests I felt compelled to take in 1986 were negative.

I had a key to a door at the back of the house that opened into the rear hallway, but after struggling with the stubborn lock for several minutes, I gave up and went around to the kitchen door. I'll have to fix that, I thought.

The ducks were paddling around on the pond, but the dogs were hysterical. I knocked, but no one answered. The garage doors were open, the garage empty. Then I banged on the door fairly hard. The latch gave way and the door swung open easily. It wasn't locked. "Hello?" I called. No one answered.

I hoisted my suitcase and scuttled through the kitchen to my door. The locksmith who had installed the bolt locks while I was in Virginia had taped a small brown envelope to the door. It contained my keys and his bill. I yanked it off. It was still sealed. Thank God, I thought, spinning around to scan the hallway for the intruder who might be inside the empty house with me. I tore open the envelope, fished out the keys, and unlocked the door. Then I lunged through it, slammed it, and locked it behind me. The envelope was sealed, I reminded myself as I started up the stairs. No way anyone could be in the attic. "Calm down," I said to myself, sternly and out loud.

I expected to find a scene very similar to the one I had left behind in Boston six weeks earlier—an infestation of cardboard boxes and great disorder. I would have to start unpacking again, just as I was doing that day. And I would remember what the act of making order had brought forth from the darkness. Lenore's open kitchen door had not helped matters.

But when I got to the top of the stairs and looked around, I choked up—not from fear, but from gratitude. My friends, who had offered to supervise the movers while I was recovering at my parents', had unpacked the boxes and carted them away. My furniture was arranged with care. My red teakettle sat on the stove and my dishes were stacked on the kitchen shelves. My friends had folded my clothes and tucked them in the dresser, hung towels in the bathroom. My bookshelves and desk had been reassembled and dusted. The boxes that were not unpacked—my books and papers—were stashed in the long closet under the eaves, out of sight. There was a note on the kitchen counter: "Welcome home!" And a postscript: "We threw away the broken stuff."

These are my things, I thought as I walked through the rooms, holding the note close to my chest, as if it were a sacred scroll.

■ ■ ■

At my request, my friends had also seen to it that the movers had disassembled and hidden the bed on which I was raped. This was not a simple thing to do, because the bed was not an ordinary bed. It belonged to my friend Pamela, whose husband had gone with me to the police station to file my report. It was big enough to hold all the mattresses required to prove that a real princess can, indeed, feel a pea at the bottom. The mahogany headboard and footboard, carved elaborately with rambling roses and butterflies, were towering, and the wood smelled of leather-bound books and beeswax. Pamela had slept in this marvelous contraption, once her grandmother's, throughout her childhood. After her marriage, the bed languished in storage until Pamela had the idea that I needed it. It was her way of comforting me. I was, at the time, getting over a love affair with a man who had an allergy to commitment. I'd finally had the strength to break off the relationship, but my self-esteem was at an all-time low.

"I loved that bed," Pamela told me. "You'll feel like a queen in it. I always did."

So I borrowed her magnificent bed.

But now the rapist had contaminated it. I felt I had stolen something from Pamela by being raped on her bed, that I had betrayed her memories of her childhood and our friendship. In a way, Pamela, too, had been raped. She didn't want the bed back, but it still had considerable financial value and we both, reluctantly, recognized this. I told her I would store it until we worked something out.

The movers could not get the frame that held the mattress up the narrow stairs to my attic. It had to be cut on two sides so it could be maneuvered around the second-floor landing. The pieces of the bed were pushed back under the eaves in a crawl space and covered with a sheet. I closed off the space, blocking the door with a bookcase. I never once looked under the sheet while I lived in Concord.

■ ■ ■

One of the saddest letters I received after my essay was published in 1994 was from a young woman who had been raped six years before, when she was seventeen. In longhand on yellow notebook paper she tracked each of her six anniversaries. She explained that she had recently started therapy and was beginning to be able to share her feelings with others, including her parents. "Still," she wrote, "it is hard for me to feel safe. I wonder if I will ever feel safe again." She closed her letter by saying that the anniversary of her rape is something she looks on as a bleak holiday. "Sometimes I simply check out for the day and sit in darkness—with my doors locked, and the guards in the basement of my building, the security cameras in the hallways, the doorman, the concierge. I pay a lot to feel safe."

The loss of the sense of safety is impossible to imagine when you still possess it, and nearly impossible to regain once you have lost it. The sense of safety is not at all like other senses—smell, taste, sight. It has no companions that can compensate for its absence. It stands alone, beneath, like the foundation below ground that supports a building. When the sense of safety and bodily autonomy has been destroyed, all that it supports crumbles. Its loss changes the relation between self and the world.

The need to feel safe can become an addiction that cannot be satisfied by external measures, although it takes many years to discover this. There will never be enough locks, security cameras, dogs, or doormen to satisfy the craving. When the sense of safety is destroyed, the temptation to construct it outside the self is itself the source of more addictions. You can spend a fortune and still find yourself sitting alone in the dark, trembling. Precautions, no matter how elaborate and sound, remain on the surface, like sargasso. No roots descend into the mysterious depths where the wreck truly lies.

■ ■ ■

"Be thou thine own home, and in thy self dwell," John Donne said. Good advice. But I could not dwell within myself as I once had. I was, I now understand, homeless. My history had been ruptured—the woman who had not been raped could never return, although I didn't know that when I walked up the stairs to my roost in Concord. And the woman who had been raped was only beginning to discover who she was. She began with a profound solicitude for *things*. Her things.

The rooms under the eaves became my new body inviolate. Its walls became flesh. Its contents, memories. Because this was all I could know of safety, these rooms became sacred and I tended them with reverence.

For several weeks I stayed locked up in my high fortress, leaving only to buy groceries and flowers. My loneliness passed for solitude, my solitude for joy. The flowers were an extravagance I could ill afford, as my funds were dwindling rapidly. Still, I bought dozens of long-stemmed yellow roses and gardenia blossoms that I put in a bowl beside the sofa bed where I now slept. I felt gardenias were protective—the floral equivalent of the vampire's poison, garlic. I so convinced myself that rapists would be driven off by the smell of gardenias that I actually slept peacefully through the night until their protection failed. This childlike thinking eventually robbed me of a small pleasure: I now associate the smell of gardenias with desperate unhappiness.

The yellow roses also had a magical property. I associated yellow roses with my mother. When I was four or five years old, my mother decided to make curtains for our living room. She couldn't afford store-bought drapes. I went with her when she selected the material, a thick cotton fabric with a pattern of yellow roses and leaves on a sage-colored background. She hated to sew and making the curtains was an ordeal sometimes punctuated by tears. It seemed to me to take forever for my mother to finish those curtains. Her black-and-gold Singer sewing machine rattled away for weeks. When they were finally hung, I thought they were the most elegant curtains I had ever seen.

I remember vividly putting the first dozen roses in an antique white pitcher I'd bought in a thrift shop in Harpers Ferry many years before. When I washed the pitcher, the image of the shop came back to me. I remembered how the floors squeaked as I wandered up and down the aisles, hoping to find a bargain. I remembered clearly, too, that the shop smelled of dusty upholstery, Johnson's paste wax, and faintly of stale beer. I'd discovered a fragment of myself in that vase, and when I finally arranged the roses, I had several fragments. It seemed a way to reach a past that I wanted to claim as my own.

I dusted, cleaned, and arranged my possessions, working carefully, like an archaeologist at an excavation site. I spent nearly two days deciding what to put on the small bookcase that now blocked the closet where the movers had hidden Pamela's bed. In the end, I put the Bible my father had given me when I was eighteen, a small bronze Buddha, and my collection of beach stones on the top shelf. I hung a framed botanical print of a lady's slipper, a flower that had given me delight as a child, over the bookcase and filled the two remaining shelves with poetry books—Stevens, Swenson, Merwin, Creeley, Rilke, Hopkins, Dickinson. I felt that these objects and the words in the books would hold back the dark memory behind the door, and it seemed at first they did.

Many of my things were gifts people had given me over the years. Each friend reentered my life through the object he or she had given me. I saw birthdays and film openings, Christmases. I polished my collection of wooden boxes, many of them gifts from my father. I cleaned pictures and hung them, took them down, rehung them. I considered myself fortunate that most of my possessions had still been in boxes when I was attacked. He hadn't seen them, or touched them. They had not been defiled.

Out of the days spent laboring to impart something of myself to the rooms, I began to remember whom I knew, whom I was related to, where I had been, what I had done in the time before the rape. The rooms began to take on an identity I could look at and recognize as my own, although something always seemed to be missing. But out of this almost mystical transformation a place I lived in was becoming my home. When I was in this dwelling, I felt safer than at any time since the rape. But I could not carry with me this sense of dwelling within myself. Forays into the outside world were excruciating encounters with vulnerability. I wanted to stay inside these rooms for the rest of my life—polishing and cleaning my things and the temple that held them.

Although this relation to things—the joys of the days and nights of seeing and touching objects that seemed to hold me with love—was not to last long, I often think of those merciful weeks and find myself wanting to add a sentence to newspaper accounts of a woman being raped in her home. It would say, "The victim's home was also destroyed in the attack."

■　■　■

But sacred objects can be dangerous, too. There came the day when my bookshelves were full and only two boxes remained unopened. The first was full of papers—unanswered letters, a folder of poems labeled "To Be Revised," a packet of my elementary-school report cards, and a bundle of love letters from my first boyfriend, Joey, who lived down the road when I was nine. His parents were divorced. It made him seem worldly, to have divorced parents, although I never had the nerve to ask him what it was like to have his mother live in another state. We planned to marry and live in a log cabin we were going to build ourselves. When his father, who was in the military, was transferred, we wrote for a few months. His letters were mostly drawings of our cabin-to-be, or of the creek where we had played, or of my dog, Poncho. A few words. "How are you? I am okay, I guess."

I read everything that had been in the unopened boxes—Joey's letters; my report cards (where "talks too much in class" was a frequent complaint); the poems in the folder, which have not, to this day, been revised; and the unanswered letters that I would not be able to answer because I would have to put into words what had happened to me. I read with the dedication of a biographer.

I finally came to the last box. It was late afternoon and a chicken was roasting in the oven, a bottle of wine chilling in the refrigerator. I'd set the table with my mother's china, a silver candlestick, and a white linen napkin. Vivaldi's *Four Seasons* was blasting out of my speakers.

The last box was heavy. Books, I guessed, as my compact edition of the *Oxford English Dictionary* was still missing. It was there, at the bottom, with the magnifying glass, an old friend. But on top of it was something wrapped carelessly in newspaper, as if whoever wrapped it up had been in a hurry. When I picked it up it felt like bones. Inside were the fragments of the wooden jewelry box my father had made for me and that the rapist had smashed. But there was something else that made me feel I had unwrapped a piece of plutonium. It was a pair of underpants. Mine. The ones I was wearing on October 11. The ones I could not find, that I thought the rapist had stolen.

I stood up slowly, as if not to wake the forces that I had unwrapped,

83

and went to the kitchen for a baking sheet, a can of lighter fluid, a box of long kitchen matches, and a soup spoon. I put the newspaper and its contents on the tray and slipped down the stairs and out the back hallway door. I carried everything outside to a corner of the garden near the pond where the ducks were gliding on the dark, still water. I placed the wood and the underpants on top of the newspaper, doused them with lighter fluid, and struck a match. I watched what happened.

Then I imagined the worst thing I have ever imagined: the man who had raped me burning up alive. I imagined his screams of agony, his hideous pain. I saw the fat under his dirty skin crackling in the flames. A terrible pleasure consumed me. "Die," I said, over and over.

Until this moment, I had not allowed myself to feel my hatred. Now my body felt huge and powerful. It felt good to be a monster, very good. My mind—all thoughts and feelings—seemed to vanish into the pleasure of the pain I gave him. His pain, my pleasure made a perfect desolation. I relished it.

The fire died. I dug a hole in the hard ground with the soup spoon, buried the ashes, and covered the spot with several large stones I lifted out of the creek. I walked to the trash cans near the garage and threw the spoon and the tray away. Then I went back upstairs, washed my hands, opened the wine, and lit the taper in the silver candlestick. I made a salad and boiled tiny potatoes. I sat down to a lovely dinner just as the light drained from the sky.

I thought I was fine now that I had killed my underpants.

■ ■ ■

In 1995 I ran across an article about a young man who had participated in the gang rape of a middle-aged woman. He said he was haunted by flashbacks of the attack, but that the images he saw were not of the woman. "It's just dark, and I'm the only one there," he said. "It's just dark. Dark, dark."

In that brief madness in the garden, I felt the darkness this young man described. I had no inkling that the bizarre and hideous rites I had just performed were a version of the rapist's story or that the hatred I'd felt for him would slowly infect my spirit. That hatred did not disappear, but it never presented itself again in such a pure form. Rather, it submerged and began to mutate in ways that made it impossible for me to recognize it for many years.

■ ■ ■

I did not tell Lenore that I had been raped when I was interviewed for the apartment. I was convinced she and Gary wouldn't rent to me if they knew. This made it difficult for me to ask Lenore about why the kitchen door had been left open the day I arrived.

I fretted about this for three weeks. I'd managed to slip in and out of the house without being noticed on the few occasions I'd left my sanctuary, but one morning Lenore cornered me as I was heading out for groceries. She invited me into the kitchen, and I could see no graceful way to decline. Olivia, who was sitting at the kitchen eating breakfast, immediately launched into one of her incoherent soliloquies, oblivious to the fact that her mouth was full of shredded wheat. Offering me a cup of coffee and a chair, both of which I declined, Lenore remarked on the fact that she hadn't seen much of me since I moved in. Busy, I mumbled. Then, to my horror, she requested a set of keys to my apartment—in case of emergencies. I had not anticipated this development. I inquired into the nature of such emergencies.

"Well, fire," she said. "I realized the other day that the only way out of the attic is the stairway. We really need to get one of those rope fire ladders—so you could get out of a window up there if the house caught on fire, God forbid."

I didn't want Lenore to have a set of keys, but I felt trapped by the reasonableness of her concern and my fear of irritating her and risking the loss of the only place I felt safe. I told her I'd make copies of my keys while I was out and drop them by that afternoon. I spent the rest of the morning, as I scurried from the grocery store to the hardware store, figuring out how I could find a way to broach the subject of why my keys were to be treated with the utmost respect. I decided that I had no choice but to tell her I'd been raped.

It isn't easy to sound casual saying, "Oh, by the way, since I was raped a couple of months ago, I'd appreciate it if you kept my keys in a safe place," but I tried when I delivered the keys to her that afternoon. Mercifully, Olivia was taking a nap.

Lenore looked stunned at my announcement but finally blurted out a response. "How utterly ghastly," she said.

"Yes," I replied.

"Did they catch him?"

"No."

"I don't even know where the key to the kitchen door is. We never lock it." So the open door on the day of my arrival was not careless, but habitual.

Her eight-year-old son came into the kitchen then, lugging his schoolbooks. Jason flopped down at the kitchen table, shoving aside the breakfast dishes that had not yet been washed, and started his homework.

"Where were you living, when…" Lenore glanced toward Jason.

"In Boston," I said.

"Oh," Lenore said, as if my choice of residence explained it away. "We never worry about crime. I mean the worst thing that happens around here is someone runs a stop sign." She laughed.

We stood in awkward silence for a moment. "Well, thanks for the keys," she said, dropping them into a pewter mug and putting the mug on the cluttered mantel over the kitchen fireplace. I turned to leave, saying something encouraging to Jason, who, tongue out and sighing repeatedly, was attacking his notebook paper with an eraser.

"I'm just curious," she said, "I mean, you know, if you knew him and whether he might…"

"He was a stranger. The police assured me it was an opportunistic thing. My phone's unlisted. There's no danger of him finding me again." I wondered then who I was reassuring. "It was just a case of being at the wrong place at the wrong time. That's what the police said." Jason looked up for a moment, caught my eye, and looked away.

"Where were you?" she asked.

"At home."

▪ ▪ ▪

A few days later I was writing an entry in my journal when what was probably inevitable happened.

Writing in my journal, which increasingly I was able to do again, seemed to calm me, although I did not write often about my feelings. I wrote about the changes in the season, the view from my kitchen window of the pond—and endlessly about what I had cleaned, where I had put things. I wrote in longhand with an ink pen, although I had previously typed my journals on an old electric typewriter whose motor seemed to be straining to keep up with the keys. I liked the scratching noise my pen made on the paper and the way words looked in my own hand, the way my hand looked holding the pen. I liked the silence of the words as they came into being. I took care with my handwriting and formed each letter carefully. I usually wrote in the late afternoon, about the time the rape had occurred, because I was most anxious at that time of day. I sat at a round, antique wooden table tucked in under the eaves in my bedroom, rather than at my desk in the other room. It had taken me two weeks to create the right place for this activity. Only my journal, my pen, a lamp, and a bud vase were kept on the table. It was an altar within the refuge of the rooms, and even when I could not write, seeing that altar was a reminder that I once had, and might again.

Before settling down with my journal that afternoon, I'd stood for a long time in the dormer window in my bedroom watching snow fall. The house below was quiet. Lenore and Olivia, I assumed, had gone out and not yet returned, as the driveway had vanished under an inch of snow and showed no signs of tire tracks.

I wrote, and as I was writing I heard a sound I had not heard before—first one, and then another bolt lock on the door at the foot of the stairs sliding into metal sleeves. Then I heard the door open and close. No one called up. No explanation presented itself except the worst one: The rapist was returning. He had tracked me, let himself into the house through the kitchen door that Lenore saw no need to lock. This was now confirmed by the sound of the stealthy footsteps on the squeaky stairs. I waited, submerged in terror. Then the terror turned to rage. I flew into the kitchen, grabbed my chef's knife, spun around, and got to the top of the stairs just as a head emerged from the shadows at the turn of the stairs, five steps below me.

What Jason and his school chum saw when they rounded that corner—a woman in a green bathrobe held together by safety pins, crouched at the top of the stairs with a chef's knife in her hand—has been a source of comic relief for me for some years since. Once, when I was hiking with Steve in the Grand Canyon, a pair of bighorn sheep suddenly leapt onto the narrow trail in front of us and thundered toward us. We had the drop into the canyon on one side, a cliff face on the other. We pressed our backs against the cliff, sucked in our stomachs, and held our breath as they hurtled past us. They *were* bighorn sheep taking a short cut, but I saw something else. I saw two enormous beasts, each with a single horn at least ten feet long in the center of his forehead, a cross between a unicorn and a rhinoceros with hair. Perhaps that afternoon Jason and his friend did not see a woman in a green bathrobe on the stairs. Perhaps they saw a green-skinned monster, brandishing a sword and thundering: "How dare you come into this place?"

To a person whose hinges are all intact, a little boy wanting to spy on a new tenant, indulging curiosity that may have been stimulated by the allure of forbidden keys in the bottom of a pewter mug, the encouragement of a buddy, and talk of police, might not come as a surprise. Such a person might be amused or slightly irritated, might, if she was fond of children and a little lonely, bring out cookies or a game of checkers. Might take the intrusion as an opportunity to provide a lesson in why it is important to respect others' privacy. But that wasn't me. Not then.

My attic was, until that moment, my outer skin. Inside my rooms,

I could be white and soft as a grub. I had no inner perimeters—no assumptions of invulnerability that could serve as boundaries between me and the unpredictable, threat-laden world outside. Experience of the world of the rape formed my entire conception of reality. Thirty-nine years of previous experience, when the last thought in my mind would have been a rapist sneaking up the stairs, was discarded, a dry and brittle shell that I could never wear again.

■ ■ ■

"You're overreacting." I was on the telephone that night with a girl-friend, sobbing my way through the Jason story. It was after midnight.

"Overreacting?" I repeated the word several times, as if it were a word in a foreign language.

"It's been over two months," she said. "It's time you got a job and stopped dwelling on what happened. It's over and done with." It wasn't, but her saying it made me feel that she was right—I should be done with it. I can trace to this moment the first time I was aware that I hated myself—because I was dwelling on what happened, because I was overreacting. The rapist had planted the seed of this self-hatred and my solitude, like a drought, had kept that seed dormant. But now the rains had to come.

"What are you going to do about money?" my friend continued. It was true. I was broke.

"I don't know," I said.

"You haven't even thought about it? How are you going to pay back all the money you've borrowed? It's not like you not to be think-ing about these things."

"I know," I said, but wondered who she was talking about.

"You've just got to put it out of your mind," she said. I noticed that she had not used the word *rape* once. "What other choice have you got?"

I had no response, nor did my friend want one.

Overreaction was to become a way of life.

■ ■ ■

Jason did not mention to his mother what I hoped was an experience that would give him nightmares for years. "Kids!" she said when I told her. "What can you do?"

"I'd like my keys back because my privacy is important to me. I think it's a good idea to get that escape ladder, and of course, with the proper notice I would be happy to let you into the apartment for an inspection." I tried to appear comfortable with this attempt to protect myself, but inside I was shaking.

"I gather you don't like kids," Lenore said, reaching for the pewter mug.

"Kids," I repeated. Then, smiling my friendliest smile, I added, "What can you do?"

Lenore said no more. "Thank you," I said when I felt the keys in my palm. Lenore wasn't smiling when I left.

■ ■ ■

Here is a story about underpants from an April 19, 1996, Associated Press article. A man named Kerry Kotler, convicted of twice raping a thirty-four-year-old Long Island mother of three, spent eleven years in prison. Then he was released. Now he might go back to prison again.

The name of the woman Kotler was convicted of raping twice was not used in the article. She is called "the victim." I want to give her a name, a face, a history. Whenever I see the words *the victim,* I want to fill in the blank. It is enough, I remind myself, to remember that she is not a blank. I know there is a good reason for the missing name. It protects her. The fact that this protection is necessary is proof, if ever one was needed, that there is still a widespread stigma for victims of rape, a stigma that is reinforced by the accumulation of unnamed names in our newspapers.

This shroud of secrecy is a matter of law only in a few states. The policy is basically social—77 percent of news organizations polled in 1991 by *Newsweek* thought that the media should not disclose rape victims' names. One of the nation's most highly regarded newspapers, the *New York Times,* was widely criticized for printing the name of William Kennedy Smith's accuser, Patricia Bowman, after NBC News identified her (without her consent) in a broadcast—and for publishing a tawdry profile that discussed her "wild streak" in high school, her mother's divorce and remarriage, and her barhopping. Unless a woman is on the Vatican's short list for sainthood, public exposure can be brutal.

The compulsion to discredit the victim, rather than to witness her pain, is almost irresistible—even in a victim's immediate circle. A few months after my rape, for example, someone I knew slightly suggested that perhaps I was raped because I had "bad karma" from a "previous life." Another person—a colleague—suggested that I had not been happy with my consulting contract in Maine and had returned to Boston with a "negative attitude" that might have "attracted" more "negativity." True, I wasn't happy with my work in Maine. Yes, I was discouraged by the experience and returned to Boston dejected. These facts were undeniable. But did they make the rape my fault? There was even the suggestion from a close friend (a friend no longer) that I had "asked for it" by moving into an apartment that was in a working-class neighborhood. What would I have heard if I had gotten drunk and been raped in a bar, like the woman who was attacked by four men in New Bedford, Massachusetts, in 1983 (the movie *The Accused* was based on her story), or raped by a blind date after agreeing to a nightcap in his apartment?

The issue of privacy in rape cases is an emotional one that divides journalists, law-enforcement officials, feminists, and rape victims themselves. Some argue that lifting the shroud of secrecy will remove the stigma by treating rape for the crime it is—a crime of violence, just like murder. Others believe that "forced disclosure" is a re-creation of the trauma of the rape and that it harms victims by reinforcing their feelings of helplessness and powerlessness. Nancy Ziegenmeyer, a rape victim who decided to disclose her name for a Pulitzer Prize–winning series published in the *Des Moines Register* in 1991, believes that going public should always be the victim's choice. I agree. Social attitudes need to change, but the pain of that change should not be inflicted on those who already suffer from the lifelong wounds of rape. According to an article in the April 29, 1991, issue of *Newsweek,* 60 percent of rape victims experience post-traumatic stress syndrome, the highest percentage of any crime. (The Crime Victims Research Center put the figure at half that—31 percent—in a 1992 report.) Kerry Kotler's victim, "the victim," is a woman with a name—and a legacy of terror. Both belong to her.

Her story is convoluted. In 1978 a man raped her at knife-point in her home on Long Island. Three years later, in 1981, he returned. "I'm back," he said. "Let's do it again." After the second attack, the victim picked Kerry Kotler out of a police file—he was now on probation for statutory rape—and then listened to a voice-identification lineup. When Kotler said, "I'm back," she collapsed on the floor. She was, the county district attorney is quoted as saying, "one of the most believable, compelling victims I had ever come across." After a trial, Kotler was convicted of both rapes and sentenced to twenty-one to forty-five years in prison.

The police kept the underpants the victim was wearing the second time she was raped in an evidence storage room. Kotler had served eight years of his sentence when DNA experts Barry Scheck and Peter Neufeld, who would use their expertise to help free a more famous client, O. J. Simpson, a few years later, decide to take on his case. Because DNA testing had not been used in criminal cases when Kotler was convicted in the early 1980s, Scheck and Neufeld think they can get him off by introducing evidence from DNA testing of semen stains on the victim's underpants. They argue that these DNA results should be considered new evidence, entitling Kotler to a retrial.

The underpants are tested and the results appear to exclude Kotler. The prosecutors argue that the DNA has been contaminated during storage, but they can't explain how. Although Kotler's conviction was based on a body of evidence that was strong enough, without DNA, for a jury to find him guilty of both rapes, a judge decides that the DNA tests (conducted eleven years later) entitle Kotler to a new trial or dismissal of the charges.

By now, the victim had moved out of state and "was reluctant to testify again." The D.A. "grudgingly" dropped the charges against Kotler, who then filed a wrongful-imprisonment lawsuit. A judge supported the lawsuit.

Scheck and Neufeld have a black-tie banquet, invite defense attorneys. When Kotler arrives they give him a standing ovation. Kotler is one of the first prisoners in the United States to be freed because of DNA technology.

Three and a half years after his black-tie party, Kotler, posing as a police officer, forces a twenty-year-old college student ("the victim") off a Long Island highway. After he has raped her, he douches her vagina with a plastic water bottle "to eliminate evidence"—the DNA in semen. The victim, however, remembers part of the license plate number. The car belongs to Kotler's girlfriend. There are hairs on the victim's clothes that match hairs in the car that match hairs on the girlfriend's dog. But even more to the point, there is semen on her clothes. "Five unique DNA markers from the semen matched markers from Kotler's blood, and the odds that the semen came from someone other than Kotler are just 1 in 7.5 million," the prosecutor states. The defense lawyers' strategy, the article concludes, will be to discredit the reliability of the DNA evidence.

According to a July 19, 1997, article in the *New York Times,* DNA evidence didn't get Kotler out of prison this time—it helped send him back. On July 18, 1997, he was convicted of the forcible rape of the college student, who wept "tears of joy" when the verdict was handed down. "The victim," however, may not want to celebrate this outcome just yet. Three weeks before his conviction, Kotler was awarded $1.5 million in his earlier wrongful imprisonment lawsuit, enough to pay for an appeal. So this case has certainly given me little comfort—and not nearly enough for me to be sorry about burning those underpants back in 1985.

Patch Work

i turn from her, shivering
to begin another afternoon
of rescue, rescue.

LUCILLE CLIFTON,
"trying to understand this life"

Concord, Massachusetts, January 11, 1986

Three months. So hard to write here. This morning was my first session with Gunilla Jainchill. I told her everything that happened during the rape. I cried the whole time.

Took a nap this afternoon, but was troubled by a dream: I had lost a tooth and was trying to keep it in my mouth, set it back in place, thinking if I could, it would take root again. But the gum around it was too abused and it fell out. Then I heard Mother calling my name, and try to find her. But I am in a dark place and can't find my way out. I wake up, crying for her.

The incident with Jason seemed to hurl me backwards into the days immediately after the rape. I was unable to sleep, and exhaustion and anxiety hobbled me once again. My friend's observation that I was "overreacting" and her bafflement at my inability to protect myself from my landlord's presumptions gave me a small window on just how unhinged I had become. Lenore began to ask me to baby-sit Jason or keep my eye on Olivia when she had to run an errand, and each request she made, although denied, presented itself as a painful intrusion that often sent me to bed in tears. Lenore seemed unable to understand that the hefty check I wrote out every month for the "quarters" meant, for example, that I was under no obligation to turn over the use of one of the closets under the eaves when she decided it would be a good place to store winter clothes. I felt violated and abused—and powerless. I was not handling matters the way the woman my friends remembered would have handled them, and they were mystified. Their confusion added to my fear that I was having a complete mental breakdown. I knew I needed help.

Soon after the incident with Jason, I found myself on the telephone with a therapist in Cambridge. I had been told by someone that she had experience in treating rape victims. It took me a long time to work up the nerve to make the call, and I was upset when—after I explained my situation—she informed me that unfortunately she was completely booked up.

"My husband is also a therapist and is available," she said.

I didn't like the idea of seeing a male therapist. But perhaps, I thought, I needed to see a man. "Has he treated women like me?" It was still hard for me to say the word *rape*.

"No, but he's very interested."

"Where is his office?" I asked, hoping she would say it was in Boston so I would have an excuse not to call him. I had ruled out seeing a therapist in the city.

"Actually, he's out your way. He works out of our home."

I wrote down his name and phone number and called him immediately, ignoring my reservations. I was numb when I made the appointment and wrote down complicated directions to his house, which was, my map confirmed, in the middle of nowhere.

But my numbness soon gave way to anxiety and dread. Alone with a strange man who lived in the middle of nowhere? Teaching him about rape? I was, I thought, asking for trouble. An image of this man and his house began to form in my mind; years later, when I saw the film *The Silence of the Lambs*, I felt like I'd designed the stage set used for the terrible final scenes in the killer's basement. Despite my fear, I seemed unable to act on my intuition that seeing a therapist who had no experience with rape victims probably wasn't a good idea.

But the day before my appointment, I woke up to what I interpreted as a terrible warning. Lenore and Gary had never gotten around to building a coop for the ducks—the only place they had out of the weather was the space under the kitchen porch, where they were occasionally fed. I had spent many contented hours sitting at a café table in my kitchen dormer watching the ducks on the pond below. They were especially beautiful at dusk, when the sky behind the bare alders dimmed and the pond was still. They were so white then, so at home on the dark water. On several occasions that autumn, I'd watched small flocks of wild Canada geese take over the pond for a few hours. The ducks quacked and raised themselves up in the water, flapping their wings in what I assumed was irritation. But perhaps it was envy.

After the first heavy snow, I started worrying about the ducks. When the temperature dropped sharply I noticed that the snow was collecting on the edges of the pond and that the circle of open water was shrinking every day. I decided to talk to Lenore.

Lenore explained that she had gotten the ducks for Jason the previous Easter. It was his responsibility to feed them, but he often forgot. "I'm trying to teach him to take some responsibility around here," Lenore said when I remarked that the ducks were often up in the yard, begging for food. "If I feed them, how will he learn? Besides, if he forgets, there's stuff in the pond." As diplomatically as possible I pointed out that the "stuff in the pond" was rapidly vanishing under a sheet of ice.

"Don't you think they need protection for the winter?" I asked, pointing out that they were vulnerable to predators out in the open.

"Oh, no," she said. "They can just fly south like those geese." I informed her that Jason's ducks were domestic and didn't know how to migrate—even if they could fly. This, to my dismay, was news to her.

It did not look good for the ducks.

I asked her if she would mind if I made an inquiry at a farm down the road about boarding the ducks for the winter. She hesitated. I offered to pay. "Okay," she said.

■ ■ ■

"Sorry, lady—got too many ducks as it is," the man at the farm said when I tried to cut a deal. The elevated coop he had built for his fowl was not only sturdy, but it was secured by a wire fence. I asked him for suggestions. He shook his head. I must have looked upset because then he offered a country comfort—of sorts. "Foxes gotta eat, too, you know."

A few days later the temperature plunged. The ducks, through some remnant of instinct, had tried to keep the circle of open water in the middle, and deepest, part of the pond free of ice by obsessive, and what seemed to me desperate, paddling. But the ice thickened and the circle of dark water grew smaller.

When I scraped the razor-thin coat of ice from my kitchen window the day before I was to keep my appointment with the therapist, the world below was white and featureless from a snowstorm that had struck in the night. Except for the center of the pond.

It was red.

■ ■ ■

With this image of slaughter still haunting me, I telephoned the therapist a few hours later, after I had smoked nearly half a pack of cigarettes. "I'm sorry, but I'm going to have to cancel our appointment," I said.

"And why might that be?" he replied. He did not sound pleased.

"I'm just not comfortable with…" I paused, unsure of myself. My palms were clammy. "With where you are," I blurted out.

97

"I gave you perfectly good directions," he said. "And there are maps."

"Yes, but, well..." I hesitated again. "It doesn't feel safe."

He was silent for a moment. I could hear him breathing. "Dealing with problems doesn't usually feel safe," he finally said. "Have you ever been in therapy before?"

"No," I admitted. Then I remembered—I had gone to see someone for a short time in my late twenties after my brother died. I quickly corrected myself.

"Uh-huh," he said. Then nothing more.

"I just feel it's too far for me to drive," I repeated.

"You knew that a week ago," he replied.

I hate you already, I thought. "I'm sorry," I said meekly.

"I require at least five days' notice for canceled appointments," he said. "You might as well come because I'm going to bill you for the session anyway."

His bullying didn't make me angry. It terrified me.

"Send me the bill, then," I said. Then I slammed the phone back into its cradle and crawled back into bed.

■ ■ ■

A week later, a friend who taught at Harvard called me to say she'd spoken to someone in the psychiatry department at a dinner party and had a name for me: Gunilla Jainchill, a clinical instructor in psychiatry at the Harvard Medical School. "She sounds perfect," my friend said. "She's expecting her fourth child and is on sabbatical this year. But she sees a few patients."

"Where's her office?" I asked.

"She's working out of her home. It's in Brookline."

"I don't know," I said.

"She has experience with treating women who have gone through what you've gone through," my friend said delicately.

"Oh," I said.

"Call her."

■ ■ ■

Gunilla Jainchill was my age and spoke with a heavy Swedish accent, although her command of the English language was masterful. She looked as if she had just stepped out of an Ingmar Bergman film. She was six months pregnant when I started seeing her, and her pregnancy gave her a serene seriousness that nevertheless turned easily to laughter.

Her approach was practical: She focused on things I could do to get back a feeling of control and self-confidence. We spent many sessions rehearsing what I might say to Lenore the next time she asked me to look after Jason. She gave me permission to ignore Olivia, who, whenever she could catch me, followed me out of the house to my car, talking at her usual breakneck pace. She helped me draft a letter to the cousin who had criticized me for seeing a therapist.

We spent many sessions discussing what I should do about work. I did not have the self-confidence or energy to resume my former freelance business. I couldn't write, and the idea of tackling another documentary film filled me with anxiety. Gunilla suggested I might consider starting with a part-time clerical job. Start small, she advised. And feel good about the baby steps. She encouraged me to eat properly and to exercise. She recommended novels and music. Sometimes we did not talk about me at all. We talked about history or literature or something we had both read in the paper. Sometimes I wept for the silence of God, and somehow she reminded me that this silence was also God.

Her home soon became another refuge, and I looked forward to our meetings. I was fortunate that she was willing to see me despite the fact that I could not pay her immediately. I was applying for victim assistance funds from the state, and she understood the process was lengthy and complicated. She trusted that I would pay her when I could. Her methods were skillful and unconventional, I later realized, as was our relationship, which soon evolved into a mutually rewarding friendship. She was the first friend I made in my new life—the one that began October 11, 1985. She is a dear friend still. Unlike everyone else in my life, Gunilla did not measure me against the woman who had died that day.

I do not remember now the content of our conversations, but what I do remember vividly was the feeling of connection with the textures of ordinary life and friendship, and it was here that I felt resonances within. I remember how her dog, a big fluffy-haired mutt, greeted me at the door, his tail thrashing in what I felt was joy. "Oh, how he likes you!" Gunilla would exclaim, pleased. I remember the way the light fell through the window behind her chair into an aquarium of bright tropical fish. Sometimes, while we talked, her two young sons waved to us from the driveway as they scampered off to the playground with the housekeeper, a grandmotherly Irish woman who offered me hot tea and cookies on especially cold days. When spring came, we sometimes sat on her back porch in wicker chairs with the dog curled up at our feet. I remember especially how clean her baby smelled when I saw him for the first time, the sweet scent of innocence and of hope.

■ ■ ■

It is Memorial Day Weekend 1986. I am sitting at my desk in the attic. It is untidy, littered with official papers and forms. I reread the explanation of the state of Massachusetts's Victim Compensation Program:

WHAT DOES COMPENSATION COVER?

a) Out-of-pocket losses over $100 for medical expenses and costs of necessary services resulting from personal injury or death.
b) Loss of wages provided there was a loss of two continuous weeks of earnings or support.
c) In the case of rape, out-of-pocket losses eligible for compensation shall include counseling and emergency funds for housing or moving expenses but shall not include funds for abortion or counseling for abortion.

Sorry, girls. If you're pregnant, we can't help you. If you can't afford an abortion, we'll just put you on welfare after you have the baby. No problemo.

I reread my documentation—thirty-five pages with all attachments. Copies of bills and the checks I wrote to pay them. Leases. A letter from Gunilla documenting her treatments. The rapist cost me more than eight thousand dollars in the first few months.

I owe Gunilla more than two thousand dollars after insurance. I think how grateful I am to her for waiting so many months for me to get on my feet financially. I am lucky now—to be working at Harvard's Graduate School of Design as a development officer, so I can pay her. I'm lucky, too, that I have had eighteen years of education so I can supply all the information required.

I am trying to concentrate on the Defendant's Interrogatories. My anger is a handicap. I go outside and sit in an old wooden chair on the dock. I think how happy the ducks would be today. The sun is warm and the pond is teeming again with life—frogs and water bugs.

When I think I am better, I go back to my desk. Thirteen questions. "Each question must be answered in writing. Within thirty days after you receive these questions you must mail your written answers to the court and mail a copy to the Attorney General. If you fail to send answers within the time allowed, your claim may be dismissed."

I am not better. I am furious. I want to overturn my desk, throw my dishes against the wall. I am so angry that I must remember like this, question by question, as if it were possible to describe. I want to write, "I am living in his hell. What more do you want to know? It cost me $8,166.35 room and board in the first four months. Please send a check to 'The Victim,' Hell. Zip 66666. P.S. I can pay my own way now."

Questions 2 and 7 are the hard ones. The others ask for lists—out-of-pocket expenses, all reimbursements from insurance. A few request information about witnesses, identity of offender, involvement of the police. Easy to answer those. Should I write "N/A" for "Not Applicable"?

2. Describe fully and completely how you were injured, including as part of your answer the date, place, time and a description of the incident which caused you to be injured.

7. With reference to your injuries, please state:
   a) the nature and extent of your injuries;
   b) the names and addresses of your physicians or physician;
   c) the date and nature of each treatment;
   d) the amount of physicians' bills and charges;
   e) if you required x-rays, please state the date thereof;
   f) if you required treatment at a hospital, please state the name and address, date of admission, date of discharge, treatment received and the total amounts of the hospital bill.

I begin to write. One paragraph for Question 2. "Just the facts, ma'am." The offender did this, did that. Injuries listed: multiple bruises, strained muscles (neck, shoulders, legs) sore/swollen right eye, vaginal tears. I look up *tear* in the dictionary. It seems odd suddenly that tears, as in crying, and tears, as in ripping, are spelled the same way. Then I write, "In addition to these physical injuries, I have suffered psychological problems since this attack that affect the quality of my day-to-day life." Appropriate understatement.

I spend all weekend answering the questions. Seven single-space pages, plus a two-page attachment: "Explanation of Lost Earnings." When I am done, I get drunk on Canadian whiskey. I put Aretha Franklin on my old turntable, weave around my rooms dancing, like a top losing spin. "R-e-s-p-e-c-t."

■ ■ ■

I am on the telephone with an official from the attorney general's office. My attic is sweltering in the July heat because the air-conditioner Lenore installed has broken—again. They are processing my resubmission of the interrogatories and my documentation. She is sorry for the bureaucratic glitch that sent my materials to the wrong office.

Sorry that it took them two months to notify me that my claim, having reached her office after the thirty-day deadline, was rejected. She has read my answers to the questions and everything appears to be in order. We discuss procedures. I should be realistic. Six months at least. A court appearance may be necessary if my claim is denied after the investigation. If so, I will need to hire a lawyer. She apologizes again for the mix-up. "I didn't realize," she concludes, "it was such a bad rape." I do not know what to say. I think perhaps I have exaggerated. That I am getting into this victim thing big time.

When I hang up, I feel ashamed for making my rape sound so bad when I know how lucky I am—not to be disfigured, brain-damaged, paralyzed.

■ ■ ■

After the first winter in my attic, I decided that I had to do something about the floor. Decades of dirt had been ground down into the cracks between the boards, some of which were nearly half an inch wide. No matter how often I washed them, they left my socks black with grime. Despite its greasy texture, this dirt still released particles of dust that swam in shafts of sunlight and settled on everything. The cracked and irregular boards were the color of marsh mud at low tide and seemed to suck in the light. And somehow the floor released great updrafts of cold air that had the musty smell of a crypt.

My offer to pay for the necessary materials dissolved Lenore's initial resistance to the idea of my painting the attic floors. She agreed that they were of such poor quality that sanding and refinishing the wood would be a waste of money she did not, in any case, want to spend. With her blessing, I spent several weekends in mid-August in the paint store, selecting colors. For two weeks I tested them on the boards in my bedroom. I finally settled on a gray so pale it looked white in the can. And on the highest gloss I could find. I wanted light, and I wanted the light to dance.

I had not slept well since the incident with Jason—for nine months my body continued to dump chemicals into my bloodstream that kept me in a state of high vigilance. Sleep had become a dangerous necessity. When I did sleep, I had nightmares. But the day I started working on the floors, I slept soundly through the night for the first time and my nightmares stopped.

I started in the kitchen in early September. With a sharp knife, I dug out the dirt between the boards and sucked it up with the vacuum cleaner. Then with a stiff, wet brush I scrubbed the cracks, let them dry, and filled them with wood putty. When the putty was dry, I sanded the boards by hand. Working every evening during the week and both days on the weekends, I slowly and carefully worked my way through the kitchen to the refrigerator, which, because of the slanted walls, was located against the central shaft of the chimney, across the room from the sink and stove. When I moved it away from the wall, I was shocked at what I found under the wads of greasy dust: a hole that was ten inches long and five inches wide. A slick of dead air oozed from it. Dropping a penny into the chasm to see just how deep it was, I heard nothing for three floors, until faintly I heard the penny hit the concrete floor of the basement. In this shaft the beam of my flashlight illuminated nests of spiders, solving another mystery that had plagued me all winter. So this was where the huge black spiders that boldly prowled my rooms at night came from. The hole behind the refrigerator seemed to stand for everything that was wrong with my life. Repairing it was complicated and took a week. I constructed a platform in the shaft from wood used to make airplane models, covered it with wire mesh, covered that with steel wool, and poured in successive layers of putty, allowing each layer to dry completely. Then I sanded the putty until it was even with the floor. The patch was a masterpiece. This done, the rest of the kitchen floor was ready for the primer. Having gone board by board, crack by crack, hole by hole, I had created a fairly smooth surface, but after I put down the primer, I could still see areas that needed caulking. In painting as in much else, preparation is everything.

The day finally came for the first coat of paint in the kitchen. The second coat went quickly. The result was even more beautiful than I had imagined. The floor was as smooth as a beach washed by waves, white with just a hint of gray, clean as a slate on which nothing has been written. All my preparations had paid off. The cracks and the filth they contained were gone, the holes sealed. Not even a dust mite could escape. The floor was a seamless expanse, a calm opaque sea that reflected light in every direction. Even at night, the light from my lamps left glistening pools in corners that had once been dark. I took three days' vacation from my job at Harvard to do the bedroom and the third room, my library and study, working late, sometimes until three A.M. When I worked on the floor, I was calm, fearless, alone in a wilderness of cracks that had a strange beauty as they vanished, one by one, because I willed it so. A peace was earned.

The woman who had been raped could submerge for a time, forget for a time. Pretend, as she swam beneath the surface, that she need never come up for air again.

Memory

Fiction, not truth, is what we humankind live in,
and truth arises from fiction, not the other way around.

LYDIA FAKUNDINY AND JOYCE ELBRECHT,
Scenes from a Collaboration

Sausalito, California, June 1993

This morning from the headlands I watched a sailboat trying to come in from the sea. Sails full of wind and outboard motor straining against the ebb tide, it was held, motionless, under the Golden Gate Bridge. Waves broke over its bow as if it were racing, but it did not move forward, did not slip back. It was embedded in the water like an ant in pine sap—going nowhere.

I began keeping a journal in fifth grade after my grandmother gave me a small, green leather diary that had a clasp with a lock. I kept the key under the plastic Virgin Mary on my bookshelf, a First Communion gift, also from my grandmother. The diary was a welcome departure from the rosaries, holy cards, bottles of holy water, and religious medals that my grandmother usually produced on my birthdays. The idea that I could have secret thoughts and feelings and that my grandmother was encouraging me to record them was revolutionary. What exactly these thoughts and feelings might be, however, required a degree of self-awareness that I did not possess. I had only two four-inch lines per day to fill in, definitely a restraining factor, and the weather, about which I seemed to be inordinately interested, took up most of the diary throughout the summer.

But as time passed I began to record feelings about how unfair it was that my brothers never had to do any housework. Only girls did housework, and I was the only girl. I was beginning to get the hang of the diary business. I would never tell my mother I was resentful. Anyone could see she was overworked and needed help, and I loved her fiercely. But it was comforting to bewail the fate my mother and I shared, to tell myself how I felt.

My first entry after school started read: "Mother Superior yelled at me today. I cried." Fifth grade was my first and only year in Catholic school, and Mother Superior, whom the boys called Mother Cruiser behind her back, plowed into our classroom like a gunboat every morning around ten-thirty to conduct our English lesson. On the first day of school, Mother Cruiser began instructing us in the art of diagramming sentences. When she asked me where in the diagram to put a certain word from the sentence she had written on the board, I froze.

"Well?" she said, twirling her rosary.

"I don't know," I finally replied. Then I excused my ignorance by blaming the public school I had attended for the previous four years, which had not seen fit to teach me about diagramming.

Mother Cruiser put her hands on her hips. Until this moment I hadn't thought she had hips—she was a square rigger, stem to stern. Then her lips compressed, her narrow mouth vanishing into a fleshy face that was pinched around the edges by her stiff white habit.

She yelled. I cried—from shame. I vaguely remember the words "How dare you?" and "Don't you ever" and other things that made it clear: A good excuse did not cut it with Mother Cruiser.

I resolved to get good at diagramming. In the process I discovered something wonderful about language: that it had structure. Words not only meant something, but they hung together in an orderly system that was, simply, the most beautiful thing I had ever seen. I began diagramming sentences in my spare time, tackling complicated ones out of my parents' books. This required looking up words in the dictionary and recording them in a notebook. I was proud of the A-minus I earned in English at the end of that year, although Mother Cruiser never remarked on my astounding accomplishment. But I have come to feel that she had more to do with my love of language than any other person. Her withering attack was an important event, and merited an entry. But I only know that it was important then because it is important now. Furthermore, it is my ever-evolving memory of that day, not the entry in my diary, that weaves this incident into the fabric of a narrative that I tell myself.

Memories do not sit inertly in our minds. They are not like the videos we rent on Friday nights or the audio books we listen to in our cars. Memories are the raw material of our personal narratives, the insubstantial and elusive elements out of which we fashion and refashion our lives into patterns of meaningful sequence.

But some memories seem to resist this refashioning and to possess a rigid, inflexible quality that resists the creation of a narrative.

The raw material I am using to reconstruct the rape and its aftermath in language consists of two quite different elements. I have what I remember about the eighteen months I lived in the attic in Concord, and I have what I recorded in my journal. When I look back on those months, I discover that, in fact, I have few real memories. And the ones I do have possess the same frozen quality as my memories of the rape and the emergency room. Jason's intrusion, for example, felt like a second rape and my memory seems to have stowed it in the same compartment as the rape itself. These memories are emotional stiffs, like unclaimed bodies on slabs in the morgue. I view them with a mixture of revulsion and fascination.

It is as if I spent eighteen months drifting in and out of a coma.

With rare exceptions, I remember my life then as a solitude as seamless as the souls of Rilke's angels. It feels as if someone else lived my life while I existed inside a sealed chamber, walled off not only from the world, but from myself as well.

But because old habit and the need to calm myself with words kept me scribbling in my journal, I can reconstruct a chronology of what happened while I was sealed in my cell. Reading my journals from the first year in Concord, I discover, for instance, that I was not as alone as I remember. My friend Chris rented one of my rooms for five months that first winter. She was a photographer who had achieved consider-able recognition for her work, but as with many artists, her resources were being consumed by the costs of mounting an exhibition at a major museum while her funders diddled around with her grants. I was equally pinched. We saw a practical advantage in sharing expenses that out-weighed the awkwardness of two adult women, both of whom had lived alone for years, sharing a space that made a sardine can look roomy.

I do remember the fact that Chris shared the apartment, but the months she was there might be a week, at most, if memory were all I had to go on. My journals are strangely silent about the life Chris and I shared. Here and there a mention: We did laundry at the laundromat, we watched a miniseries on television, we took a walk. I can only spec-ulate that having occasional company—Chris often traveled—was com-forting. I do not remember ever talking to her about the rape, and my journal makes no mention of it as a subject of discussion between us.

But I do have two memories of the months Chris was living with me, and both feel like real memories—memories that are flexible and that can be woven and rewoven into my narrative. They were moments of reconnection.

Chris, who was out of the apartment before I got up, usually made her breakfast in the blender—a high-protein concoction with a banana, raw egg, and protein powder. I remember opening the refrigerator one morning and finding a glass of breakfast on the shelf. She had left it for me. I remember reaching into the refrigerator, holding the glass in my hand, and feeling myself come together for a moment. And the sensation of briefly, fleetingly being connected to myself through a connection with her forged by a small gesture of concern still seems miraculous. In those days, such moments were rare.

In late April, my journal informs me, Chris's grants came through and she moved out. Waiting for me on the kitchen table when I got back from work the day she left was a gift—a black-and-white photograph that she had taken that winter on a Cambridge street. The image is a rose blooming in the snow, shot from an angle that suggests the camera is in another dimension. The background is a flat plain of white—overexposed, glaring, inhospitable. On the right side of the picture a tree juts out of the snow. It seems to be cut off at the knees and about to fall backwards. On the left side stone steps ascend out of the frame. The pale gray rose rises on a single dark stem, a black line that runs top to bottom in the foreground center of the picture. The earth from which it rises is out of the frame, so that it seems to be floating. The rose seems untouched by the cold, although below the stem the remnant of leaves are twisted and curled in death.

She left no note, nor was one needed. I often think that of all my possessions, Chris's photograph would be the hardest to lose in a fire or a flood. Her vision connected me to myself because it connected me to someone else who saw me as I was—a woman trying to survive.

This photograph is an antidote to the sense of failure I have carried with me from those months in Concord—the failures of nerve, of judgment, of faith. These were, Chris reminds me, the failures of a broken vessel to hold water—although the shards still held something. Someone else saw a kind of strength, or at least the will to endure in the inhospitable emotional conditions that were the legacy of my rape. And because she did, I can as well.

The photograph hangs on the wall in the room where I write, and over the many years of silence since the rape I have clung to its message, hoping one day to plumb its stark truth, a truth that Chris saw clearly and that I am only beginning to see.

It reminds me of something the painter Georges Braque said: "Art is a wound turned to light." It still gives me hope.

■ ■ ■

It wasn't pleasurable to reread the journal I wrote in Concord. It left me with a new pain that I had not anticipated: I felt little connection with the person who had written it. I encountered a fastidious text, an archive of sorts, a book of days that provides a dull record of daily life. But like my fifth-grade diary, it is missing the real story—and I *cannot fill it in*. I am missing the most important text of all—the text that is written by memory, that makes meaning out of "Mother Superior yelled, I cried." There is no mention of the incident with Jason or my conversation with the male therapist the morning the ducks were killed.

This is what I learned about the woman who kept that journal: After a month of therapy, she was able to get a part-time clerical job in a large insurance company which she held through the winter. I remember nothing about that job except being tormented by a man who kept pursuing me for a date. By spring, she had gotten a full-time job, working at the Graduate School of Design at Harvard. Again, I do not remember much about my work, except that I was terrified of the dean—a problem, since my job was writing letters to major donors for him and he was not easy to please. I discover that by the time she was working at Harvard, she kept herself frightfully busy and overcommitted, as was her former habit. The journals are full of complaints about her not having any quiet time, alone. She did a lot of organizing and reorganizing in her rooms, and this ceaseless shuffling seemed to pass for peace, happiness. Indeed, some days she writes she is perfectly happy now that she has organized her desk, her kitchen, her socks. She mentions difficulties with her landlords, but only in passing. She did seem to handle business with her former diligence—doing taxes in a timely manner, submitting insurance forms, paying bills. She went to movies, concerts, art openings, dinners. She took a trip to Colorado with a friend, where she white-water rafted for the first time. In July she celebrated her fortieth birthday. Friends, many of whom traveled long distances to mark the occasion, gave her a party and a Univega bicycle she pedaled alone down deserted country lanes, although she admits riding her bike alone made her "horribly anxious." This woman, I see, was getting on with her life.

But who, I ask myself, was she? I don't really remember her. Only here and there are passages, fragments, that stir a feeling in me. For example, when I reread the dream I recorded on January 22, 1986—about the lost tooth and hopelessly damaged gum—I wept. I think it is because only now am I beginning to understand what it means.

■ ■ ■

The writer Patricia Hampl has remarked that she doesn't write about what she knows. "I write in order to find out what I know." I don't know what I know about myself as a raped woman. I don't know how I got here, in this room, on this afternoon with these shadows of trees on the curtains, writing about this woman. That is what I must discover. Are words the only possible medium of thought? Maybe I still want to believe that by writing about the rape I will be able to close the door on it—someday. Perhaps be able to forget completely what is behind that door—the rape itself and how it shapes me still. Perhaps even someday forget there is a door.

But I am discovering, word by word, that if the self, as Milan Kundera said, is "the sum of everything we remember," the annihilation of my past would be a suicide. Yet years of repressing what defies narrative constantly push against memory and language. I am exhausted and full of doubts about the value of the effort.

This does not seem like writer's block. This is confronting again and again the limits of language as it struggles to create meaning out of what is incomprehensible. The rules of narrative—synthesis, continuity, causality—do not apply to ruptures of the moral order. Survivors instinctively understand that what they experience is different in kind from all other experience. This difference seems to destroy the threads of narrative the moment one tries to weave them.

Is this what I am trying to do by writing this book—construct my identity, my self? But the self that is engaging in this construction, the sum of all I remember, is a self in which repression has been a factor in survival and, dare I say, sanity. I am by now accustomed to trying to forget not only what happened that afternoon but, perhaps more significantly, how what happened shaped me and is still shaping me.

Freud noted that the process of repression is not something that takes place once and for all, "as when some living thing has been killed and from that time onward is dead." Repression demands "a constant expenditure of energy, and if this were discontinued the success of repression would be jeopardized, so that a fresh act of repression would be necessary." What is repressed exercises a "continuous straining in the direction of consciousness, so that the balance has to be kept by means of a steady counter-pressure. A constant expenditure of energy, therefore, is entailed in maintaining a repression...."

I read my journal and see that I did "get on with my life." Yet the "I" who wrote page after page, trying to record as faithfully as possible not only external events, but whatever internal states she could express, was an "I" that had lost its identity—that is, the narrative thread of the past. The only past she possessed was a recent past that could not be synthesized. The rape distorted not only what came after it, but all that went before it as well.

What is this self I am writing into being, this sum of everything I remember? It is not flesh. If the rape taught me anything even remotely metaphysical, it taught me that my self is not body. Does my body remember being beaten and raped any better than it remembers a skinned knee when I was eight? My brain, which is body I suppose, still occasionally remembers the terror in that back-alley way that Daniel Goleman describes, but these memories bypass words and do not, therefore, belong to the self that is this sum of memory. No, my body does not remember in a way that will help me reconstruct my history.

I think about something the psychiatrist Leonard Shengold wrote—that the mind is a history-making organ. "We weave our memories into narrative, from which we construct our identities, despite our faulty registration of what goes on around us and within us." What happens in our inner and outer worlds may be "ultimately unknowable," but our sanity and survival depend on registering both worlds.

"There was a past, however imperfectly we have registered it and however impossible it is for us to communicate it or recapture it completely." Shengold believes human beings have an intense need for psychic synthesis, continuity, and causality. In other words, a need to create narrative. From the moment the first cave painter said to an astonished buddy, "Now, that's a damn good antelope!" human beings have been talking their heads off, and for the last ten thousand years writing it down.

But it seems my rape impaired my ability to create this synthesis, to weave memories into the myth and history of my self. Do other rape survivors share this injury, and is this damage part of the reason for the nearly seamless silence about rape, I wonder? I know of less than a dozen personal accounts by rape survivors, despite the "sex war" statistics.

One writer who has explored the way rape affects our history-making mind is Pat Conroy, whose novel *The Prince of Tides* turns on the relationship of each of its characters to a moment of terrifying too-muchness—Tom Wingo's rape, and the rapes of his mother and sister by three escaped convicts who break into their home. "Rape," Tom Wingo tells the reader, "is a crime against sleep and memory; its after-image imprints itself like an irreversible negative from the camera obscura of dreams. Throughout our lives these three dead and slaughtered men would teach us over and over of the abidingness, the terrible constancy, that accompanies a wound to the spirit. Though our bodies would heal, our souls had sustained a damage beyond compensation."

Conroy's metaphor of the afterimage of rape as an "irreversible negative"—a photographic negative that cannot produce a positive image—that is imprinted, like some genetic code, in the memory is striking. It is the dark chamber of dreams that produces this irreversible negative. Forgetting is itself a kind of remembering, but a remembering that is both hopeless and destructive. Conroy's protagonist plays out this destructive remembering for much of the novel, which is set into motion when Tom, a cynical, disillusioned Southern football coach, learns that his twin sister, Savannah, a poet who lives in New York City, has tried to kill herself for a second time. Tom is a disconnected man—he is unemployed, his marriage is crumbling, and his life has become a raging defense against his own acts of repressing pain. "I had a limitless gift," Tom tells the reader, "for turning even those sweet souls who love me best into strangers." But it is Tom Wingo who is the stranger haunted by his family's past, not because he has forgotten something, but because he remembers it as if it had happened to someone else. It is not part of his narrative.

Tom goes to New York to try to help his sister, and meets and falls in love with his sister's psychiatrist, Susan Lowenstein. Functioning as his catatonic sister's memory, her "window to the past," Tom gradually reveals the truth about their childhood. The secret that he finally articulates for Lowenstein is the rape of his family, their murder of the rapists, and the family's reaction to the horror of these events. Each of the characters expresses one dimension of the impact of this event on memory. Lila, Tom's mother, exacts a promise from the children never to mention what happened. She reacts the way society itself reacts—with silence. When Tom tells his mother that he intends to reveal their secret, Lila reminds him of his promise. "Where did you come up with the idea," Tom asks his mother, "that if you simply pretended something didn't happen, then it lost its power over you?" She responds, "When I say good-bye to something in my past, then I just shut the door and never think about it again." Savannah, whose memory of the rape and murders has evolved into a death instinct, suffers from "white intervals," blank periods from the past that "seem to exist outside of time or space or reason."

When Tom Wingo finally tells Lowenstein about the rapes, he is released from the burden of holding his memories outside the ongoing narrative of his life. He not only reconstructs his past but gains a future. Unlike his sister, Tom Wingo has not "forgotten" what happened, but he has not fully remembered it either because he has not put his memory into words. Conroy suggests that this act of articulation is itself a restoration of Tom Wingo's history. But Tom Wingo is not a new man. He is a man with a memory—a man with a story he can tell himself.

The burden of holding the memory of rape outside their personal narrative is one that I believe nearly all rape victims carry to some degree. But not all have a Lowenstein, nor does life often provide a set of circumstances that compel a victim, as Tom Wingo was compelled by external events, to articulate the unspeakable. Perhaps because Tom Wingo is a fictional character, it is easier for us to accept Conroy's condemning him to a soul damaged beyond compensation. And he had Lowenstein, who, I couldn't help noticing, did not charge him for their meetings.

Although Nick Nolte's performance in the film based on Conroy's book (also called *The Prince of Tides*) was sensitive to the complex emotional legacies of rape, the Hollywood version of "getting over it" drifted slowly but inexorably—and alas, predictably—into *Love Story*.

Rape, like other experiences of terrifying too-muchness, is, first and foremost, a crime against memory, a crime against the self. The fact that rape is a sexual violation tends to make it harder for others to understand this crime's impact on memory and identity. Sex—or what seems like sex—has a way of grabbing our attention.

Dr. Bessel A. van der Kolk devotes a chapter in his 1991 book, *Psychological Trauma,* to the case of a fifty-five-year-old woman identified as Melody D., who survived the November 28, 1942, Coconut Grove nightclub fire that killed 492 people. After testifying at hearings a year after the fire, Melody D. did not think about that night for the next thirty-nine years. "When she did recall the tragedy, it was not in the form of a memory," van der Kolk writes. Her "memory" of the fire metamorphosed into psychotic states that led to a series of hospitalizations beginning in 1981. One day, for instance, she was arrested for pulling the fire alarms in supermarkets: "Run, run. Gas from the ceiling is going to kill you," she screamed as she was led away by police. I wonder how many of the deranged people I see sometimes on the street are simply trying to reconstruct their own narratives.

"I'm talking things over with myself," Melody D. explains to van der Kolk during a rare moment of lucidity. "Which would be better—to continue this struggle to recall piece by piece the parts of my memory I have forgotten, or to live my life peacefully and let the pieces pop up? Each piece I remember just tells me how much I have forgotten." Although Melody D.'s case may be dramatic, I feel it differs from my own only in degrees. I view those degrees of separation as a blessing bestowed on me for reasons I shall never know, although I often think of my mother's response to me in the weeks immediately after the rape as the benevolent margin between me and a locked ward. Like Tom Wingo, I have not forgotten what happened, but I cannot weave the memory of it into my personal narrative. Like Melody D., each piece I remember just reminds me how much I have forgotten.

I have discovered as I write that my memories of the thirty-nine years I lived before the rape—years of ordinary life experience—are not only insubstantial, as they were before the rape, but they have an added quality of unreality because they also seem to belong to someone else. The woman who was raped—the woman who came into being on October 11, 1985—wants to have a story that reaches back into the past of the woman who was not raped. But the loss of an identity—more than a loss of innocence, although it is that, too—seems to preclude this possibility. I wonder: Is my history-making organ "damaged beyond compensation"?

In an essay about the art of memoir writing, Annie Dillard makes a point about what happens when you bring language to the formless stuff of memory. "After you've written, you can no longer remember anything but the writing." Writing does not, she says, preserve your memories. It replaces them. Is this what I hope will happen as I sit at my desk, day after day, over these many months? I cannot seem to construct a comprehensive view of reality that includes the rapist and the woman he left behind—the woman who cannot make a story, but must have one.

EIGHT

The Woman
in the Amber Necklace

It takes two to speak the truth—
one to speak, and another to hear.

HENRY DAVID THOREAU, *A Week
on the Concord and Merrimack Rivers*

It is early February 1994, a few months after my essay appeared in the *New York Times*. My rape is out of the closet now. I am sitting at a banquet table in Chez Panisse, Alice Waters's highly acclaimed restaurant in Berkeley, California. I have added another eight years to the journal I wrote in Concord—several more handwritten notebooks have taken their place on my bookshelf—and I am writing again.

I have just been served the first course—a rocket salad with pine nuts. Women, some of whom I know, have gathered to say good-bye to a friend who is moving "back East," as people in the West call it—a vestigial reference to life on the frontier. Baked steelhead salmon with Meyer lemon salsa verde and passion fruit sherbet will follow the second antipasto, Belgian endive with mustard vinaigrette.

I introduce myself to a woman sitting to my right who is wearing an amber necklace. The beads are the size of walnuts and there are a great many of them. She is an energetic woman in her early fifties who is a well-known supporter of the arts. She recalls the guest of honor mentioning me and tells me she's read my essay. We toast our friend, who is taking an important post in Washington.

The rocket salad is taken away and the Belgian endive is served. The woman with the amber necklace turns to me again and says, as if she's been thinking about it while the toasts were being made: "I thought your article was well-written." I am smiling. "But let's face it, no one wants to hear about such terrible things."

I stare at my salad. I can't think of a reply. I am ashamed, but not for her.

■ ■ ■

The next day I can't get back to the book, which I have been working on for several months. And the day after that. A week passes, then six. When I do sit down in front of my computer, the cursor blinks like a caution light at a dangerous intersection. I am afraid to pull out into the traffic. I hit a stretch of insomnia. I sit up late after my husband has gone to bed, watching television, not asleep and not awake, not thinking and not wanting to think.

One night I catch a rerun of the popular television series *Cheers*. Frasier, the psychiatrist, asks the affably dense bartender, Woody, if he ever gets angry. "Oh sure," Woody replies. "I get angry sometimes, but I just keep forcing the pain down and clamp it in." Frasier pauses, grins wryly. "Tick, tick, tick!"

The audience laughs because Woody's solution is familiar. They know denying painful feelings is like swallowing a time bomb. Yet it seems to me that this is what is asked of survivors of terrible things, and that survivors can't help swallowing.

For weeks I didn't know that I had swallowed the silencing words of the woman in the amber necklace. But they were inside, ticking.

Steve noticed I wasn't writing—or sleeping. One Sunday morning he asked me what was going on.

"Nothing," I said.

"I noticed," he replied.

"I've been thinking about getting a real job, a trade. Like dental hygiene."

"Okay," he replied, "what happened? You were going along fine."

"Nothing."

"Let's talk about nothing, then," he said.

"Look. No one wants to read about such terrible things," I shouted, angry at him and relieved, for a moment, to displace my true anger.

He put his arms around me. Then the ticking stopped and I wept.

■ ■ ■

I went back to work and tried to figure out how the remark made by the woman in the amber necklace had both shamed and silenced me. What was she really saying? I sensed her words had the punch of truth, but I was getting in my own way. I could only hear them as a woman who had been raped.

In *Trauma and Recovery* Judith Herman writes that the normal response to terrible things is to banish them from consciousness. "Certain violations of the social compact are too terrible to utter aloud: this is the meaning of the word *unspeakable*." These violations are unspeakable because they are too terrible for words. But words, after all, are all I have. The conflict, it seems, is built into my attempt to fashion my memories into a sum of everything I remember, my attempt to reconstruct myself.

Herman says that "the conflict between the will to deny horrible events and the will to proclaim them aloud is the central dialectic of psychological trauma" and that this dialectic of trauma operates not only in individuals who survive unspeakable horrors, but also in society. Her notion of dialectic seems to be Hegelian—that trauma creates a process whereby the contradiction in denying terrible events (after all, they *do* happen) causes denial to turn into its opposite, truth-telling. Hegel was discussing a purely logical process; the idea of contradiction is central to his philosophy because reality for Hegel was a world of conflicting truths, each containing a contradiction that sets in motion the dialectical process (thesis-antithesis-synthesis) that he took three nearly impenetrable volumes to describe.

I found Herman's use of the term *dialectic* in relation to psychological processes appropriate because of the notion of contradiction that it contains. Life as a rape survivor is full of contradictions and layers of shame. Before I sat down to write about the seventh anniversary of my rape, I had come to the conclusion that my continued silence was a wounding disguised as a healing. Denial had been ticking, and when the timer went off—seven years after the rape—and words finally came, I was discovering that truth-telling could be a healing disguised as a wounding. The truth, or the best of it you can muster, is something no one wants to hear. If no one wants to hear about such terrible things (and why should they? I asked myself), why am I writing this? How can I make a sum of everything I remember—a self—if that self does not exist in relation to others? It is easier to go numb in front of the television set.

I started thinking about my family—what I had learned from them that had made it so difficult for me to break my silence. The conflict between the "will to deny horrible events and the will to proclaim them out loud" was, I realized, something I felt intensely. The habit of silence was deeply rooted in my family.

My mother's father was a farmer who raised tobacco as a cash crop. He and my grandmother, who died while my mother was pregnant with me, raised ten children on a farm in Virginia. I was named after my grandmother. Even as a child I looked up to my mother's family. They were self-sufficient and direct, practical people of few words and many deeds.

Two of my mother's sisters married local boys and settled down on farms near their home, and every summer we visited them for several weeks. My mother's sister Lace was eighteen years older than my mother, and I thought of her almost as a grandmother. Her farm, which had been occupied by her husband's family since the mid-eighteenth century, stood with its house, barns, and mysterious sheds on a broad ledge that was open on one side and enclosed by a long graceful hill on the other. The rutted driveway was steep, weaving through fields of corn and patches of hardwoods, until it straightened out at the family cemetery.

The first floor of the house—the cold larder, the kitchen, and a sitting room—was a half basement with thick stone walls. It was always cool, even on July days when the cicadas were deafening and the air shimmered in the heat.

Although she had an electric range, Lace preferred to bake in a wood-burning stove. The kitchen smelled of biscuits, blackberry rolls, apple pies, spoon bread, and wood smoke. She canned lima beans and beets from her vegetable garden, cured her own hams, put up strawberry and peach preserves, tatted, crocheted, wove rugs out of scrap wool, raised bees and collected honey, milked cows, chopped firewood, collected eggs from the chickens, and cooked three hot meals a day. I was in awe of her.

Lace had one child, a son who was killed in the waning days of World War II. My brother Edward was named after him. A picture of him in uniform stood in an ornate wooden frame on the sideboard in the ground-floor sitting room. He was buried in the cemetery on the hill behind the barn and sometimes I went to his grave, trying to put it together with the picture on the sideboard. Once I asked Lace about Edward. "He was a good son," she replied. I waited for more, but there wasn't any.

When the relatives gathered in Lace's sitting room after dinner, there were long stretches of silence. The squeak of wooden rockers on the hardwood floor might go on for ten minutes at a stretch. There were no confidences exchanged among the sisters. No one complained about anything worse than the ravages of a thunderstorm. There were stories, but they were always funny stories. They never mentioned the alcoholic brother who died one night in a shed, the horrible death of the youngest brother, who was killed when he was run over by the horses dragging a harrow. When Lace's husband got Parkinson's disease, she nursed him at home until he died, just as she had his mother and her parents. Without complaint. Nothing seemed to disturb the rhythms of their days and nights, and whatever pain and losses they carried, they carried silently. They never spoke about unpleasant things. Their stoicism was matched only by their tirelessness.

I wanted to be like them. I wanted to be practical, like they were. I wanted to carry my pain alone and secretly. As a child, I felt criticized for being too sensitive, too softhearted. I cried when Lace killed a chicken, ran when my uncle slaughtered a hog, let fish go after I caught them, agonizing over the pain I'd inflicted. I was told I had to learn to toughen up: Life was "no bed of roses," "no bowl of cherries."

After my rape, my silence was reinforced by the values of my mother's family, values I associated with people I loved and admired. My mother and I did not tell her family I had been raped. We discussed it briefly and agreed that it was just "too complicated." My mother carried my rape alone and silently for years. Eventually she did tell Lace. Although I knew Aunt Lace knew about the rape—and, of course, she knew I knew my mother had told her—we never mentioned it. I never brought it up, nor did she. My mother sent Lace and her other surviving sister my article after it was published, but they never mentioned reading it. I never had the courage to ask about it. Aunt Lace, whose mind showed no diminishment with age, died before I could finish this book. She was ninety-six. Her last words, spoken clearly at the moment of death, were plain: "It's over," she said.

The tension between denial and truth-telling seemed to increase the more I spoke about my rape. I had made a decision not to stay silent about it, in part because I was rebelling against the rapist's command to "shut up." But my reaction to the woman's remark at the luncheon—my retreat into silence and shame—seemed to confirm my anxieties that I would never be up to truth-telling. Was the book I was writing a symptom of my failure to "integrate" the rape into my life? Because I had written before the rape, I wanted to go on writing after the rape. But every word I wrote engaged me in contradictions. Truth-telling produced reactions that silenced me, but staying silent was a betrayal of my own memory. At the same time, my silence was also safe—if I did not write about my rape, I would not have to feel the shame that reactions such as the one from the woman in the amber necklace still seemed to produce in me. Silence was living up to the standards of my mother's family. Being strong.

▪ ▪ ▪

After my essay was published, I had other experiences that illustrated not only how deeply Herman's trauma dialectic operates, but also how laborious are the mechanisms for changing attitudes about rape. Judith Herman's book represents two decades of research and clinical work with victims of sexual and domestic violence, and reflects the growing body of research on other traumatized groups such as combat veterans and victims of political terror. It is an important work because its goal is to restore connections between "the public and private worlds, between the individual and community, between men and women." By examining commonalities between rape victims and combat veterans, between victims of domestic violence and political prisoners in a book that is written with the general reader in mind, Herman has performed an immeasurable service for people who have been raped. By being associated with other survivors, rape victims gain a measure of relief from the burden of shame that they have always borne. Rape victims are part of a larger community of survivors who are not to blame for their trauma.

Yet new clinical and theoretical work on trauma seems to be as isolated from group awareness as individual trauma victims are from their own groups. Unless you are a trauma survivor or a highly motivated friend or family member of a survivor, Herman's book, despite its excellent review in the *New York Times Book Review*, probably will not be on your bookshelf because the normal response to terrible things is to banish them from consciousness. The rate at which information filters down from the growing body of literature about rape and other traumas is appallingly slow.

Soon after my encounter with the woman in the amber necklace, I was invited to dinner with a group of professional women. I had met a few of the other guests but did not know anyone well. After we had taken our places, the hostess tapped on her wineglass with a spoon and suggested that we each take a few minutes to discuss our current work before dinner was served. I dreaded my moment in the spotlight. Telling everyone what I was working on meant announcing to perfect strangers that I had been raped. And, perhaps worse, that I was still thinking about it. The "confessional" nature of the book might easily be viewed as a form of narcissistic exhibitionism, only one step removed from the sensationalism of a daytime television talk show.

Although all of the women in the group were highly educated people with well-developed social sensitivities, the tension of the "dialectic of trauma" that Herman describes operated even here. As soon as I started talking about my work, a hush came over the room.

I stated my belief that individual stories like mine could play a small role in changing attitudes about rape, which were still enmeshed in societal anxieties. I said that I had not yet found any Jungian analysis of rape from the perspective of the victim and I was growing more curious about how psychological theory treated the subject. A few days earlier I had stumbled on a book by Bradley A. Te Paske entitled *Rape and Ritual: A Psychological Study,* published in 1982. Te Paske viewed the impulse behind actual rape (as well as male fantasy of rape) as "the dynamic drive of the [male] individuation process." There were, I noted, studies on the meaning and function of rape for men, but I had not yet discovered anything comparable for victims. I found this curious. After all, there were so many of us.

Everyone listened respectfully. After I finished there was a long silence. Finally, someone said, "What about Susan Brownmiller's book *Against Our Will?* It seems to me she covered these issues." Several women around the table nodded their heads in agreement. Was this comment, I wondered, a version of "no one wants to hear about such terrible things" or was I being oversensitive? Brownmiller's book was published in 1973, over twenty years earlier. It seemed no one in the room was familiar with recent studies of rape and that there was no context, even among educated women who cared deeply about history and culture, for individual stories of the rape experience. One book "about rape" was enough, they implied. It was unnerving. I realized, too, that had I not been raped, I might be as baffled as they.

Against Our Will: Men, Women and Rape established the subject of rape as a matter of public debate. As Herman points out in her book, rape became the feminist movement's "initial paradigm for violence against women in the sphere of personal life." Eventually the initial focus on rape—spearheaded by Brownmiller's meticulously researched study—led to the exploration of other forms of public and private coercion—from date rape to incest, from domestic violence to sexual harassment in the workplace.

But Brownmiller's political agenda and her redefinition of rape as a method of political and social control that preserved male power meant she had to avoid psychological considerations of rape as an experience. Ironically, this still left the individual rape victim's journey shrouded in silence and mystery. Brownmiller's study and the feminist movement out of which it was born generated an upswelling of research and stimulated new social response to victims—rape crisis centers sprang up across the country and studies on the psychological effects of rape on victims were undertaken. Rape survivors were talking to one another and to professionals who were beginning to understand the real nature of rape trauma. A few brave souls were telling their stories and a few publishers were printing them. But my own experience convinced me that rape survivors were still cut off from their communities because truth-telling was a complicated and painful plunge into the dialectic of trauma that Herman described so well. "No one wants to hear about such terrible things."

"Brownmiller's book was a landmark achievement," I said. "She looked at rape in its historical and political context and redefined it as an act of power, not sex. I'm trying to look at rape as a meaning-bearing experience for the victim." I felt I was beginning to sound both muddled and defensive. I was probably both.

"Well," our hostess said, smoothing out the napkin on her lap and turning to the person on my left. "Shall we get off rape to something…" She paused, apparently at a loss for words. I feared the next word would be "agreeable." It was.

■ ■ ■

Several days later I received a gracious note from the hostess, encouraging me to persist with my book "for all our sakes." I had not been offended by her remark because I understood what she felt, something simple and true: It is hard to hear about "such terrible things," especially when they have to do with genitalia. I faced that truth every day when I sat down to write. I felt her discomfort, and a part of me still felt guilty about causing it.

I could well imagine her lying in bed that night, feeling confused by her remark, wishing she'd said something different, yet feeling she had spoken the truth. Her life was dedicated to decencies. It mattered to her that she had a vase of fresh sunflowers on the hall table and that they be in the blue vase with gold flecks so when guests arrived they would feel welcome. Because life could be wretchedly ugly after all and one must do the best one can. Perhaps she sorted her confusions out in her sleep and sat down the next morning at the old postmaster's desk that stood in the corner of her kitchen to write me. Perhaps she saw the truth in what she had said. No one wants to think about terrible things—except perhaps the terrible people who bring terrible things into being. About them, perhaps she thought, one simply can't think. But terrible things do happen. We hope to be spared. That is only natural. When we hear about terrible things, we are hurt. Perhaps she thought along these lines before she took out her pen.

I pinned her note up on my bulletin board, next to a quotation from Virginia Woolf's *The Voyage Out* that I've had over my desk for almost twenty-five years. "One doesn't want to be things. One wants merely to be allowed to see them." It's typed on a faded blue index card; the ink is thin with age, bleached by sunlight that has fallen through windows in more rooms than I care to recall. The note from my hostess deserved, I felt, that honored place. Seeing it made me feel less ashamed.

One winter many years ago I spent a week alone in a cottage on the coast of Maine. It was perched on a small rise fifty yards from the shore of an inlet, facing the sea. The ocean was icy even in August. When I looked at it in February through the picture window, the sight made me shiver. The waters of the inlet were gray at the shore, but further out, where the water was deep, they were the color of the spruce at twilight. Sometimes the wind came up at night, picking up cold from the water, and pushed it through cracks around the windows.

The weather was clear that week, short days of bright sunshine on snow with temperatures just below freezing. Then toward the end of the week the temperature began to drop. One morning it was well below zero, according to the radio weather report. By late afternoon it was sixteen below. The earth and cloudless sky felt brittle and the sunshine itself seemed as if it would shatter to the touch.

The next morning I awoke to find the inlet and the ocean beyond transformed. Mists were rising up from the waters. The ocean was like a cup of steaming green tea, not cold at all.

All along the heat had been there, but I hadn't realized it.

It was like this with my shame. Words seemed to make it visible. But speaking, even when it embarrassed me, also slowly freed me from the shame I'd felt. The more I struggled to speak, the less power the rape and its aftermath seemed to have over me. A few months later, for example, while helping a friend look over a house she was considering buying, I suggested that if she did buy it, she install an alarm system. Her older brother, who was also giving the place a once-over and whose opinion was weighty, objected. He thought an alarm system was an unnecessary expense. I said matter-of-factly, "I was raped in my home, and since your sister is going to be living here alone, I think it's a good idea." He blushed and seemed uncomfortable; we'd known each other for years and I'd never mentioned my rape.

Afterward, I realized that his reaction—embarrassment—did not make me feel ashamed, although it once would have. My concern for his sister's safety was reasonable. It was based on my own experience, which I felt was appropriate to share in this context, and my research. A study funded by the National Institute of Mental Health in the mid-1980s, for example, found that 29 percent of victims were raped in their own homes. The only place that posed greater risk was the street—34 percent of victims were initially attacked on the street (and raped elsewhere) and 2 percent were raped on the street. Once my shame would have silenced me. Now revelation seemed to be freeing me from my shame.

. . .

The compact edition of the *Oxford English Dictionary* devotes eleven columns to definitions of shame and related terms. The first definition is "the painful emotion arising from the consciousness of something dishonoring, ridiculous, or indecorous in *one's own conduct* [italics mine] or circumstances...or of being in a situation which offends one's sense of modesty or decency." *Webster's* agrees that shame is a painful emotion and that it is caused by "consciousness of *guilt, short-coming or impropriety* [italics mine]."

That shame should play such a profound role in rape began to strike me as curious. Why did I feel such shame? Until I began writing about my experience, I had not known the extent of it. I had told myself a thousand times that what happened to me was not my fault, but I did not really believe it. Those comforting words bobbed on the surface of my mind like buoys broken from their moorings.

Shame is the only emotion discussed at any length in the biblical story of Adam and Eve. They feel shame even before God notices that they aren't frolicking about as usual.

"Why are you hiding from Me?" God says.

"Because we are naked," they reply.

At this point, God puts two and two together. It is not because they are naked that they are hiding behind the fig leaf. They've always been naked and it never bothered them before. It's because they *know* they are naked—quite a different matter. And they wouldn't know they were naked unless they'd eaten the forbidden fruit. They are self-conscious—something God apparently intended or he would not have put the tree of knowledge in Eden in the first place. They feel shame; indeed, they are nothing *but* shame from the moment they taste the fruit, and that, the story suggests, is dangerous: "for on the day thou eatest thereof, thou shall surely die...."

Theorists from evolutionary biology, clinical psychology, and psychiatry have been thinking about shame since Darwin first observed that human beings are the only species capable of blushing, a physical manifestation of shame. Darwin and his fellow Victorians were fascinated with blushing, I suppose because they did a lot of it. Blushing requires self-consciousness, a quality that distinguishes us from the beasts. But, if one of the manifestations of shame is the desire to hide or disappear, I'm sure a friend's dog, Trouty, has felt it.

Trouty learned how to open the cabinet door under the kitchen sink to get at garbage when she was still a puppy. Although she is severely disciplined for this behavior, from time to time my friend comes home to find splayed ice cream cartons and chicken bones mixed with coffee grounds smeared across her shiny linoleum. I happened to be with her after one of these lapses. When we walked in the door, Trouty was trying to hide under a kitchen stool, which rode on her back like an undersized seashell. With her head down between her paws, her eyes averted, her tail between her legs, Trouty had "Bad Dog" written all over her body. Even after she'd been forgiven, Trouty kept making herself smaller, hunching up between her tail and her nose.

The desire to hide, disappear, or die is one very important feature of the phenomenology of shame, according to Michael Lewis. In his 1992 study *Shame: The Exposed Self,* Lewis notes that this desire is an overpowering component of the experience of shame. Other elements include intense pain and a feeling of worthlessness that Lewis describes as "a global statement by the self in relation to the self." When we feel shame, we are both its subject and its object.

According to Lewis, this results in "the disruption of ongoing behavior, confusion in thought, and *an inability to speak*" (italics mine). The physical states that accompany shame include a shrinking of the body, "as though to disappear from the eye of the self or the other." The state of shame is so intense and has such a devastating effect that "individuals presented with such a state must attempt to rid themselves of it. However, since shame represents a global attack on the self, people have great difficulty in dissipating this emotion." I could attest to that.

Shame is often confused with guilt, but Lewis notes that whereas shame is "the complete closure of the self-object circle...in guilt, although the self is the subject, the object is external." Guilt is produced when you evaluate your behavior as failure, but the focus is on what you could have done differently—and what you can do to repair the damage. Guilt is less intense than shame and less negative because the focus is an "action of the self rather than the totality of the self." When corrective action is impossible, guilt is converted to shame. Rape, by definition, is a situation where corrective action is impossible.

The feeling of shame is so intense for rape victims that many never tell anyone what happened to them. Even in psychotherapeutic settings, victims of rape often avoid talking about what happened to them. Despite more than two decades of change in social attitudes about rape, I still found it difficult not to feel ashamed when others reacted to me with embarrassment or discomfort. And this feeling of shame silenced me. Lewis notes that an intense feeling of shame can actually cause loss of memory. Shame silences because it encloses the entire self.

Rape shame is hard to escape, as I learned from the woman in the amber necklace. Attempts to dissipate the shame by giving words to the unspeakable seem only to increase it. The shame is mirrored by the listener, sometimes quite obviously by a blush, an averting of the eyes, or a hunching of the shoulders, sometimes by silence. The telling then feels like a confession, an admission of wrongdoing, and the sense of shame is deepened. Shame is what the rapist, not the victim, should feel. Yet his shame is transferred to the victim, and her shame renders her mute. And her muteness seems to confirm the moral rightness of this transfer. The feeling of shame seems to make being the victim of rape an act of wrongdoing. When others ask her to "hide" or "disappear," she has no hope of "corrective action."

The loop can become even more vicious. Causing others to feel shame is to wound them. I felt guilty toward the woman in the amber necklace, because she had read my article—and it had upset her. I felt guilty about introducing a "disagreeable" subject at a dinner party where everyone was having a good time. Guilt piles up on the shame with each disclosure.

Lewis notes that there is little agreement on the specific external triggers of shame. "No particular stimulus has been identified or is likely to be identified as the trigger for shame and guilt....There is no simple class of events that precipitates shame." Nowhere in his book does Lewis mention rape—an omission I found remarkable. Rape seems to be one of the few triggers for shame that operates in all human cultures.

■ ■ ■

I ran across a curious twist on rape shame in *Demonic Males: Apes and the Origins of Human Violence* by Richard Wrangham, a professor of anthropology at Harvard University, and the writer Dale Peterson. In a chapter on orangutan rape, chimpanzee battering, and gorilla infanticide, Wrangham and Peterson cite a case of orangutan rape witnessed by Biruté Galdikas, a scientist who spent twenty years studying orangutans in Borneo. In her 1995 book *Reflections of Eden,* Galdikas describes the rape of a human female, an Indonesian cook at the research camp, by a young male orangutan named Gundul, who had been born in the wild and taken captive. Living at the camp, where he was allowed to roam about freely, Gundul had lost his fear of people; although he had frequently charged male assistants, he had never threatened a woman. When the attack began, Galdikas, who tried unsuccessfully to fight off the animal as it grabbed the hysterical cook, feared the ape was trying to kill the woman. But then Galdikas began to realize that the orangutan "had something else in mind." Apparently the Indonesian cook had a similar realization that the only way to avoid serious injury or death was to submit. Galdikas writes: "The cook stopped struggling....Gundul was very calm and deliberate. He raped the cook."

It would seem that to the shame of rape would be added an even deeper shame—the shame of being raped by an animal. But apparently the victim, who was not seriously injured, was not stigmatized. Her friends and family did not blame her. Her husband reasoned that since the rapist was not human, the rape should not provoke shame or rage. "Why should my wife or I be concerned? It wasn't a man."

If it wasn't a man, it also wasn't sex. It was not a "sex crime." It was an "act of God" similar to Livingstone's mauling by an African lion. Gundul was a dumb animal. All of the issues that the cook would have had to face had the orangutan been a human being were irrelevant. He could not be seduced, encouraged, or "driven" to sexual passion by anything the cook said or did. She was not implicated in a crime because no crime had occurred. No one was going to suggest that she was raped because "she asked for it."

My rapist acted like an animal, although he was not "calm and deliberate" like this wild orangutan. But because he was a man, even I—the victim of an aggravated rape by a stranger in my own home (about as blameless as any rape victim can be)—could not escape from the shame of having been raped. The blame, embarrassment, and silence that characterized how others responded to my rape were "shaming" punishments this Indonesian cook apparently did not have to endure. No one told her that being depressed about a contract that had disappointed her "caused" her rape. I found this both ironic and enviable.

■ ■ ■

Oddly, Freud had little to say about shame, and according to Brownmiller, he was "struck dumb by the subject of rape." She notes that the man "who invented the concept of the primacy of the penis was never motivated...to explore the real-life deployment of the penis as weapon." Once Freud abandoned his early conclusions that "hysteria" in his female patients was the result of actual premature sexual experience and embraced the view that their traumatic symptoms were the result of sexual fantasies based on repressed Oedipal conflicts, rape victims for decades to come would carry a burden that would deepen and complicate their shame. "Though he continued to focus on his patients' sexual lives, he no longer acknowledged the exploitative nature of women's real experience," Herman writes in *Trauma and Recovery*. "With a stubborn persistence that drove him into ever greater convolutions of theory, he insisted that women imagined and longed for the abusive sexual encounters of which they complained." In effect, these "convolutions of theory" turned women into masochists. (They also present another problem I mention only in passing. The other victims of rape—boys and men—were, theoretically at least, inexplicable.)

I am old enough to remember when someone could say "If you're going to be raped, you might as well relax and enjoy it" without being censured. I remember vividly when I first heard it—in 1962 when I was in seventh grade. This conventional wisdom was bestowed upon me by a tenth-grade boy who was on the football team. I can still picture the school corridor where we were standing, although I cannot remember how the subject came up. I took it as a confusing warning. A warning because the implication was I might not be safe around him. Confusing because he seemed to be telling me something about my own sexuality—based, I assumed, on his extensive experience. I had seen *Gone With the Wind* twice and the big "sex" scene had not escaped my attention—Rhett Butler, drunk, angry, and threatening, carrying his protesting wife up the grand staircase, and raping her—or something. Scarlett O'Hara wakes up the next morning in a good mood for the first time in reels. Whatever he did that she didn't want him to do, she certainly seemed to enjoy it.

Brownmiller credits Helene Deutsch, a Viennese psychoanalyst whose *Psychology of Women* appeared in the mid-1940s, with the construction of an "epic thesis of female masochism." Brownmiller writes that Deutsch's belief in "the fundamental rightness of rape as an archetypal female experience rested primarily on her view of sexual intercourse as an essentially painful encounter for an essentially passive woman." Brownmiller comments that in the 1950s when she was in her early teens Deutsch's "pronouncements" were "piously quoted in all the popular books and magazine articles...that purported to teach women how to 'accept' their female role." Things had not changed much when I was in my early teens a decade later. Deutsch was firmly rooted in the Freudian psychoanalytic tradition and found further evidence for her views of feminine masochism in the conscious and unconscious rape fantasies and dreams of adolescent girls. Deutsch's treatment of this "unmistakable masochistic content" ignores the possibility that these fantasies and dreams are evidence of fear, not unconscious desire for abuse—a point Brownmiller is quick to make in her commentary on Deutsch's work.

The idea that women derive some kind of erotic pleasure from "forced sex" has drifted down from the stratosphere of psychoanalytic theory into our attitudes toward rape like rain that carries imperceptible toxins down into the drinking water. Despite the fact that Brownmiller and others in the women's movement redefined rape as a crime of violence and challenged the idea that rape was a sexual act that fulfilled women's deepest desires, and despite changes in our understanding of female sexuality, this idea is not yet extinct—although it may, mercifully, be politically incorrect. How else can we explain a comment I heard one night in 1996 from a police detective interviewed on television who said, in reply to charges of indifference brought against the San Diego Police Department by two rape victims, that the attitude of some cops in the department about rape was that it was "assault with a friendly weapon"? When I mentioned this comment to a friend, she summed it up beautifully: "Some people are incapable of imagining that a penis could be unwanted. Just ask Freud."

■ ■ ■

Brownmiller's thesis that rape was "nothing more or less than a conscious process of intimidation by which all men keep all women in a state of fear" redefined rape as a method men have used "from prehistoric times to the present" to maintain male power. This harsh conclusion was central to her radical political agenda because she viewed rape as the enforcement of the subjugation of women through terror. But political agendas aside, Brownmiller also challenged the idea that rape fulfilled women's desire for abuse. Severing sex from rape was a form of vigorous intellectual weeding, long overdue. As long as female sexuality was defined as fundamentally masochistic and rape was viewed as sex, female rape victims were trapped in shame that silenced them—and this very silence implied that they had reason to be ashamed.

Brownmiller reminded us that rape has always haunted human life, and she believed that it was unique to humans. "No zoologist, as far as I know," she wrote in the introduction to *Against Our Will*, "has ever observed that animals rape in their natural habitat, the wild." But not long after her book was published, scientists were beginning to observe rape in other primate species. (Indeed, finding an exception—a sister species to the chimpanzee, the bonobo, who "make love, not war"—is now challenging the idea that violence, including rape, is biologically inevitable for primates.)

The documentation of rape in the wild may actually support Brownmiller's fundamental point that "patriarchy" and "rape" are connected. Recent studies of violence among chimpanzees suggest that social organization may play an important, if not central, role. In *Demonic Males* Wrangham and Peterson observe that only two animal species—chimpanzees and humans (each other's closest relatives)—are known to live in a patrilineal, male-bonded society with "a system of intense, male-initiated territorial aggression, including lethal raiding into neighboring communities in search of vulnerable enemies to attack and kill." Both species also have similar patterns of other forms of violence—"political murders, beatings, and rape."

The authors observe that a "plausible alternative" to the view held by some researchers that rape in nonhuman mammal species may be a "fertilization tactic" (a way to increase an individual male's success in passing on genes to the next generation) is the hypothesis that "in some species rape may be an evolved male mechanism whose primary

aim is not fertilization in the present, but *control*—for the ultimate purpose of fertilization in the future." The immediate purpose of rape is
not, according to this line of speculation, necessarily fertilization.
"Instead, much as many feminists have long argued, it may be domi-
nation."

According to statistics compiled by the National Victim Center in
1992, 78 percent of rapes involve a person who is known to the victim.
Wrangham and Peterson wonder if such rapes, "by reminding a man's
partner of his physical power, may increase his sexual control over her.
Society's growing sympathy for rape victims may thus be working to
end a system that has deep evolutionary roots." This is a disturbing and
intriguing speculation. For society to acknowledge the truth about rape
and its legacy in the lives of millions of victims, it must also contemplate
a continuing profound revolution in the organization of society itself.
The recoil against feminism that the Pulitzer Prize–winning journalist
Susan Faludi documented in her 1991 book *Backlash: The Undeclared
War Against American Women* suggests that facing up to this challenge
is not going to be easy.

■ ■ ■

The silencing nature of the emotion of shame and the dialectic of
trauma that Herman has identified, when combined with societal inertia that could have "deep evolutionary roots," may keep the discussion
of rape at a standstill for some time to come. In the first years after the
rape, when those closest to me denied the reality of my experience, I
understood that they did so because they loved me. Their denial was
hope, and I consented because I, too, hoped that eventually something
I could recognize as myself would crawl from the debris of my former
life. But as the years went on, I began to see that denial in others is also
an effect of trauma as it moves outward from a single individual into
society. Like a stone thrown into a pond, rape has ripples. After my
encounter with the woman in the amber necklace, I began to feel that
I was looking down through muddy water at submerged debris. I
needed to understand what I saw in order to understand the effect of

my truth-telling on the woman in the amber necklace—because truth involved both of us.

Herman calls one side of the dialectic of trauma "the will to deny horrible events," but it may be even deeper than will. Will implies choice, volition, taking an action one can choose to take or not. Perhaps the woman in the amber necklace could not help her recoil from the fact that a rape survivor can never forget her anniversaries. Perhaps it is a psychological response to trauma that mirrors my own.

This woman's words have other dimensions. I wonder if they state a truth about the pain that witnesses feel when they encounter another human being's suffering. Is the pain of the witness the pain of the survivor? Perhaps the psychological devastation of trauma is similar for both witnesses and victims. Although we are not all survivors of an overwhelming life experience, we *are* all witnesses. And witnesses are also in some measure victims.

While I was writing this book, a federal building in Oklahoma City was destroyed by a terrorist's bomb. A gaping tomb of twisted metal and broken concrete rose out of the choking dust and smoke where, seconds before, a building had stood whole, its windows reflecting the gray skies of an overcast April morning. Millions of Americans sat helplessly in front of their televisions watching the aftermath minute by minute, day by day, until the last body was extricated from the chaos and delivered to those who would bury it.

We saw the strangely solemn faces of the children as they were carried away in ambulances to yet more incomprehensible experiences. They stared into the cameras, their eyes like the eyes of soldiers on the battlefield in photographs—"the one-thousand-yard stare," dry, round eyes focused on something in the distance no one else can see. I wonder if this is how my eyes looked that night in the emergency room. I wonder, too, if a trace of this look was in all of our eyes as we watched the wounded and dying children on television that night.

As I worked through my response to the remark made by the woman in the amber necklace, I realized that she was subject to Herman's dialectic of trauma just as I am. My rape wounds her, and like me she is hurt. Did I cause her trauma by writing about my own? Did I owe her an apology because I had been changed forever by a single overwhelming life experience? Was it my fault that atrocities harm us all? Did silence make the atrocities go away?

Judith Herman argues that remembering and telling the truth about dreadful events are "prerequisites both for the restoration of the social order and for the healing of individual victims." I think she is right. But the act of speaking or writing about the unspeakable is difficult and painful because remarks like the one made by the woman in the amber necklace imply that the decent thing to do is to remain silent. And the resistance to truth-telling, one side of the trauma dialectic, is constantly exerting itself inside me because of the nature of shame itself. My silence is further reinforced by my guilt at "causing" this woman pain, reminding her that terrible things exist.

The woman in the amber necklace was right—no one wants to see or hear or read about such terrible things. Or experience them. Psychologically and biologically, we are not made for such stress. And when it happens to us, we are not as we were. Herman writes that traumatic events "shatter the construction of the self that is formed and sustained in relation to others." The destruction of the psychological structures within the self includes burning out the lines that link an individual to her community.

Like a building fused by expert demolitionists to fall in upon itself, the inner self is reduced to rubble. It is the traumatized self that emerges from the dust, not like the Phoenix, the mythological bird that rose from its own ashes every five hundred years to live on as before, but more like an alien creature bearing little resemblance to the earlier one. It is a metamorphosis. Although the event is external, it is quickly incorporated into the mind, where it replicates itself, like a virus. There is no defense. And yet life goes on.

But it is not the same life. The failure of society to acknowledge this may be the result of the trauma of the witness. Because society is not the same either. The damage cannot be confined because the self cannot be confined. We exist in relation to others.

NINE

"Victoria"

Behold this little Bane–
The Boon of all alive–

EMILY DICKINSON

Sometimes even the devil slips up and something good happens. The rapist brought Victoria back into my life—I can thank him for that. And because of that, my life improved. The Buddhists have a saying: From the mud grows the lotus. This is a story, then, about the lotus.

Victoria and I became friends in the late spring of 1974, the first year that the word *gate* was attached to nouns to denote a scandal. A few weeks after the House Judiciary Committee began closed hearings on whether or not to recommend that the full House impeach Richard Nixon, Victoria joined the staff of the nonprofit media education organization where I'd been working for two years. We were the same age—twenty-eight—and had similar backgrounds. We'd both been raised Catholic and had mothers who were Southerners. Because of our fathers' work, we'd both spent our adolescence in Europe—she in Italy and I in Germany.

Watergate was our backdrop. The final act of the drama unfolding in the city we called home made the national crisis feel intimate, a neighborhood affair. We often saw the special prosecutor, Archibald Cox, striding in and out of his nearby office building, and occasionally we'd join the crowd in the lobby for one of his news conferences. As the President of the United States dribbled out the tapes that would destroy him, the city began to feel like a stage set for a Greek tragedy, with ordinary citizens—coworkers, cabdrivers, and grocery store clerks—acting the part of the chorus. On Victoria's first day in the office we discovered that between us we had an impressive collection of Watergate jokes and that we each had had nightmares about Nixon. I dreamed I was attending a reception in the Rose Garden, shaking hands with the President, who suddenly began to melt, like the witch in *The Wizard of Oz*. She dreamed that she was trapped in the White House, running from room to room with H. R. Haldeman, who was dressed in a Boy Scout uniform, in hot pursuit. We had an instant rapport that withstood the pressures of nonprofit work, not the least of which was never being sure where your next grant was coming from.

Our respective duties required us to work closely together, and we were often in and out of each other's offices, reviewing drafts of grant requests, massaging numbers, or figuring out how five people could do the work of ten and still like one another at the end of the day. She was graceful under pressure, smart, and direct—an excellent colleague. Our professional relationship evolved easily into an intimate friendship—we usually took our lunch together, eating sandwiches in a nearby park when the weather was decent, or in a dingy hole-in-the-wall café with booths and checkered tablecloths around the corner from the office. We discovered interests besides Watergate—movies, modern dance, Roberta Flack, reading the *National Enquirer* when we couldn't sleep, and cats (we both had two overweight males we admitted were substitutes for the children neither of us had, or even wanted). She, too, wrote poetry and, like me, was serious about it. We began meeting after work to comment on each other's poems, and on the weekends for a movie or a dance performance at Wolf Trap.

Although we delighted in the process of getting to know each other, it seemed like a formality. In retrospect, our friendship seemed fated from the beginning, as if our story had already been written and nothing more was required of us than to turn the next page. Neither of us could have cooked up the plot.

Victoria took the first risk in our friendship—only many years later would I understand how big a risk it was. We were having dinner at the Hawk and Dove on Capitol Hill on a typical Washington summer evening—the humidity had a sickly, swampy taste and walking even a few blocks left us feeling poached in brine. That day the Supreme Court had ruled that Nixon could not hide behind executive privilege and would have to hand over more tapes. The other tables were crowded with congressional staff, mostly men. Everyone looked exhausted. We took a table in the corner as close to the air-conditioner as we could get, ordered vodka tonics, and decided not to dwell on the spectacle of the President of the United States trying to extricate himself from the unrelenting undertow of cover-ups. We got into what interested us more—each other.

It didn't take long to get to the subject of men. Victoria told me she'd been engaged to a man named David when she was nineteen.

"He was killed in Vietnam. It was a terrible blow. I had my whole life planned. Then it felt over."

I felt sad, and said so, although the words seemed inadequate and I was uncomfortably aware that the only person I had ever grieved over was myself. She talked about David, their time together before he was shipped out, the letters he wrote, the call from his parents, the funeral.

"There hasn't been anyone else since then. Nobody special, that is." Victoria was a beautiful woman—one of those women who did not have to work at it, and usually didn't. "I'm sure it's not for lack of admirers," I said.

"I suppose I hold back. David's death and…other things."

"In a way, I do, too. I got married when I was nineteen. It ended badly. My divorce came through about a week before my twenty-second birthday."

"I was traveling in Europe then," Victoria said. "That wasn't a

great year for me either." She seemed to drift off, then catch herself.
"Anyway—why did you get divorced?"

"He was the boy next door, believe it or not. We got married the
summer after my freshman year in college. He'd just finished Harvard
and had been accepted at the Iowa Writers Workshop. I transferred
credits to the University of Iowa, deciding on philosophy as a major,
and off we went to Iowa City. Ernest Hemingway was his idol, so he
grew a beard, wrote in a coffee shop downtown, and had affairs. I think
he wanted to become a writer because he thought it would spice up his
seductions. Of course, I had no clue he was running around on me.
Then I came home one afternoon and found another woman on my
side of the bed. That was it. I packed up, rented a room in a boarding-
house, and hired the cheapest divorce lawyer in town."

"You must have been devastated."

"I was hopelessly naive. I was a virgin when we got married—you
know, saving myself for Mr. Right. I felt terribly betrayed."

I confided that a month earlier I had broken up with a man I'd
been seeing since graduate school. Jake was, I told her, a philosopher
who made his living as a carpenter. He was a good carpenter, but what
he really loved was philosophy.

"Jake's interested in Truth, with a capital T. The more absolute, the
better. Me, I look for little truths. Things get complicated when you're
trying to talk about your relationship and he comes up with a quote
from *The Critique of Pure Reason*. We're still friends—he has wonderful qualities."

"Nice that you could stay friends," Victoria said.

"I worry about him—he's drinking more than he should—or I
think he should. I guess we're just going our separate ways, but it's
hard to accept."

The waitress, who was having a hard time keeping up with the
crowd, finally presented herself and scribbled down our orders. After
she left, we sat silently for a minute. "There are things I can't accept
either," Victoria finally said. "Something happened when I got back
from Europe that summer, the summer you got divorced. I was finally

getting over David's death. I was back in Washington just two weeks—first apartment, first job. Then…" She seemed to be assessing me. I couldn't think what was harder to accept than having the man you love die.

"If I tell you, you've got to promise me you'll keep it to yourself."

I said I would.

"There's no easy way to say this. I was raped," Victoria said. "In my own apartment."

I must have known other women before Victoria who had been raped. But no one had ever told me. I was shocked. Since puberty I'd carried around a fear that was so low-grade I was hardly conscious of it. Passed-down fear, from mother to daughter. Shapeless fear that I resented and tried to ignore. I'd seen this fear in other women's eyes, but never once in the eyes of my brothers or boyfriends. It seemed to be part of being female, like having a menstrual cycle. Somewhere was the vague thought that if I paid attention to this fear, if I ever once said to myself that I wasn't going to do something because I was afraid of being raped, that I would make the thing I feared happen. That was why I didn't want to think about it. Somehow the obvious truth that it is the fact of rape that creates the fear, and not the other way around, was never clear to me until that moment. Victoria was an intelligent, capable, talented woman, a friend and colleague whose judgment I respected. How could this have happened to her?

I didn't know what to say. My impulse to comfort was paralyzed by my ignorance. There was nothing in my own experience to draw upon, nothing at all. Nor could I imagine what she had experienced.

"That's every woman's worst nightmare," I blurted out.

"It was worse than a nightmare," Victoria said.

I could sense a struggle going on inside her—she wanted to tell me what had happened, but she was nervous about it. And I was struggling with my own questions. The rape myths emerged from somewhere in the back of my mind: that *real* rape rarely occurs because women secretly want to be raped; that if rape is inevitable, a woman should lie back and enjoy it; that rape happens to women who are seductive, ask-ing for it; that boys will be boys and Eve is responsible for Adam's sins.

I know better now.

I think that Victoria felt my anxiety and remembered when she did not understand either—a time when rape was an unimaginable night-mare that happened to other women who were, somehow, different from her. But if she felt my fear, she must have felt my affection as well. She decided, I suppose, to trust it.

She told me about her summer in Europe—how free, confident, and self-assured she'd felt as her long season of grief over David's death turned. I didn't understand for ten years—until my own rape—why she seemed to be talking about herself in the third person. This confident girl who felt invulnerable and self-assured seemed like a character in a book she had read. When the waitress appeared with our meals and another round of drinks, Victoria seemed to reconsider her decision to tell me what had happened the night she was raped. The myths were, perhaps, tangling her up, as they would tangle me up a decade later. They would still be there, squeezing through cultural crevices like moray eels when it was my turn to tell.

That night in 1974 I thought she hesitated because telling me about her rape would be like living it over again, as if her memories were asleep and speaking would wake them up. Now I understand that the tension came from her awareness that rape focuses attention on the victim rather than the victimizer. She'd been raped seventeen years before I was—before rape crisis centers, before the American women's movement redefined rape as a crime of violence rather than a sexual act, before post-traumatic stress had a name—back in the Dark Ages when rape jokes were funny and women were expected to laugh at them. I was luckier than Victoria. I was to have the benefit of two decades of research and discussion that raised public awareness of rape and that changed social response to its victims. Still, there were plenty of moments when I felt implicated in the crime against me.

She did go on to tell me her story. It had an uncanny resemblance to my own, but I didn't know that yet. Her demon, unlike the one that awaited me, came out of the darkness, not the light. She woke up, and he was there. This happened. That happened. I tried to imagine enduring what she described, but it was unimaginable. I tried to imagine what she felt, but I could not.

"I went to work the next day," Victoria said, "as if nothing had happened. I didn't tell anyone. I couldn't sleep for months. Finally I told a close friend, but it made me feel worse. I don't like to tell people really."

It was selfish of me, but I asked anyway. "Do you feel worse now—for telling me?"

"No," she said. I must have looked relieved, because she squeezed my hand and smiled.

It was nearly midnight when we finally paid the tab. The night felt even more oppressive after the hours we'd spent deluded by air-conditioning. We hurried to my car, scanning the shadows. I had always been alert on the streets at night. But now I was truly afraid. Rape happened—to women just like me.

Looking back on our conversation that night, I credit myself for listening. I didn't change the subject or tell her no one wants to hear about such terrible things. That fact alone implied that I felt there was nothing shameful in what had happened and what she had done to survive. Listening without trying to protect myself from what she had to tell me must have been enough because our friendship endured and deepened. Her story was part of our connection, a secret we shared. I never told anyone, and Victoria rarely spoke about it again. I sensed her strength and respected her more because of it, but I could not see its dimensions until I myself was raped.

■ ■ ■

The next April I was to have my own lesson in grief. My twenty-three-year-old brother had a severe reaction to medication his doctor had prescribed for a sprain. He slipped into unconsciousness and in the ambulance on the way to the hospital his heart stopped. Although the emergency room staff managed to get his heart going again, his brain was irreparably damaged. I remember the way the doctor drew the picture on a napkin in the hospital coffee shop—the little reptilian brain stem at the bottom, all that was left. The words, *brain dead*. The doctor's tone of voice when she said he could hang on for years. Mercifully it was only four months.

I leaned hard on Victoria in those months, and on Jake, who showed up for old times' sake. They were thrown together as my brother was moved from the hospital ICU to a room with a respirator, to a room without one, and finally to a nursing home where he spent his days strapped to a chair. They comforted me, waiting together in sterile corridors while I sat beside my brother, bewildered and enraged. Not one of the machines that had pulled him back from death could restore his brain. I went through the motions at work, shifting my load to Victoria, who carried it without complaint. While I floated away, weightless in my capsule of grief, Jake and Victoria had to keep their feet on the earth. They were down there together, in the beautiful muck of living where I could not follow.

I took a month's leave of absence from work after my brother's funeral in late July, renting a cabin in the mountains, where I slowly realized that his death had made me a stranger in my own life. Driving back to Washington, I decided I hated my job. I was tired of developing film study curricula for high school teachers, who seemed to spend most of their time bickering about funding. I called Victoria that night and rambled on about my determination to work at the National Endowment for the Arts, a fairly new federal agency dedicated to supporting the arts. Art in America was undergoing a renaissance, I told her, and I wanted to be part of it.

Victoria was, as always, supportive, helpful. Then she stunned me. She'd wanted to tell me, she said, but there was never the right moment. She and Jake were in love. They were engaged. She couldn't hide it any longer. Their relationship was predictable, but I hadn't seen it coming. Although my love affair with Jake had run its course, I felt betrayed and rejected. By the time they were married in mid-

September, I'd quit my job and Victoria and Jake were barely speaking to me. It was easier that way for all of us, although as I look back on it, I can't think why. Someone once said you must lose a fly to catch a trout. At the time, I suppose, the fly mattered.

A few weeks later, I passed the civil service exam (which did not, on its two-page list of possible college majors, have a category for philosophy) and a few months after that I was hired by the Endowment. During the six years I worked for the agency, I ran into Victoria and Jake only once—in a crowded department store one Christmas. I'm not sure they saw me, but I pretended I hadn't seen them.

After I moved to Boston, mutual friends sometimes mentioned Victoria in passing. Her career had taken off—she'd made several documentary films, and although none of her feature-length scripts had gone into production, she was making a living from options and teaching. Her marriage, on the other hand, was troubled. I was not surprised—I suspected Jake's drinking had become a problem. Then I heard she was getting a divorce after eight years of marriage. I wrote her a kind letter but didn't have the courage to mail it. Our estrangement was a habit now. Two more silent years passed.

■ ■ ■

Then my worst nightmare came true. While I was recuperating with my parents in Virginia, Victoria tracked me down through a mutual friend in Boston who had heard about the rape. I was raking leaves one morning when my mother, looking worried, hurried from the house.

"Victoria's on the telephone," she said.

"Victoria?"

"If it's going to upset you to talk to her after all this time, I'd advise against it." My mother rarely gave advice, so I thought about it for a few seconds. Then I ran inside, still carrying the rake. I was crying when I picked up the phone. To my relief, so was Victoria.

We had the trout on the line.

■ ■ ■

"Victoria"

The next afternoon she made the two-hour trip from Washington in a VW bug that looked as beat up as the one she used to drive, except that this one was yellow. We spent the afternoon together on the deck, drinking coffee and stuffing ourselves with Oreos. I told her my story. She did not offer advice. She did not pretend to have a map in her hip pocket. Knowing her story made the telling of mine feel like an exchange rather than a confession. We shared an exile, not an island. She was on her own island, a different shore. She saw me—as I was—and that was the comfort.

We spoke of other things as the afternoon wore on—Jake, her divorce, her work, and Michael, the new man in her life. In the late afternoon my father stuck his head out of the sliding glass doors and wanted to know if the chatterboxes would like a drink. She declined, saying she wanted to get back before dark. In the early days of our friendship I'd found it strange that Victoria was reluctant to drive after dark. If we went out in the evenings, I usually picked her up and brought her home. Even after she told me about her rape, I didn't fully understand her anxiety, the immersion into vulnerability that is rape's legacy.

"I know. I never really understood before," I said, close to tears again, ashamed of myself.

"There's no way you could have," she replied. I knew she was right.

■ ■ ■

From then on, Victoria and I called each other often. I was now settled into my rooms under the eaves in Concord. I called her in the blackest hours because I knew her own rape made her incapable of judging me. She never once said I was overreacting, never made suggestions on what I should or shouldn't do, never questioned my decisions or lack of them, never promised that somewhere over the rainbow I would find myself as I once was. She knew better. And her own life was evidence that grace and humor were still possible. Her existence itself was a promise.

That spring Victoria called with news—she and Michael planned to marry in October. She asked me to be her maid of honor. Of course, I said, I'd be there. But as her wedding day approached, a crippling anxiety seemed to take control of me. Her wedding fell just before the first anniversary of my rape. The leaves were turning again, and the peace I had found seemed to be splintering. The fear crept back. I gave it shape, texture, because it was shapeless and penetrating. Making it resemble something was better than living with its amorphousness. My plane would crash. I'd get lost trying to find the church and end up in an alley in the wrong part of town with my throat slit. I'd be raped and murdered by a maintenance man at the hotel. The cabdrivers might be serial killers. I'd be alone surrounded by strangers. I lay awake at night, watching my own horror movies. In the year since the rape I had hewn out a narrow rut for myself with as few unknowns as possible. I felt too vulnerable to handle a trip.

In its return orbit my fear had the added nastiness of making the tremendous effort of the past year feel like a shameful and humiliating defeat. After a year, I was right back where I started. Fear was the enemy, and it was winning. But if I backed out on Victoria, whose friendship had sustained me, I was giving in, giving up. The fear that returned with the season seemed to be inseparable from myself, like the color of my skin. To hate it was to hate myself. How could I feel proud of myself for what I had achieved in the past year? Who was I one year later? I was a woman who was afraid of fear itself. This was the rapist's first anniversary gift to me.

Thoreau is on record as the first to observe that the only thing we have to fear is fear itself, although Franklin D. Roosevelt usually gets the credit. Fear of fear, Roosevelt said in his inauguration speech at the height of the Great Depression, "paralyzes needed efforts to convert retreat into advance." The fear of fear had made me psychically rigid, an arch-conservative. Dr. Lenore Terr, who has studied trauma in children, refers to the fear of fear as "traumatophobia" (from the term *trauma to phobia,* first coined in 1942 by a psychoanalyst studying battle fatigue). Traumatophobia is a phenomenon that springs from psychic trauma. "Being psychologically overwhelmed," she writes in *Too Scared to Cry,* "is such a hideous feeling that the victim seeks never to experience that sensation again." According to Terr, the fear of fear explains why sexually abused children almost universally are silent about their abuse while it is going on—they are so afraid of what has already taken place that the unknown, what might happen when they tell, paralyzes them.

It also explains the inertia that overcomes people who believe they are hopelessly trapped. An FBI hostage specialist once asked Terr what she thought he could expect from children who were held hostage. Adult hostages, he said, stayed exactly where they had been put by their captors, even when they were in a position to escape. The FBI's problems with adults were identical to what Terr had learned from her follow-up study of twenty-six children kidnapped from their school bus by three armed men in the small farming community of Chowchilla in California's Central Valley in the summer of 1976. The children, all of whom survived their eighteen-hour ordeal, were entombed alive inside a truck trailer that the kidnappers had buried under the ground. The victims made no attempt to escape until the ceiling of their metal coffin began to crumble, a change in conditions that released only a few of the children from their paralysis, permitting them to dig their way out of certain death and find help. Terr makes the point that only a change inside the traumatic situation itself seems to trigger action, and even then not always.

The experience of utter helplessness, established during the first moments of trauma (when the natural fight-or-flight response is blocked completely by inescapable circumstances that cannot be changed, only endured), is a toxin at the core of the self. Although Hollywood action films suggest that helpless human beings spring into action in traumatic situations—indeed, this most popular of genres relies on the formula that a human being plus a crisis equals edge-of-the-seat action—real human beings rarely do. Perhaps the popularity of these films lies in our wish for them to be accurate images of human behavior. But the fear of fear is the most paralyzing of venoms, the psychic equivalent of the poison injected by certain wasps of the American Southwest into their favored prey, the tarantula. The venom paralyzes the spiders so completely that they can be dragged without protest into their own burrows. There the spiders wait for the wasp's eggs to hatch into larvae that will eat them alive. Poison lasts long after the stinger that injected it has been withdrawn.

In the days before Victoria's wedding, I felt the larvae were about to hatch. I called Victoria in tears. The woman I had been was dead, I told her. I was ready to bury her. A person I loathed had taken her place—a woman confined to her rooms by the fear of fear.

Victoria reminded me it was my first anniversary. I had not recognized this before she commented on it. "It always comes back," she said. After eighteen anniversaries Victoria was, after all, an expert. Her observation gave me a way to think about what I was feeling, a moment of self-reflection that released me from the vise of fear. I wasn't loathsome. I was having my first anniversary. She did not try to talk me out of my feelings. She understood them only too well. Because she didn't judge me, I could stop judging myself. I began to think of the fear as the rapist's ghost, and I decided that this time, I would fight to the death. Victoria, meanwhile, set about lessening the unknowns, working out complicated arrangements so that the only thing I had to negotiate alone was the airplane flight. I was to stay with a mutual friend whose parents lived in Washington. The friend would drive me to the rehearsal dinner. And to the wedding the next day.

The alpinist Roger Marshall once said that he believed in an extra-consciousness that looked after him, but "it only comes into play in extreme circumstances, which for me is in the mountains." Victoria's wedding was my mountain and it seemed that while I climbed it a benevolent wisdom beyond my own began to take the place of my fear. This conversion of feeling was not accompanied by tongues of fire or blasts of trumpets. If grace descended, amazing or otherwise, it fell gently, like a dew. As I boarded the plane for Victoria's wedding, I felt that the rapist, and all he represented—the darkness itself—was gone. I leave it to mystics to explain the peace that was mine.

At Victoria's wedding, I met Steve, Michael's best friend. We agreed after we were married that it was love at first sight, across the table at Victoria and Michael's rehearsal dinner. It happens. At least it happened to us.

■ ■ ■

There is a coda to this story. Without Victoria's friendship, I could not have packed my bags and boarded the plane to Washington that October in 1986. The story I write now would be a different story, and I am not sure I would be writing any story at all had Victoria not come back into my life. Over the many months of work on this book, she has been a harbor from the storms of self-doubt that have plagued its voyage. Although our shared experience of rape is a deep bond, she has taken another path for herself. She is still careful about who knows she was raped.

Victoria, the bravest woman I know, asked me not to use her real name.

The Good Ground

between the grains of change
blue permanence

one short step
to the good ground

MAY SWENSON, "Love Is"

It was two days before the first anniversary of the rape, and Victoria and I were making repairs in front of the mirror in the hotel bathroom. I was relieved to find that the rehearsal dinner was small and informal— about fifteen people. She began filling me in on Michael's side of the guest list, coming last to Steve. He was divorced, she explained, had two children—a nine-year-old daughter and an eighteen-year-old son who was a freshman at Berkeley—was forty-three, and ran a national environment foundation in San Francisco. "He's been divorced for five years," she said, "so that's good—he's not on the rebound. Not that I'm matchmaking." She blotted her lipstick and stared critically at herself in the mirror.

"Stop," I said. "You've never looked better."

"I like Steve. He's solid, you know—an 'old soul.' And I think he's awfully handsome."

"You are too doing it," I said.

"Doing what?"

"Matchmaking."

"Well, maybe just a little." She grinned sheepishly.

We hurried back through the lobby to the small banquet room Victoria had rented for the occasion. Weddings make old friends of strangers, and the gathering had the atmosphere of a family reunion, with hugs replacing handshakes and everyone talking at once. Victoria and Michael's happiness was contagious and I felt perfectly at ease. Michael introduced me to Steve only moments before someone managed to be heard above the din directing us to find our assigned places at the table. Victoria was right—he was handsome.

Steve was seated diagonally across from me. Between us was a centerpiece with lilies and ferns that was beautiful, but a conversational bundling board. Still I felt Steve was flirting across it and I could feel myself blushing. Steve had the bluest eyes imaginable, and they were hard to ignore. They were warm, intelligent, and slightly mischievous, as if he were looking out on a world that might tumble at any moment into something that could amuse him. When he looked at me I saw appreciation and interest. For the first time in a year I felt that I looked attractive. It felt damned good.

Steve delivered a toast to Victoria and Michael halfway through the main course that impressed me because it made them both laugh but not blush. I was struck by how at home he was in his body, which was compact and trim. There was self-confidence, but it was cut by a vulnerability that I sensed came from a distant season of pain he had put behind him.

As dessert was being served, Steve got up and came around the table to my chair. "I'm sorry we were seated so far apart," he said. "It's difficult to talk through the undergrowth."

"I hardly recognize you out here in the open," I said.

"I was wondering if we could have brunch tomorrow. The wedding doesn't start until two."

For an instant I hesitated.

"That would be lovely," I replied.

155

∎ ∎ ∎

I remember that small moment of hesitation as a long pause. When I looked into Steve's eyes, I saw a different woman than the one who had called Victoria in tears. I saw a woman who smiled and blushed and flirted and felt the small tug of a future that held—she knew not what. I saw a part of myself that I had not seen since the rape. For a year I had believed that any reconstruction of myself that resembled what had existed before was impossible. But here was a shard, a remnant of a woman who felt curious about the future, rather than fearful of it. Life had not just flowed around me, like a stream around an immovable tangle of debris. I had moved with the stream. In Steve's eyes I could measure the distance I had covered.

I didn't really know Steve, yet my intuition told me he would be part of my life. Intuitions are mysterious, sudden leaps over rational processes to understanding. Before the rape, I had not only valued my intuition, I had trusted it completely. It was a way of knowing that was both discovery and recognition; it did not replace more plodding rational processes, but only invigorated them. But after the rape I no longer trusted my intuition. I asked myself over and over again why I had not sensed that something evil was close. Why had my intuition failed me?

The question did not present itself in this way—it did not fit neatly into a sentence that, once written, is obviously absurd and that casts light only on the sunken hulk of self-blame. If I had articulated this question, I might have been able to see how cruel, muddled, and unfair it was. But it was beyond language, a dense core of feeling that I had betrayed myself by not anticipating what was going to happen to me. It was a deeply rooted belief, and such beliefs are neither entirely rational nor easily demolished by argument, especially those that hold up an even more elemental need. The sense that I was responsible for the rape supported a more important belief, one that I could not give up, although it had been severely damaged. It was the belief that I could control what happened to me, that my actions had a bearing on the outcome of my life.

Helplessness seems to me to be the first and last indignity of human life, one we strive to hurry past in childhood, one we dread to think we might meet again in old age. I remember where I was and what I was wearing on the day I finally learned to tie my own shoelaces. Control over one's own body is the model for the more complex tasks of autonomous and authentic human existence where we may speak meaningfully, for example, of the destiny of planet Earth being within our collective control. To give up belief in control is a redefinition not only of the self, but of the world outside the self. How shall the world outside the self be conceived if it cannot be controlled, managed, brought into line with our image of its purpose? When the eastern tribes of American Indians began dying from European diseases transmitted by inland trade in the seventeenth century (sometimes well before they encountered the white man himself), they lost something more devastating than population. As healing rituals failed, they lost the belief in a meaningful relationship to their physical and spiritual world. Whatever our conception of the world may be, it is both unbearable and inconceivable without the belief in control.

Believing I was responsible for what happened to me that October afternoon actually supported the belief that I could be in control of my own life. It was the sole buttress for the span that could link my future and my past after the rape because regaining a sense of control over my life was the only way forward. It was that or ceasing to live a meaningful life. But there was a costly toll for crossing the bridge—years of self-blame and guilt.

The belief that my intuition had let me down was reinforced and strengthened by the overwhelming fear and loss of identity I continued to experience in Concord. Losing confidence in my own intuition was the loss of a function that I believe is innate in all human beings. In that year I was left with only rational processes that were barely recognizable because they were continually twisted by fear, which was itself a protection against the rage that I could not allow to surface. It would eventually rise from the depths, the behemoth I had caught a glimpse of in my father's workshop and seen again in the garden in Concord when I burned what was left of the physical traces of those terrible hours.

■ ■ ■

This brings me back to a moment of hesitation, a clock's second hand moving from one dot to another. Recalling that moment, I cannot escape my knowledge of the destination I perceived in that first meeting, a destination that is now my daily life, and a good one on the whole. The details were missing then, and just because I have them now as part of my history and part of Steve's does not make the intuitive leap less astounding. To decide to trust an intuition—in this case, a feeling of connection with Steve—was an act of self-forgiveness, one that I would have to repeat many times before I could finally demolish altogether the belief that I was responsible for the rape. It implied that the self that had let me down—the intuitive self—did not deserve eternal damnation and punishment. It had to be forgiven, and trusting an intuition was an absolution.

The belief, however, that I was responsible for the rape was not destroyed with a single absolution, nor could I have described what was going on within me at the time. For many years to come it thrived within, and my self-blame grew cell by cell. By the time I could see it, it was a malignancy on my spirit.

There is another aspect to this belief that compels me to venture beyond my experience into the historical moment in which I live, the world outside myself. I see this world differently now than before I embarked on the long journey of discovery that has been my life since the rape. For it is in this world, and not some other, that I must find a place beside the hearth. I view it now with the eyes of a refugee, and find companions where I least expect them.

Recently, a close friend in her mid-forties suffered a stroke. After several months of tests, her doctors discovered that she had a hole in her heart, a congenital disorder called ventricular septal defect that had gone undetected since birth, as well as a rare problem that caused her blood to clot too readily. This hole let a clot pass into her brain one morning while she stood in her shower, getting ready for work. One day, many months after the stroke and while she was still struggling to regain the use of the left side of her body, she called me in tears.

"I feel like I did this to myself," she said.

"You gave yourself a hole in the heart and cooked up a clotting disorder to go with it?" I replied. "I'm impressed."

"Why me, then?"

"Is that a medical question?"

"No. I just wonder what I did to deserve this."

"Just guessing," I replied, "but probably nothing at all."

"Maybe I was working too hard...." She rattled off a long list of accomplishments that under any other circumstances would have filled her with pride. Then she started in on possible flaws in her personality that might have caused her illness—her short fuse, her perfectionism. I knew only too well where she was going.

"Ever hear of bad luck?" I said.

"I'm not sure I believe in bad luck."

"Maybe you're going to have to start," I replied.

"Why?"

"Because the alternative is very unattractive."

She was comforting herself by thinking she had control over the cause of her misery. Her guilt and self-blame seemed easier to bear than the thought that she was a helpless victim of a genetic weakness that had ambushed her one morning in the shower. Perhaps it was unkind of me to try to talk her out of it. Some mutual friends did hint that she had "caused" her stroke somehow. There were those unresolved issues from childhood (always a safe bet), and she was impatient, a perfectionist when it came to her work. True, she didn't smoke or drink and was a bit of a health nut. Still...

Everyone seemed to have a theory about the cause of her illness that ignored the obvious one her doctors had spent months investigating. Somehow, in some mysterious way, my friend was responsible for her illness, as if illness itself were unnatural. I recognized their censure as a need to protect a belief that she and I, for different reasons, had been forced to abandon—that you can control what happens to you. I wondered whether, had my friend been the victim of an epidemic illness that affected many individuals in the community at the same time—a plague caused by bacteria in our drinking water, for example—anyone would have wondered if she was responsible for her illness.

Bad luck. It does not seem so radical a notion. Yet it appears to go against the cultural grain. My friend was blaming herself, just as I had done, with as little cause. It seemed to me that being a victim (defined as "one that is acted on and usually adversely affected by a force or agent," "one that is injured, destroyed or sacrificed under any of various conditions," "one that is subjected to oppression, hardship or mistreatment") was no longer perceived as a fact of human existence, a fact of life—like illness and death. I began to wonder if blaming victims for their misfortunes had a cultural function, just as individual self-blame has a psychological one. It denies the conditions or agents that create the suffering and protects the belief in control. If we ban victims, we can also deny the forces or agents that make them.

When you become a victim of certain types of illness—depression and chronic fatigue syndrome come to mind—or of certain kinds of crimes, especially rape, this subtle but pervasive interpretation of suffering makes being a victim feel like some kind of personal failure. I wanted to give my friend the notion of bad luck because with it comes a blameless suffering, a path toward acceptance of the cause of suffering, itself a way to become a survivor and a witness. There is an odd humiliation in feeling I must defend my suffering while I am suffering, that I cannot grant, even to myself, the right to pain I cannot escape. More is required than understanding my own suffering. I must also understand how it is perceived by others if I am to reconstruct another self and take a new place in society.

How to believe in bad luck when the invisible forces that once administered it hardly exist any longer in collective consciousness and the comfort afforded by collective rituals of protection are mostly meaningless relics? Reconnection with the self will always be incomplete as long as it remains a private, personal task. Despite a very real effort by society to acknowledge victims of abuse and oppression, and thus the conditions that cause the abuse and oppression, there seems to be another, more subtle tide moving in the opposite direction. My friend and I have both felt its tug, and we must deal with it if we are to forge this reconnection with self and community.

Perhaps not all rape victims blame themselves as I did, although all rape victims do find themselves adrift in a sea of silence that makes those who do not blame themselves astonishing marvels of sanity. But I believed for many years that I caused my own rape—by being disorganized and losing my car keys, by failing to intuit that the rapist was present, by my physical incapacity to overpower him, and by my failure to find words that would magically make him go away.

I have come a long distance from that single moment of decision—the moment I chose to trust my intuition again, Steve standing beside my chair, looking hopeful. It was a small, grand moment, a beginning without fear. Slowly trusting my intuitive self over and over again as Steve and I found our way together was a reassembling that would bring self-forgiveness to a level that allowed me, eventually, to see what I had not yet forgiven.

"That would be lovely," I said to Steve, knowing that all futures from now on would be futures where evil was possible, at any moment, and from unseen dimensions. Yes, I knew this very well. But I knew, too, that evil was not the only possibility. Life seemed to me then to be desirable simply because it had gone on. It had carried me to this moment, and I felt Steve was there in it with me.

■　■　■

We have a photograph on our dresser that was taken at Victoria and Michael's wedding. Steve and I are standing close together, facing each other. He has placed his hand on my elbow, as if we were about to turn and walk away arm in arm. I am laughing at something he has said, and he is smiling, leaning toward me, looking pleased. Victoria's father is in the background, slightly out of focus. He is smiling, too, a wistful smile. We are oblivious, focused on each other. The joy that caught the eye of the photographer has become deeper and wider than it was at that moment, but no less intense.

We did walk away arm in arm soon after the picture was taken. We had dinner together in Old Town Alexandria, and afterward we walked. I cannot remember what we talked about, only that there was nothing in our way. After we had walked a long time, we passed a stone house whose many windows glowed dimly in candlelight. We heard chamber music, the tones of a bass viola. We stood in front, watching guests gather in small groups on the front lawn, where lanterns cast flickering pools of light on the garden. Time seemed round, as if we were circling back to a place where we'd been before.

As we stood there, an awkwardness passed briefly between us for the first time. There seemed to be a destination for this day, but we had old scripts and none of them were right. The words we exchanged are forgotten now. Even Steve, who is much better at remembering who said what, when, has forgotten them. Only our intentions are still vivid.

I look back on that night with astonishment. A few days before the first anniversary of my rape I decide to spend the night alone in a hotel room with a man I barely know. It seemed that the substance of fear that had tormented me for a year had become the substance of faith, as if a transsubstantiation had begun at Victoria's wedding and was now complete.

Before the rape I believed that the opposite of fear was courage. With the danger or difficulty fully in view, I believed that the best tactic for a risky situation was a combination of perseverance and brute strength, mental or physical. When I was a kid, for example, I was afraid of snakes, especially water moccasins, because they tended to congregate at a narrow bend in the creek where my brothers and I swam. The tea-colored pool that formed there was only waist-deep on an eight-year-old, and its bottom was slimy from rotting vegetation, but it was all we had. On summer days it was irresistible. We drove the snakes away by throwing stones into the water and beating the banks with sticks. Although my brothers thought these precautions sufficient, I still had snake thoughts, which I banished from my mind by closing my eyes and imagining the swimming hole I wished we had—the one without snakes. Only then, still afraid, would I throw myself from the bank. That was courage.

But I was not being courageous when I walked into Steve's hotel room. I wasn't taking a risk of any kind. Being courageous implies resistance against something that is present—fear or difficulty or danger. But there was no danger or difficulty.

The opposite of fear is not, I think, courage. It is faith.

We held each other all night. For many hours after he had fallen asleep I lay awake listening to his breathing and the rattle of leaves tumbling over cobblestones in the street. No man had held me since the rape. The rapist had violated my most basic human need—my bodyright. By destroying my ability to control my own body, he had made my body an object. I lost a sense of it as the boundary of self, the fundamental and most sacred of all borders. A self without boundaries is like a weak country that has been overrun by a stronger one. Once the borders are violated and the invader is entrenched, inhabitants can do little more than go into hiding and hope for outside aid. Touch that respects bodyright is healing; it restores the autonomy and authenticity of the self. Although Steve did not know that I had been raped—I didn't tell him until the next morning—he seemed to understand the role he was to play in this restoration.

At dawn I slipped away to the little balcony and watched the eastern sky fill with color. It did not matter to me at that moment whether I ever saw Steve again. I had made a choice. I had trusted my deepest feelings about Steve. I could go on alone.

The next morning over breakfast I told Steve about the rape. I wanted him to know that I was grateful for the good, solid ground I had found. A harpist was playing in a corner of the restaurant, and I remember thinking that I'd feel the scene was overwritten if I read it in a novel. But there she was in a blue gown, strumming away like an angel.

Telling Steve about the events of that October afternoon wasn't complicated. I saw myself and the rape differently now. I thought of the rapist as a defeated enemy and myself as a heroine. What shame was there in my victory? I was a survivor. I was proud of myself for trusting my feelings about Steve, and this pride spilled over as I rewrote the story of the rape and the year that followed it. The facts were the same, but my relationship to them had changed, and so the story was different because a different person was now telling it. This I observed as it was happening, and it interested me. I was not only a survivor, but a witness to my own survival. I saw, too, that however painful my feelings of the past year had been, the pain had not, after all, replaced other feelings, but only hidden them from sight. It was like being inside the house under bright lights at night. You look out the window, and the darkness is thick and covers the stars. But if you leave the house and walk out into the night and look up, after a time you can see one star and then many stars. They were there the whole time.

■ ■ ■

Victoria's wedding was the beginning of what seemed to be a total remission from the effects of the rape. I still think of that weekend as a mystery, an encounter with grace that I do not question. My apparent remission was accompanied by an inner contentment that was all the more profound because of the misery that had preceded it and that, indeed, seemed to be its source. My perception of this relationship between pain and joy transformed my feelings about the rape. It felt like the fire that forges the blade, not the all-consuming inferno that destroys it. I believed that I had been given a numinous gift, the formula for turning straw into gold. The rape, for all its horror, was a path, not a sentence. I believed I was stronger than I had ever been and that I was leaving the rape behind me forever. It was Gerard Manley Hopkins's "that night, that year, of now done darkness," and it was over. While the harpist played, I wrote an ending to the story that I wanted to read. But it was not the one I would live.

■ ■ ■

I had made plans to spend a few days with my parents after the wedding, and my mother and brother Ed were driving in from Virginia to pick me up that morning. After breakfast Steve and I sat on a bench in front of the hotel waiting for them to arrive. I was glad he was going to meet my mother. I knew she'd be reading between the lines from half a block away and it comforted me. My mother and her sisters often joked that my grandmother chose their husbands for them. "Mama could size somebody up quicker than anyone on this earth," Aunt Lace told me when she was close to ninety. "When she didn't like a beau, you knew it because she never said a word about him—one way or the other. She could do right much with silence. When Mama paid a man a compliment, it sank in without you even knowing it. Of course, we didn't figure it out until we'd all married the men Mama liked." With a sly smile, she added, "I've got to hand it to her—she did a pretty good job when I look back on it."

My mother used the same technique with me, although when I leapt into marriage at nineteen I wasn't wise enough to listen to her. Like her mother, she had a sixth sense about people and I came to respect it more and more as I grew older. Although she was gracious to the man I considered marrying when I was in my early thirties, her polite silence put me on alert. When I told her I had broken off the engagement, she finally said. "I'm relieved. I never felt he was right for you."

"I noticed."

"It was something in his eyes," she said.

Ed's silver Celica pulled up to the entrance of the hotel just as Steve was telling me he'd like to visit me in Massachusetts later in the fall. Well, maybe, I thought to myself, he'd come. If he didn't, I still had my foot on new ground. I introduced my mother and Ed to Steve and the four of us stood around on the curb chatting about the wedding for a few minutes. Then my mother offered to take Steve to the airport for his flight back to California. They fell into an easy conversation on the way. Steve's quirky sense of humor amused my mother, just as it did me, and she was smiling warmly when he turned to wave good-bye before disappearing into the crowd at the terminal.

She didn't mention Steve until we were nearly home. Then, after we'd exhausted every other conceivable subject, she announced, "You know, I really like Steve's eyes." The significance of her remark was not lost on my brother, who, slipping his right arm back between the bucket seats, flashed me a private but enthusiastic thumbs-up.

"I do, too," I said.

"I noticed," my mother replied.

■ ■ ■

A month and many phone calls later, Steve did come to see me in Concord. The odor of burned pecan pie (his favorite) wafted from my oven down the stairs and into the hallway. (I've never tried to make another.) He stood in the smoky haze at the top of the stairs and looked around at what I suddenly thought he might find appallingly humble. He'd described his apartment over the telephone—a view of San Francisco Bay, orchids on the balcony, antiques he'd inherited from his parents. I'd been less than forthcoming about mine. He put his bag down and pulled a box out of the side pocket. "Now that I see where you live," he said, "I feel I made the right choice." After digging around in voluminous layers of bubble wrap and tissue paper, I finally felt something. It was a crystal vase, a very elegant crystal vase.

"It's beautiful," I said.

"Like these floors. They're wonderful!"

We visited each other four more times—once more in Concord, once at my parents', and twice in San Francisco—between Victoria and Michael's wedding in October and the following March when he proposed, formally, on his knee in the garden of his family home. I accepted, and we danced a wild polka among the camellia and around stately white oaks, until we fell breathless onto the grass. We figured it out the other day—excluding the phone calls, we'd spent less than a month together.

The Good Ground

Although Steve's children lived an hour's drive from the city with his ex-wife, he shared custody and was deeply involved in their daily lives. Without needing to discuss it at any length, I understood that Steve's moving to Boston was out of the question because of them. If we were going to be together, I would have to move west. Before meeting Steve, I had never even visited California, nor had I ever imagined I would live there. Boston was where I planned to live for the rest of my life.

If it is possible to fall in love with a city in a single moment, I had done so with Boston ten years earlier. It was as if I'd always had a Boston inside my heart and only discovered it when I set eyes on the real city for the first time. The moment of this recognition is still clear in my mind. I was taking the Red Line from Cambridge into the city for the first time. The subway emerged from the tunnel to cross the Charles River and stopped in the middle of the bridge, waiting for a signal. The sun was setting upriver and the water was glassy and glowing in evening colors. Crew boats glided upriver in long thin files; their oars, rising and falling in harmony, left slender wakes of gold behind. The stillness lasted only a moment. The train lurched forward again and the moment passed. But in it I discovered that I would never feel a stranger in this place.

Leaving Boston, abandoning the friendships and professional connections I had formed over a decade, should have been more conflicting than it was. But Boston felt like a friend who had betrayed me. Only recently have some of my feelings of affection for the city returned. After the rape I saw the city differently. Somewhere on the streets of Boston skulked the man who raped me. If our paths crossed, he'd recognize me, but I was still blindfolded. For many months after I was raped, I could not get on the subway or stand in line at the bank without asking myself whether the rapist was sitting next to me or standing behind me.

But after a few months I noticed that some men frightened me more than others—overweight, stocky, fair-haired white men in their twenties were especially upsetting. Although I did not see the man who raped me, perhaps in some sense I did know what he looked like, as if the information about him gathered by my other senses, which terror had heightened to the point of excruciating sensitivity in the first minutes of the attack, somehow formed an image in my brain. My visceral reaction to a certain physical type was immediate and produced flashbacks of the rape that had a peculiar vivacity.

I saw a man meeting the rapist's "description" getting into a car at a supermarket in Cambridge nearly a year after the rape, and my physical reaction—a paralyzing recoil—was instantaneous. Everything about him was horribly familiar—his shuffling gait and the way he held his body over his legs, his hair, his feet, his height. The rapist's odor came back to me, as if I were catching his scent on the air from across the parking lot. Raw feeling of this intensity has a compelling truth that my rational mind did not know what to do with then, and still doesn't. Perhaps I invented a mental image of the rapist out of a psychological need to fasten a human shape onto the formless thing that I had not seen and that seemed, therefore, to emerge from another dimension in an inhuman form. Perhaps my construction—the fat, fair-haired man— was a way of cutting the external threat down to a manageable size, from all men to only some. Perhaps my "description" was drawn from a long-buried memory of a schoolyard bully.

As I write these words I remember an incident when I was thirteen that I had, until this moment, completely forgotten. An American boy who was several years older and lived across the street from our house in Germany threw a baseball at me as I pedaled my bicycle past his front lawn. It hit my buttocks with such force it knocked me off my bicycle. I remember his derisive laughter at my tears and the yellowish bruise radiating from the blue-black point of impact that lasted for weeks. I knew there was something sexual going on, because he had made crude references to parts of my body on several occasions before this. It was from him that I first heard the shocking four-letter words that so many years later I heard the rapist say. I can see him now. He is fat, blond, and stocky.

Unless the man who raped me is caught and admits to his crime, I will never be certain if the man in the supermarket parking lot was the rapist, or even if my image of him is accurate. But I cannot shake the feeling that my body does not lie. I still react to men meeting this description differently than I do to other men—the memory of the rape returns. Only now do I wonder if the image I carry of the rapist is an image formed not at thirty-nine but at thirteen.

Of course, there would be overweight white men in their twenties in San Francisco, and rapists of every other description on its streets. But as I prepared to leave Boston I began to anticipate how good it would feel to know that my chances of encountering one particular rapist would be cut by three thousand miles. Worrying about earthquakes (and before long experiencing one) seemed a fair exchange.

■　■　■

The day before Steve and I were married, we drove out to Concord from Boston in a rented van. We'd come for Pamela's bed, the only thing left in my apartment, the only aspect of my move that I could not face alone. We extricated all the pieces from the closet and carried them down the narrow stairs. With borrowed tools Steve repaired the frame, first gluing the severed pieces together and then securing them with metal strips hammered into the wood over the cut at quarter-inch intervals. Pamela's aunt owned the only unconverted carriage house still standing in the city of Cambridge, a sturdy building with wooden floors and horse stalls, and it was here that we deposited the bed. I polished the headboard and footboard, wrapped the mattress in plastic, carefully stacked the pieces in a stall, and covered everything with a sheet. I didn't tell Steve anything about the bed, nor did he ask.

"That's the last of it," he said as we drove away.

We were married the next day on Cape Cod in an Episcopal ceremony witnessed by his children, my family, and a few close friends. It was late June 1987, a year and eight months after the rape. Victoria was, of course, my maid of honor.

■　■　■

We settled into married life in Steve's apartment on Russian Hill, not far from North Beach, San Francisco's "Little Italy." After a year and a half in the city and months of looking, we bought a small, run-down house in a ravine in Sausalito, a picturesque town clinging to hills just north of the Golden Gate Bridge that was famous in the early days of San Francisco for its abundant supply of fresh drinking water. Three of its many springs, we were to discover, issued from the blackberry-infested hillside behind the house that would eventually become our garden. We moved in with construction crews who arrived every week-day morning at eight A.M sharp, boom boxes blaring, for six months. When they finally left, we had a home together.

Throughout this two-year period of change and construction, con-scious thoughts of the rape disappeared completely, although, of course, I had not forgotten it had happened. A journal entry recorded on October 11, 1987, focuses only on the pleasures of a family outing with Steve's daughter, Elizabeth. But three days later I record a dream that I describe as deeply troubling. In the dream I am exploring a land-scape near my parents' home, one I seem to recognize as a dream land-scape in which I have ventured before. It is beautiful country with rolling hills, protected glens, and great outcroppings of black rock. As I walk I remember that access to this landscape is through the basement of a large house, although I cannot remember where the house is or when I entered it. I come upon a place built of stone and I know that below the ground is a complex set of rooms, caverns, and waterfalls. The atmosphere is "profoundly threatening" and the stones seem to have a power or energy within them. "Suddenly," I write, "a lion approaches. It guards this place. I see it coming toward me and begin to fight it. In the course of the fight I am bitten by snakes. I kill the lion, somehow, by hitting it with its own limbs, but it won't fully die, although it is now in pieces. I am poisoned by the snakes, but I, too, do not die. I cannot enter the chambers below. This is a known yet unknown place—full of dangers, unexpected."

A year later, I am still silent about the rape but again record a dream of threats encountered in a submerged world. I describe a landscape that I feel I have seen before "in another dream." Again the dream begins close to home; this time Steve and his children are nearby. But I leave them to follow dark horses along a twisting path among jagged dark rocks that look like "ruins" to the edge of a cliff. I plunge with the horses into the sea and swim into an underwater room where I find I can breathe. The horses are at first shy and cautious as they flit about in the air/water "like birds." But soon they become bolder and more threatening, "no longer birdlike but beastlike." One horse attempts to grab my face in its mouth as I peep out of a window. "I wake up," I write, "with the sense of having drawn to myself, as if to tame, a force mindless and untamable."

These dreams, recorded without comment, seemed at the time to be dreams someone else was having. In these years I lived my daily waking life in the state of blessedness that had begun at Victoria's wedding. I recorded its textures faithfully in my journal from this period. Only these dreams hint at what was to come. I ask myself now what was really going on during these years. Was this a textbook case of denial? My remission, after all, did not last. Isn't that evidence that the pain, fear, and anger were merely submerged beneath the surface, as the dreams I recorded suggest?

Yet the feeling of being whole and connected with myself and therefore with Steve, his children, and a community of new friends and colleagues in San Francisco was no illusion. I was happy. Not middling happy but profoundly happy. I do not mean to suggest that making the adjustments this new life required was effortless. When life goes on, it goes on with lumps. I was profoundly happy simply because life was going on.

I did miss my friends and parents three time zones away, and stepfamilies are complicated—perhaps even more complicated than original ones. I had to learn how to conduct the daily negotiations of family life after years of living alone. Steve and I argued, said things we didn't mean, made up. The usual stuff.

I felt the strangeness of the land itself, and that I would always be a stranger in it. I seemed never to know what season it was, and I was always cold. Summer was winter. October was summer. February was spring. The light was stronger, cleaner, untarnished, exposing, and the sun setting over the ocean (rather than rising from it) seemed like a different sun altogether. I was disoriented by the feeling that I was losing the distinction between indoors and outdoors, that rooms were permeable membranes. The dramatic beauty of the Bay Area stunned me out of metaphors. I missed the green of eastern summers yet experienced true green for the first time when winter rains transformed the browned headlands into pastures fit for paradise. I missed the hush of white in winter on city streets, the dream time of snow. When we lived on Russian Hill a flock of squawking parrots flew by our dining room window every morning and seals barked at night from the bay, their sharp calls punctuating the mournful bass chorus of foghorns. Our windows in Sausalito didn't have screens—and didn't need them. It rained for months, and then not at all.

Finding work in a city where I had few professional contacts was discouraging at first, but within a year I was busy freelancing for private foundations and nonprofit arts groups—writing annual reports, catalogs, grant requests. I was productive, content. At the same time I associated myself with an arts center located in the Marin headlands, part of the Golden Gate National Recreation Area, and through its artist residency program rented a studio at the beach where I retreated to write. On clear days I could see breakers smacking the beach and dignified processions of pelicans flying between the lagoon and pinnacles of rock through the window over my desk. In the summer when the fog pouring over the scrubby hills drove away the sun-worshippers, foxes came down to hunt for scraps on the deserted beach.

The other tenants in the building were visual artists. I envied them their tubes of color, their brushes soaking in thinner, the music they played while they worked. Why not? I thought. This is California. You can re-invent yourself. When one of the artists moved out, I bought her workbench and started painting, something I had not tried since third grade when my picture was rejected for the bulletin board next to the principal's office. Painting was to become a way through the dark time to come when the beasts of dreams and the underworld they inhabited began to seek the light.

Almost overnight, soon after we finished the renovation in Sausalito, the unity within turned to anarchy; the inner calm that had made it possible for me to embrace changes with confidence and optimism turned to a feeling of isolation, and the isolation soon warped into a depression far worse than anything I had experienced before.

When memories and feelings of the rape began to surface two years after my marriage, I did not recognize them. They seemed to have undergone a complete metamorphosis, like the water tigers, the predatory, underwater larvae of the diving beetle, which seem to be another species from the hard-shelled, winged adults they become. The beetles did not look like water tigers at all. This metamorphosis of trauma has a name in psychological literature—dissociation—and except when related to brain injury, it is always a response to traumatic life events. Memories and feelings connected with the traumatic event are seemingly forgotten. They return not in their original form but as intrusive flashes of distorted recollections, as overwhelming anxiety and panic unwarranted by current experience, as emotional stupors covered over by acting "normal."

In light of what came after my brief walk in paradise, can I still believe that remission had actually happened to me? Was I "repressing" the trauma or had I experienced something else? And if it was something else, what was it? Why do I still feel that calling this experience "dissociation" is an easy way out of my own incapacity to describe it? Yet what other words do I have if I abandon the language of psychology, a discipline that may someday soon be understood as biochemical phenomena, reactions in the cells and synapses of the brain that can be altered by a pill?

I am left with the words *pardon* or *mercy,* the archaic meaning of the word *grace* according to the *Oxford English Dictionary,* which in scriptural and theological language is God's temporary exemption— "the divine influence which operates in men to regenerate and sanctify, to inspire various impulses, and to impart strength to endure trial and resist temptation." I believe I was granted (by whom or what I cannot say) a full but temporary pardon that permitted me to construct the hull of the vessel that would carry me here, to words themselves, the witnessing of my own survival. It is a mystery, one of many in my life. I am content with the words of the old Gospel song:

> *My soul looked back in wonder,*
> *how I got over,*
> *how I got over.*

ELEVEN

A Fall from Grace

and the path starts
nowhere and drops off sheer

D. M. DOOLING, "Transition"

In Daniel Defoe's *Journal of the Plague Year,* a novel written in 1722 that poses as a true account of the ravages of the Black Death in London fifty-seven years earlier, the narrator, H.F., relates the story of a man running all day and night through the streets of London to escape from his own infection. His cure included a mad swim across the Thames. The man made a remarkable recovery—and survived his cure.

The image of a man trying to outrun his fate came to mind recently when I began to look back on my first two years in California. Although I made no resolve to stay in perpetual motion, to fill each hour with something productive, useful, helpful, I may as well have. And had I given any thought to describing my life at the time, I might have agreed with my mother, who worried that I was overdoing everything. But my energy seemed boundless. I was getting on with my life, and the busier it was, I thought, the better.

My consulting work was soon nearly full-time. Still, I volunteered at the arts center that was renting me "a room of my own." No matter that I never had time to use it.

I knew I would have to earn the affection and respect of Steve's children and I worked at it diligently. Steve and I often drove over to Berkeley to visit his son, Sayre, a student at the university. We visited his daughter, Elizabeth, two nights a week, a two-hour round trip on congested freeways. We attended school plays, parents' nights, softball games, and piano recitals. Elizabeth spent every other weekend with us, and I tried to make each one memorable. We baked cookies, bicycled in Golden Gate Park, visited museums, hiked, picnicked. I organized slumber parties, birthday parties, and monthlong summer vacations at Lake Tahoe, where Steve and his sister had a house.

We entertained new friends frequently. Although the kitchen in our apartment was little more than a galley, I thought nothing of tackling formal dinner parties. Steve and I went to the theater and concerts, attended art openings and fund-raisers. I accompanied him on environmental site visits with his board of trustees and their spouses—to the rain forests of Costa Rica, the Florida Everglades, and the deserts of Utah. We even managed to squeeze in a belated honeymoon in the Caribbean. I traveled frequently to Virginia to see my family, and called and wrote old friends in Boston regularly, determined to preserve the intimacy that distance threatened to dilute.

I cleaned, shopped for groceries, cooked—happily organizing every nook and cranny of our lives. I insisted we go into family counseling with Steve's ex-wife to work out joint-parenting issues. In my zeal to maintain old ties, I devoted a month to helping a friend from Boston move to San Francisco, finding her an apartment and helping her settle into it. I cheerfully chauffeured her around the city, as if she were incapable of finding her own way. She wanted a canary. I drove her to Oakland to buy one. The canary didn't sing. I drove her back to Oakland to get another. That canary's singing drove her crazy. I drove her back again to Oakland to return it. I cleaned her stove, installed pan racks in her kitchen, and took days off from my own projects to take her sight-seeing.

For a year, I spent my "spare time" house-hunting. Finding one that had to be rebuilt from top to bottom did not bother me, although

Steve worried we were taking on more than we could handle. Steve's assessment, as it turned out, was more accurate than mine, at least about the amount of work involved. The renovation required more time, money, and energy than either of us would have guessed. However, I was right about our being able to do the job.

Living in the house while it was being torn down around us added to the challenge, but at least that way I could busy myself in every detail of the construction. I woke up in the middle of the night to rain falling through open skylights onto new hardwood floors. We went for a month without a kitchen. While Steve was at work, I stayed close to the action, cheerfully taking on the role of project manager. I was there to call pest control when the carpenters refused to work because of an infestation of fleas, hangers-on from the former owner's dog. I noticed if a light switch had been installed upside down and when the painter had used the wrong color in the guest room—birch white instead of antique white. I stayed busy, busy—buying faucets, wall sconces, toilets, sinks, tile, window shades, carpeting. Together Steve and I stained the new hardwood floor upstairs, working board by board on our hands and knees. It rivaled in effort and result that other floor I had refinished alone in my attic although at the time, surprisingly, I did not even think of it.

I met work deadlines, despite the pounding and sawing, the roar of the compressor, and the cacophony of boom boxes tuned to country western music (the carpenters), hard rock (the roofers), AM talk (the plumbers), classical (the electrician), and pop (the painters). When the house was as finished as any house can ever be, we started work on the garden and adopted a cat.

I was making a new life, one that left behind the woman who had been raped.

■ ■ ■

In early August 1989, a few months after we finished the house, I recorded a nightmare in my journal. In the dream I crash-land a "box-like vehicle" in a "vast swamp teeming with fish, frogs, and strange

177

aquatic creatures." A crab emerges from the ooze, grabs hold of something I am holding—"a book or a picture"—and tries to pull me under. I wake up, terrified. "This scene," I write, "is connected with a landscape of swamp and river I feel I have seen before in another dream—a place somewhat familiar, associated with raw, submerged forces." Then I asked myself a question: "What might have happened if I'd let the crab drag me under?" I would not have to wait long for the answer.

Two months later, on the fourth anniversary of the rape, I mention the rape in my journal for the first time since my marriage. Even in my most private and intimate dialogue with myself, the rape had vanished from my radar screen without a trace, a fact that astonished me when I reread my journals. But on the fourth anniversary I describe a "sudden and intense" fear that strikes "out of the blue" while I am cleaning the house. Then I "remember" that four years earlier I was raped. "I could never have imagined the change in my life," I write. "My life with Steve and the children—this house, our many friends, our dear, sweet cat, Minette, the garden, my studio—seems too good to be true. Today I remember it was born from something too bad to be true. I am on edge—remembering, and not, the day my world changed."

A few days later, I crossed the threshold between "remembering, and not." It was only a short step in physical space—a few inches off a doorsill in San Francisco's Chinatown. But for my spirit, it was a long plunge into an abyss. Looking back now on this dream, and the question I asked myself at the time, I wonder if I was giving myself permission to stop running. Only then could I begin to remember what was "too bad to be true."

■ ■ ■

Chinatown is a twenty-four-block nook of three- and four-story buildings with pagoda roofs and ornate balconies constructed after the earthquake and fire of 1906. Chinatown's busiest intersection—Broadway and Stockton Streets—was two blocks from the Italian café in North Beach where Steve and I were regulars. On Saturdays we often followed our morning espresso with a plunge into the river of shoppers that converged, five or six abreast, at this intersection and let ourselves be carried along south on Stockton Street, the bustling heart of the Chinese neighborhood.

Here we bought vegetables and fruits that spill from stores in bins along the sidewalk—boxes of eggplant, long beans, snow peas; crates of pomelos, tangerines, bananas, and bitter melon. Sometimes we bought takeout—glazed duck or dim sum—or browsed curio shops for gifts.

I missed Chinatown after we moved to "the Mediterranean resort side of the Golden Gate Bridge," as the visitors' bureau likes to describe Sausalito, a town that has dedicated its shopping district to T-shirts, refrigerator magnets, and upscale souvenirs.

Chinatown, on the other hand, is a tropical forest—dense and brightly colored, a confusion of time and place. A visit to Chinatown woke my senses—the scents of roast duck, fried onions, and roof tar; the music of Cantonese or Mandarin overheard in an incomprehensible tangle of sound that twists itself into English when you least expect it. And in the pedestrian alleys—a maze of narrow passages connecting sections of the neighborhood—a brooding stillness, broken only by the sound of footsteps.

In the surge of people flowing through this tropic of neon fanned by crimson and gold banners, the eye discovers a thousand small details. Gold dragons snake around a street lamp or glare from the roof of a phone booth. A middle-aged woman in a short quilted jacket and loose black pants frowns into a basket of red onions, as if she's lost something there. A German-speaking couple stand dumbfounded at the door of an apothecary shop watching herbalists fill prescriptions from floor-to-ceiling drawers containing mysterious bark, roots, and leaves—dried sea dragons, angelica root, isatis leaves.

It was into this city within a city that I ventured one day in mid-October four years after the rape. My errands—dried chrysanthemum blossoms (which when steeped in boiling water render a delicious tea), vegetables, and whatever else caught my eye—were, for the first time in many months, of no importance. This was a rare day of luxury, a day without a purpose.

After parking in a garage near Union Square, I entered Chinatown under the Dragon Gate on Grant Avenue, stopping to admire the green-tiled monument that is a clear dividing line between Chinatown and the retail district. "Everything in the world is in just proportion," if we are to believe the four gilded Chinese ideograms that hang under the central archway. In this imperial-looking construction were more dragons and globes on pedestals, and two fish, each with its tail swung high into the air, holding the edge of the cornice in their open mouths.

I distanced myself from the tourists on Grant Avenue after a few blocks, turning left and walking deeper into the neighborhood. Stockton Street was, as always, impacted with pedestrians piling up on the corners, waiting for the light to change. An old woman wearing scarlet socks and a bright green baseball cap sat with her back against the wall selling tiny packets of dried stems, oblivious to the feet of passersby that missed her by inches. I asked her what they were, but she did not speak English, nor I Cantonese. But she smiled sweetly, as if she was genuinely pleased that I had inquired.

I meandered, stopping frequently, causing shoppers who were more single-minded to pile up behind me or to squeeze between me and crates of produce or lampposts. I filled my plastic shopping bags with fruits and vegetables and moved on, to the window of a meat shop. I stared at a tray of tiny birds, then stood for a time with my back against a wall, looking up at a tier of three balconies across the street, each with a set of red double-doors. The metal railings were painted green and elaborately worked, like lace. I imagined living above such bustle, the peaceful interior behind the doors where families shut out the world.

Drifting on again, I passed a fishmonger's shop. Every inch of space the owner could claim as his was in use. On the sidewalk an elegantly dressed young woman was picking through a wooden crate of blue crabs with a pair of tongs. The crabs seemed dead, but they came to life as she tossed them about, thrashing their legs with alarming energy. Next to the crabs was a mesh cage of live bullfrogs who stared, I thought, resentfully at shoppers who got too close. The frogs had grouped themselves together in an orderly clutch, as if panic were beneath their dignity.

The walls of the shop were lined with tanks, stacked one atop the other. Large fish swam in brackish water that was frothing with bubbles on the surface from their efforts to gulp oxygen from the air. There were tanks of Pacific crabs, stacked with their claws curled inward, like the paws of dozing cats, and tanks of lobsters. Bins of squid, prawns, shrimp, conch, clams, and turtles created a narrow aisle that led to a central table of both fillets and whole fish. Giant flies buzzed about in what seemed a mad determination that was not diminished by the swats of the shopkeepers or customers.

The shop was popular, and people poured in behind me as I made my way toward a tray of prawns. I soon found myself wedged in and pressed on all sides. There was no line to speak of—women spoke up over the heads of the women in front of them to clerks in white bloody aprons, who netted fish from tanks or fetched them from trays. After allowing myself to be shoved aside several times, I vowed to hold my ground and, pushing hard, wedged myself between two women at the counter who seemed to be arguing with each other and the clerk, who was holding a large chef's knife in his right hand. The problem appeared to be a fish head that was lying on a wooden cutting board in a pool of watery blood. It was gray and the size of a football. A real monster. Its mouth was torn, as if death had been long in coming, and its open eyes, protruding from their sockets, struck me as having a weary, defeated look.

The argument escalated. The clerk turned the head around several times impatiently. Suddenly, he grimaced, raised the knife, and delivered a single deft stroke to the head, splitting it in half. The force of the blow sent a fine spray of gore into the air and forced the fish's eyes from their sockets as if they had been poked out from behind. Grinning, the clerk gestured toward the split head with a look of satisfaction.

I did not wait around to see if his Solomonic solution to the problem of one fish head and two customers satisfied the women. Overcome by an inexplicable panic, I turned and began clawing my way through the crowd behind me. All I could think of was escape. My heart seemed to be turning over inside me. I struggled for the open doorway. But at the last minute I lost my footing. Letting out a wail, I fell headlong onto the sidewalk, facedown. Vegetables flew from my pink shopping bags and for a moment I believed these and the many pairs of shuffling feet that gathered around me would be the last thing I ever saw on this earth. So this, I thought, was a heart attack. Unable to take a breath, I gasped for air as a passerby lifted me up.

"I'm okay. Thanks. Just tripped. Yes, that's my eggplant. No, leave it. Thank you." Words came out of my throat. I was breathing. Talking. Standing up. I was fine—and deeply embarrassed. I disappeared into the anonymity of the multitudes and hurried back toward the Dragon Gate, shocked at my reaction—the sudden panic and suffocation. I had no explanation for it.

After a few blocks, I noticed a delivery truck double-parked in front of a butcher's shop. As I approached, the driver, as if he'd been waiting for me to appear, swung open the doors. Inside, stacked neatly in cords, were at least fifty fleshly slaughtered suckling pigs. The driver reached in, yanked a pink, supple body from the top of the pile, swung it over his shoulder, and trotted into the shop. The piglet's head bobbed up and down, and its forefeet gently struck the man's chest in a gesture that passed for protest. A sob clawed its way out of my throat, which had contracted involuntarily in a futile attempt to hold it back. It seemed I had been holding back this sorrow for years, and that if I did not release it, I would suffocate. Tears I could not control followed.

Somehow I drove home. When Steve returned from work that evening, he found me crumpled on the couch in the living room, crying still, as I had been all afternoon. What is it? he wanted to know, holding me and soothing me. Tell me, tell me.

I could not tell him. I did not yet know that the clawed monster in my dream was pulling me under.

TWELVE

A New World

How shall the heart be reconciled
to its feast of losses?

STANLEY KUNITZ, "The Layers"

There is a Persian proverb that observes, "A drowning man is not troubled by rain." On October 17, 1989, when the Loma Prieta earthquake struck, only a week after the earth had given way beneath me in Chinatown, I hardly noticed. I remember getting a telephone call from a friend in Japan who had spent days trying to get through on jammed circuits. I described the way the house heaved upward and sideways at the same time, the way books and china hopped about on shelves as if possessed by a poltergeist. I told her how, seconds before the quake, the cat had stared at me, eyes wide, pupils dilated, her hair bristling. I told her how I had laughed out loud, thinking Minette was playing some absurd game of feline make-believe, and how I realized in the quake's aftermath that her animal senses had perceived what mine had not. I told her how Steve, who was driving home from work, had no explanation for his car radio suddenly going dead or for the odd wobbling in his tires. He didn't suspect an earthquake until he got to the Golden Gate Bridge and noticed southbound cars bunched together and honking as drivers, anxious to get off the bridge, confronted always-diligent toll takers determined to exact their fee.

But I said nothing to my friend about my own plunge days before—one that had for me far greater consequences than the earthquake. I didn't tell her that I felt out of control, that I was being turned inside out. I didn't tell her that the unreasonable terror I had felt, what seemed a very long time ago, when I lived in an attic and two little boys had crept up the stairs—that terror over a childish prank, over nothing really—had returned.

■ ■ ■

Although the earthquake had catastrophic consequences for many in the city, Sausalito rode it out on its cushion of fractured bedrock with only minor damage. Our contractor had done his job, and the house stood firm—a flower pot broken, a few books on the floor, a cat who ran away and then came home, the telephone ringing at three in the morning, worried people on the other end. A few friends carting perishables from the still-dark city piled into our enclave, where power had been quickly restored. We cooked, drank, smoked cigarettes (even those who had quit), and watched television like people everywhere else. The televised images of destruction across the bay, presided over by network anchormen in expensive safari suits, by sheer repetition turned our individual and fairly benign experience of the earthquake into a respectable catastrophe through which we had all, miraculously, lived. We assembled our respective earthquake-preparedness kits in the weeks that followed, kits that still languish, untouched, in the backs of closets with their dead flashlight batteries and expired jars of peanut butter. Denial, the best medicine for living in earthquake country, soon set in again.

But I could deny no longer the woman who was beginning to remember.

■ ■ ■

In her *New York Times Magazine* article about post-traumatic stress in nurses who served in Vietnam, Laura Palmer cites the case of a nurse named Jean Roth who was raped by an Air Force colonel the day after she arrived in Vietnam. Then, some months later, she was raped again by a Catholic priest who held her by the ankles over the edge of a water tower to silence her. Roth forgot these and other horrors of her war experience for twenty-two years while achieving impressive professional success in her medical career. But after a back injury she slipped into a severe depression that eventually brought her to a trauma recovery program for women in Menlo Park, California. "What Roth finally found at Menlo Park," Palmer writes, "was one place where it was finally safe enough to feel terrible."

According to the program's clinical psychologist, Judith Stewart, overinvolvement and overachievement—strategies that hold rage and guilt at bay—are common in women she has treated for post-traumatic stress disorder. Many of these women have been able to hold the symptoms of PTSD off "by working three jobs, getting multiple degrees, and being extremely active." But when these patients are immobilized, for whatever reason, "PTSD comes rushing in."

I did not know about this syndrome in 1989, nor did I suspect what was rushing back into my life. I was both unable and unwilling to see that my identity as the woman who was getting on with her life— the one who was happily busy, busy—was only a partial identity. The woman who had been raped was still there, but I wanted no part of her.

And there was another problem. I could not connect the intense feelings that overpowered me that day in Chinatown with the rape. They did not "come with a story," a linear narrative, the way non-traumatic memories do. They had no verbal context, and seemed to occupy another dimension, parallel to, but never intersecting with, language.

Some trauma researchers speculate that in states of high sympathetic nervous system arousal, such as those produced by trauma, the linguistic encoding of memory is actually deactivated, causing the central nervous system to revert to sensory forms of memory, such as those that characterize early life. I call them memories only because, like memories, their origin was in past experience. But strictly speaking they were not memories. They were sensations and emotions—of vulnerability, rage, blame, incredulity, fear, helplessness, shame, and grief. And like the event that created them in the first place, they had struck me down in a great fury, out of nowhere.

These sensations were even more disturbing the second time around. In Concord at least I knew that what I felt was linked to the rape. I had not yet constructed an identity that precluded that connection. Once I had stitched together the woman who had gotten on with her life, watching her fall apart at the seams created another layer of rage and sorrow.

Confucius said, "To be wronged is nothing unless you continue to remember it." Before the rape I felt this was as concise a statement as one can find of why it is a good idea to forget wrongs, and for normal experience it is not a bad rule of thumb. But for traumatic experience, "forgetting" is impossible, yet "remembering" is the last thing you want to do. And defenses, no matter how well-built, cannot hold the raw, submerged forces of traumatic memory at bay forever.

Denial is a trickster, capable of astonishing disguises. I've come to think of the capacity to deny as something sinister, although I realize it also has a good side, or at least a useful one. It helps you cope with the practicalities of life—and it is essential if you choose to live on the San Andreas Fault. But my experience with denial in 1989 had the feel of a science fiction plot: An unidentified life form takes over a space ship; it assumes the shape of whatever will ensure that it is not detected—the captain, a bulkhead, the life-support system. Invisible, it sets about its destructive business. Denial is a presence disguised as an absence. You cannot see it even when it is staring you in the face.

Perhaps if I had not been blessed by a strong constitution, an illness might have immobilized me, as it did Jean Roth. As it was, I was physically able to stumble on for another year as I resisted the painful descent that victims must eventually make to become survivors.

And so this year of "remembrance" disguised itself. Where was the hero of the story I had told Steve so long ago? She was, in fact, falling back into the rapist's hell, but I needed to believe that she was still on terra firma. No hero falls from glory without a struggle. The heroic ideal—ultimate triumph over adversity—was the only map I had that seemed to offer a way out of the pain and confusion that had characterized the first year after the rape. Perhaps no idea is more culturally cherished than the idea that "when bad things happen to good people," they overcome their adversity by heroic acts. They "snap out of it" and get on with their lives. Hadn't I done just that?

As these traumatic "memories" overwhelmed me, the activities that had kept them at bay themselves became overwhelming. I began to retreat from the life I had worked so diligently to construct. But I had to find a reason for this retreat that would preserve the fantasy hero who had, after all, made a damned good life for herself in California. I attributed my "memories"—the sensations of helplessness, loss, rage, and blame—to my present circumstances. I began to experience the gains of my new life in California as losses—of privacy, independence, control, and context. I resented the complications and obligations that were part of it. The pleasures of family life began to feel like debilitating demands. And even the simplest chore—paying a bill, responding to an invitation, making dinner—felt like a burden. I turned down work, avoided friends. As happiness drained out of my life, I began to feel retroactively resentful until I had rewritten my new life and turned the previous two years inside out.

What I needed was to get away from everything that was making me miserable—from my family, the house, my friends, my work. I hoped by this retreat to preserve the only self I thought I had—or wanted.

■ ■ ■

After the earthquake, I sought out the only safe place I could find—my little-used studio at the beach. It was a small, drafty room at one end of a former enlisted men's barracks, one of twenty or so buildings, only

187

yards from the beach, that were thrown up by the army in 1941 just before the Japanese attack on Pearl Harbor. Soldiers stationed here during the Second World War manned artillery batteries with sixteen-inch guns—concrete-and-steel fortifications half-buried in the hills and cliffs above the sea. But the great cannons on the ridges above the beach had long since been dismantled and their bunkers abandoned. Swords were being slowly turned back into the earth by wind and rain and the roots of grasses that seemed to prefer cracks in the concrete to more hospitable ground.

I craved solitude but was lonely. Sometimes I sat at my window facing the lagoon and wept. Sometimes I slept all afternoon on a camping mattress, wrapped in an afghan that my aunt Lace made when I married Steve. Sometimes I roused myself to write in my journal, which was now only a vessel for my self-pity. Eventually I dug up the unfinished poems and stories I had written before the rape. I tried to work on them again, but I felt a stranger had written them.

Then shortly after Christmas I stumbled upon a University of New Mexico Press edition of Cabeza de Vaca's *Adventures in the Unknown Interior of America* in the library. It was written in 1542 as a semi-official report to the king of Spain under the title *La Relacion*—"the telling" or "the tale."

Cabeza de Vaca, generally acknowledged as the first European to cross the North American continent, came to America in 1527 as part of a Spanish expedition that was intent on conquering whatever lay north of the Gulf of Mexico. But de Vaca's exploration party of three hundred lost contact with his ships. Setting out northward on foot, he spent the next eight years finding his way back to what he could call civilization. Only four of his party survived the six-thousand-mile odyssey.

I was particularly affected by an observation de Vaca made in an introduction addressed directly to the king: "Although everyone wants what advantage may be gained from ambition and action," de Vaca wrote, "we see everywhere great inequalities of fortune, brought about not by conduct but by accident, and not through anybody's fault but as the will of God. Thus the deeds of one far exceed his expectation, while another can show no higher proof of purpose than his fruitless effort, and even that effort may go unnoticed."

I immediately started work on a long narrative poem with the title (which in retrospect seems almost sadly pretentious) "Mundus Novus." New World. Looking back, I now understand why the unnamed narrator of my poem was not de Vaca, whom history tells us survived by becoming a healer among the native inhabitants, but one of his anonymous companions who never made it back to Spain. Telling the story of this unrecorded, unheroic life of "fruitless effort" compelled me. I labored through the winter, many hours a day, revising endlessly. Then I began a series of small abstract paintings, one for each stanza, and assembled a handmade "book."

After months of work, I decided to read the poem to two friends whose literary expertise and judgment I respected. I was so moved by the despair of my narrator in several stanzas that I wept as I read. When I had finished reading, there was an awkward silence. The powerful emotions I longed to express in words were not in the words I had written. They both told me this—gently but firmly. I was devastated. That night I cut the book up into tiny pieces with a pair of scissors. I felt that I had cut out my own heart.

Although this attempt to explore my feelings of loss was doomed, it was, nevertheless, a first step toward "remembering." Therapists would say that my creative impulses were enslaved to emerging traumatic sensations that I did not recognize as traumatic memory. I was reliving my experience of the loss of self, and the expression of it in my writing was as incomprehensible as the feeling itself.

Like Cabeza de Vaca, I would have to wander in the wilderness. On that journey I would lose the fantasy self I was trying to preserve—the kind and resilient wife, mother, and friend—and find another woman. The self I had been denying was beginning to emerge from the denial my fantasy hero had spun around her. But her emergence was fearsome, graceless, and nearly cost me my marriage.

In my studio that year, facing creative failure, I did not recognize that my work was a step in the right direction. My failures, rather, confirmed what I feared most—that the rapist had silenced me for life. I felt he had robbed me of the transformative power of language. I saw my inability to create something whole and sensible as a final and bitter defeat.

■ ■ ■

That summer our adored and pampered cat, Minette, died of a rare cancer. I grieved inconsolably for her, as if I had lost a child. Steve buried her in the garden with her blanket, her name tag, her toys. But nothing could bury my grief. Its intensity at first baffled Steve. Then it alarmed and finally angered him. Once the cat was gone, the house seemed to have lost its center. It was now a place of absences and vacancies. Loss was all I could feel.

■ ■ ■

On September 4, 1990, I ran across an article in the health section of the *Washington Post*. I happened to be in Washington for a conference that week; otherwise I would have missed this bold-faced headline: "Post-Traumatic Stress Disorder Common Among Women Who Have Been Raped." I was trying to drum up consulting work again, having given up on my writing, and was sitting in the dining room of my hotel having breakfast, dreading the day that lay ahead—a long meeting in a windowless conference room to be followed by an evening reception, then dinner for hundreds and speeches. My depression made the necessity of being charming and intelligent feel like torture. I was wearing a personality that felt like a suit of nails, acting as if I were who I wanted to be. I forced myself to behave as if I cared about the topics that so interested my fellow consultants and that had once equally interested me. As I read the short article, a sense of relief and—however impossible a companion—despair came over me.

Rape, it began, was a significant health problem for American women. Statistics followed: 11.8 million women are raped sometime in their lives; of these, 3.9 million suffer from post-traumatic stress disorder, "a debilitating and often long-lasting psychiatric problem traditionally associated with combat veterans." Experts quoted. Dean G. Kilpatrick, director of the Crime Victims Research and Treatment Center at the Medical University of South Carolina: "Women raped by strangers, by their husbands or by former boyfriends viewed their rapes equally as violent.... The victims were equally likely to have feared serious injury or think they might die during the rape.... The trauma can last a lifetime."

A lifetime? Not me, I thought. I just hate my life. Choking up, I thought of Minette, how she used to sit in the window waiting for me to get home. I ordered more coffee, stared at the waiter's back as he walked away.

Then I kept reading. Long-term studies show that as many as half of rape victims never fully recover and suffer lifelong chronic depression. Was I chronically depressed? I asked myself. The idea that I might be terrified me. I was forty-four years old. Could I take another, say, thirty years of living as if I were living? Maybe, I thought. More studies showing that 75 to 80 percent of women blame themselves for their rape. Did I blame myself? Patricia Resick, a professor of clinical psychology at the University of Missouri at St. Louis: "We have women here who are just now dealing with the fact they were raped 30 or 40 years ago." The average victim, she notes, does not seek help until five years after the attack.

Five years? I counted the years since 1985 on my fingers. Maybe I'm nuts, I thought. Maybe I'm normal. Five years.

I stuffed that section of the paper into my briefcase as if it were a stolen national security document. I'll read it again, I told myself, when I get home. But I didn't. I put it in my in-box and buried it. But I knew it was there.

■ ■ ■

Perhaps nothing is more threatening to a person who believes he or she is happily married than to discover that his or her spouse has become suddenly and inexplicably miserable. My instincts had led me to a withdrawal from our life, a season of wandering in the wilderness. But I did not understand this myself and so could not reassure Steve. For his part, Steve attempted to resurrect the energetic, involved woman he had married while I needed to let her die an honorable death. We were soon locked in a fierce struggle for dominance that played itself out in the arenas of everyday married life. Who had control of the television remote or the grocery cart was no longer a laughing matter.

Steve's reasonable complaints were, it seemed to me then, violent assaults on my being. I responded with verbal barrages. Steve fired back. My need to give shape in language to the emotions that swarmed up from the past was an obsession. Often Steve withdrew to sulk in silence.

I regarded his retreats as cruel and manipulative attempts to silence me. I now refused to shut up. Our disagreements, although once easily defused by humor, were becoming dark, disguised replays of the rape itself, although at the time I did not recognize this. In this version we both got to play the part of the rapist as well as the victim. We both raged. And we both felt helpless, vulnerable, afraid, and guilty.

The phenomenon of reenactment, I have learned, is well documented in the literature of trauma. It is another of the so-called intrusion phenomena, like flashbacks, nightmares, and "storyless" memories. Like "memories" that are not really memories, the recreations of the trauma are usually disguised. Judith Herman, for example, cites in *Trauma and Recovery* the case of a female incest survivor who engaged in compulsive risk-taking that was often dangerous. The woman describes routinely playing chicken on the highway with men, until finally she had an accident: "A male truck driver was trying to cut me off, and I said to myself with the crudest of language, there's no f——ing way you're going to push your penis into my lane." Both the accident itself and hearing herself make a verbal and conscious connection between her childhood abuse and her dangerous driving were a turning point. It was a moment of recognition, alerting her to the need to explore the emotional legacy of her abuse.

Not all reenactments are so pointed or dangerous, but all do have what Herman describes as a "driven, tenacious quality...a feeling of involuntariness." Freud called reenactment a "repetition compulsion." Most contemporary theorists speculate that the repetitive reliving of the traumatic experience "must represent a spontaneous, unsuccessful attempt at healing." Psychiatrist Mardi Horowitz sees intrusion phenomena, including reenactments, as a completion principle that "summarizes the human mind's intrinsic ability to process new information in order to bring up to date the inner schemata of the self and the world." By definition, traumatic experience is "new information" that the human mind is not prepared to process. It is incomprehensible experience that shatters the inner conceptual framework, what I think of as the "summary" of our lives, the personal narrative that we each carry within us. Horowitz suggests that traumatic experiences are stored, therefore, in a special kind of active memory that is highly kinetic and repetitive. It plays the same scene, over and over, but this scene defies attempts to integrate it into the main text of the narrative. Because the scene can never be discarded, the story itself must eventually be rewritten.

Other researchers discussed by Herman in her book suggest that reenactments are emotionally (rather than cognitively) driven attempts to master the overwhelming too-muchness of the traumatic experience. The compulsion to relive is an attempt to master the terror, helplessness, and rage of "mortal danger."

Lenore Terr examines in considerable and riveting detail the way traumatized children reenact their experiences through games and play, an adaptive strategy that adult survivors do not often employ. She was surprised to find that the post-traumatic games of some of the children who survived the Chowchilla kidnapping had actually been passed down to younger, untraumatized children.

"One wonders," she writes, "if the old 'traumatic anxiety' stays permanently affixed to such games." Her four-year-old daughter, for example, refused to play Ring Around the Rosie because the game "made her feel funny." Why? Terr asks, reminding her reader that the "rosie" is the lesion of the Black Death that ravaged Europe in the Middle Ages; "A pocket full of posies" are flowers for the dead and amulets to ward off the disease; "Ashes, ashes" represent the charred corpses that were burned in the streets; and "we all fall down" is, of course, dying itself. She speculates that her daughter had "picked up the traumatic feelings that were still attached" to this old verse, even twenty generations removed from "the traumatized originators," a compelling speculation.

What is without question is that this verse, born of medieval trauma and one I vividly recall from my own nursery school days, has lived on into the twentieth century. Is it not reasonable to suppose that such traumatic experience might just as well be transmitted or reenacted in less playful ways? Might not an individual re-create personal trauma in disguised forms in much the same manner as the society has? My own experience suggests that all of these reenactments can be, and often are, a part of the attempt to make trauma survivable. There are aspects of my own behavior since the rape that I can explain in no other way. The trauma, for one reason or another, resurfaces. Feelings such as dread, failure, helplessness trigger it. Sometimes the resurfacing is straightforward and I can identify my dread as a remembrance of the rapist. Other times, the trauma resurfaces disguised, and all I know is that I feel helpless and out of control.

It is still difficult for me to see clearly how my unassimilated feelings—rage or helplessness—affected my marriage during this year. Any intimate relationship has its share of conflicts and disagreements, and all carry to some degree the elusive legacies of the past. No human being is ever free from the accumulation of buried motivation and desire that make the Socratic commandment "Know thyself" a particularly challenging assignment. Traumatic experience makes it difficult to distinguish between "normal" and "abnormal" conflict. I still have to work at determining whether a feeling of anger is legitimate or whether it is inflated by the "abnormal" rage that is the "normal" response to trauma. I can never reclaim the woman who was not raped. In a very real sense, I cannot remember who she was nor can I hope to experience the marriage she might have had. It, no doubt, would have had its own conflicts.

A New World

After a year of unhappiness and tension, Steve and I knew that something was terribly wrong, but neither of us knew what it was. Our willingness to fight, and fight hard and mean, may have saved us, although at the time we both felt our fights were the prelude to divorce. One Saturday afternoon in early autumn we had a violent argument. I cannot remember what set us off, but by this time it didn't take much. I accused him of complete disregard for all my feelings. Clearly, he'd never loved me. I was a thing, not a person. I traced this crime back in a catalog of insensitivities and abuses that was astounding for its attention to detail. Steve exploded. "You're turning me into a monster," he yelled. "I'm not your rapist!"

"Well, you're acting like my rapist," I screamed back, stunned that he was using the rape, the worst thing that had ever happened to me, against me. Now he really *was* a monster. But in the shocked silence that followed this exchange, we both caught a glimpse of the beast who was haunting our home.

■ ■ ■

A week later we were sitting on a love seat in the office of a psychiatrist whose specialty was couples counseling. His office was beige and Danish modern, well-appointed with boxes of Kleenex on end tables on either side of the couch. The complaint on which we had finally settled and which we presented calmly to the doctor, whom I shall call Dr. Blanchard, was that we were having trouble "communicating," a euphemism that he accepted with a slow blink, one of his more animated expressions.

We visited Dr. Blanchard once a week for ten weeks. Over these weeks he said almost nothing that could pass for a suggestion. We had the slow blinks, occasionally punctuated by an "Uh-huh" or a nod, and the inevitable question that followed my long-winded and Steve's more succinct descriptions of our latest argument: "And how did that make you feel?" He took no notes, expressed no opinions. With one exception, neither Steve nor I remember anything he said. But that exception fascinates us both when we look back at it. We still cannot decide whether it was an example of gross insensitivity or a stroke of professional genius.

In our first session, Dr. Blanchard asked us each to say something about our backgrounds. Steve later told me that I concluded my remarks by mentioning that four and a half years earlier I had been raped in my own home. I provided no details and observed only that "they never caught the guy."

"Was it," Dr. Blanchard asked, "a particularly bad rape?" I responded instantly and without any emotion. "The guy was there for a number of hours. I wasn't cut up, if that's what you mean."

Dr. Blanchard nodded his head, and the session went on without any further reference to the rape.

It was Steve who drew my attention to Dr. Blanchard's question afterward. As odd as it seems now, I had nearly forgotten it.

"I think that question about rape was strange," Steve said as we were walking back to the car.

"What question?" I replied, thinking only that Steve was looking for an excuse to get out of therapy. Steve repeated Dr. Blanchard's question.

"Oh, that," I said, as if I had noticed it. "What does he know? I should have said, 'Oh no, it was one of those gentle, make-you-feel-good rapes.' "

"Do you think we need to find someone else?" Steve said.

"No," I said. "My rape is not the problem here."

■ ■ ■

Although I pretended not to be bothered by Dr. Blanchard's remark, it set me on slow burn. I projected my anger away from Steve onto Dr. Blanchard in what I now regard as a case of transference that belongs in the psychiatric *Guinness Book of World Records*. I belittled Dr. Blanchard behind his back and treated the sessions like business meetings. I never once reached for a Kleenex and never expressed a feeling. He was an insensitive dolt, but I believed that he might have some tips for Steve, who was, as far as I was concerned, the designated patient.

In hindsight I can see why I could not react to Dr. Blanchard's question. It seemed to discount rape by implying that some rapes were not all that bad. On the one hand, I wanted to dismiss my experience. On the other, I wanted to claim its brutality. But to do that would force me to claim as well the consequences of that brutality. Between these opposing needs—to deny and to affirm—I felt trapped and hopeless. Each session with Dr. Blanchard left me more and more depressed. My answer to Dr. Blanchard's question downplayed my actual experience— because I wasn't stabbed, I seemed to be suggesting that the rape was no big deal. At the same time, I hinted that it was a very big deal ("The guy was there for a number of hours").

If Dr. Blanchard intended to force me to face my own denial, he deserves more credit than I gave him. All I know is that I interpreted his question then as another example of the insensitivity that isolates and humiliates women who have been raped.

One night ten weeks after we started seeing him, I found myself sitting in a bathtub with a razor blade in my hand. I was crying uncontrollably. It was time to put my hero out of her misery. Her wounds, I felt, were mortal.

Steve, frantic on the other side of the locked door, told me he was calling Dr. Blanchard's emergency number. A few minutes later he returned, demanding that I open the door.

"I just called Dr. Blanchard," Steve yelled.

I stopped crying. I felt for Steve in that moment. I knew he loved me and that he was hurting.

"What did he say?" I asked. I got out of the tub. And opened the door. "I'm sorry," I said when I looked into his eyes. "I don't know what is happening to me."

"I know," Steve said, wrapping me in a towel.

"What did Dr. Blanchard say?"

"I told him you were threatening to kill yourself. That you were hysterical. He thought maybe I should come in to see him and asked me how I felt about what was going on."

For a moment, we stared at each other. Dr. Blanchard wanted to see Steve, not me? Then we started to laugh. Laughter shook us as we each imitated Dr. Blanchard's slow blinks, repeating "And how does that make you feel?" over and over again in as many variations of tone and emphasis as we could invent.

After we'd exhausted ourselves, we sat on the bed holding hands while I called Dr. Blanchard back.

"I'd like a referral," I said. "I think I need to see someone who has treated rape victims." Dr. Blanchard had a name handy—a woman he'd known in medical school, a "specialist." Perhaps he'd been expecting my call. Then again, maybe not.

THIRTEEN

Blackberries

You open your eyes
and you're locked in the woods—
bare woods like barbed wire
thickets, tangled twigs.

FREIDA CHAPMAN,
"Look Again into This Day"

Sausalito, California, September 1993

An odd clipping from KS yesterday: "Romania's law frees convicted rapists who marry their victims." What does it mean? Is it an old law, out of the feudal past, created by patriarchs to get damaged goods off their hands—no one will marry her now that she's been raped? Except, of course, her rapist. I can't imagine any woman willingly marrying her rapist. Amusing to think of the marriage proposal:

"Bitch. I know you have not forgotten me. Jail is no fun. The place is crawling with rapists and rats. It makes me hate you even more. I have no reason to hate you, but my hatred is pure and you can count on it. If you marry me, I will hate you forever. Please say no again. I'll know what you *really* mean. With all my hatred, forever, your Rapist."

I give up trying to understand the Romanian law or why it's mentioned in the paper.

Blackberries are notoriously hard to get rid of—they grow from a crown deep in the earth that sends fast-growing roots out in all directions, like spokes radiating from a hub. From these roots, new shoots head for the surface, where, very quickly, they push out leaves. Each new shoot then exerts the utmost energy to produce its own crown. Blackberries grow in poor soil and mind neither drought nor flood. They do everything but flower and produce berries in the shade. Shade, in fact, increases their energetic search for sunlight, which must, they seem to think, be just around the corner. If a blackberry branch stays on the ground long enough, roots will grow from it, too. Each berry contains many seeds. New shoots seem to be capable of strategic thinking—they come up around half-buried boulders, making them impossible to dig out. They grow close to desirable plants, where they often go undetected until they are so firmly established that extricating them usually involves an unwanted sacrifice. To protect themselves they grow briars that can pierce leather work gloves. Blackberries live in what are euphemistically called patches, but in truth their plots are impenetrable, chaotic tangles that ensnarl and wound even the most cautious of berry pickers.

"You'll never get rid of these," the man Steve hired to cut the blackberries down said as he topped off the third pickup truckload of cuttings. He elaborated on why he would be back in a few months. With this gauntlet thrown at his feet, my husband, whose stubborn streak can come in handy, set about to prove the expert wrong.

Steve didn't want to work with something that had a skull and crossbones on the label, so weekend after weekend over a year he shouldered his pickax and dug out blackberry crowns. I collected them, dried them, and set them out in the garden shed in a cardboard box. They are, in their way, very beautiful—twisted, sculptural knots of determination, some twice the size of my fist. Someday, I think, I will do something with them—sand them, paint them in bright colors, and set them out on my bookshelf.

In the shade garden that Steve and I have made, now nearly mature, I still find new healthy shoots every spring hiding in the sweet woodruff or growing among the Australian violets. Blackberries growing far up the hillside on our neighbor's property creep to the edge of our garden, and these sometimes take root if I am inattentive. I can't help but respect them. I know if I abandoned the garden, the blackberries would be back half-strength in two years, and in three they would be choking the ferns, impatiens, and calla lilies to death.

Some ideas are like blackberries. It's good policy to respect them. I have one idea in particular in mind when it comes to rape. It's a thorny one.

■ ■ ■

In 1996 a woman seated next to me at a New York dinner party discovered I was writing about rape in the first person. "I just can't imagine how you can write about something so..." She paused, searching for the words. "So very personal."

"Why is it more personal than writing a book about having a life-threatening illness or a wretched childhood?" I replied.

"Because rape is a sexual act—such an intimate invasion."

"The most personal part of my rape," I said, "doesn't have to do with my vagina." I was angry, and my voice had a nasty edge.

"Why is talking about being raped any more personal than talking about being mugged on Central Park West?" I continued. "People talk about being mugged *all* the time. They aren't ashamed—it isn't too personal to bring up. Why should I or other rape victims be any different?"

"But rape is different," she said.

"I beg to disagree," I replied. Then I thought for a minute. "You're right," I said. "It is different—but it shouldn't be."

I immediately felt sorry about directing my anger at this woman.

She was only saying that it was embarrassing for her to imagine how she, as a woman, would feel about such an intimate invasion of her body. I'd reacted without thinking, without checking whether my anger was a reasonable response or an overreaction.

I realized that I loathed the notion that sex and rape were conceptually related and argued against it whenever I got the chance. I wanted a precise distinction, a syllogism: Rape is violence. Sex is not violence. Therefore, rape is not sex.

But what about sadomasochistic sex? someone is likely to ask. Isn't that violence?

I know nothing about this subject personally. I'm one of those people who prefers to be put on nitrous oxide when I get my teeth cleaned. But I've had friends over the years who get sexually turned on by "pain" of one sort or another—being spanked or bound. One friend liked to be tied to the bedposts with men's neckties and "tortured" with ice cubes. She screamed "No, no, no" so loudly one night that her neighbor called the police. But "No" meant "Yes" and both she and her willing (and enthusiastic) partner knew it. People have all sorts of "fantasies" during sex and sometimes they are comfortable acting them out. A "fantasy" is a fiction created by the imagination over which its inventor has control, just as she has control over acting it out. It is "enjoyable" precisely because it isn't real.

It seems there are "rules" to sadomasochistic sex, and unlike rape, it *is* consensual. In rape "No" really means no. Only one party thinks otherwise. The difference between being a "sexual partner" and a "victim of rape" may be as simple as a three-letter word—*fun*. Whatever kinky or rough modalities human beings invent for sexual pleasure, being raped is not one of them.

■ ■ ■

I believed when I started this book that the idea that rape is about power and control, not sex, was well-established. I thought it was clear, not only to me, but to my circle of friends and acquaintances and to their circles of friends and acquaintances and so on. In other words, to everybody. This was one blackberry patch I would not have to tangle myself up in—because in the decades since Victoria's rape I believed it had been completely eradicated. Thus, it was both a bafflement and an irritation to encounter what appeared to be thriving shoots among the lilies.

I have a friend who is skilled at hunting mushrooms. One summer I visited her in Canada's province of Quebec and for a week I accompanied her on daily mushrooming jaunts. It was the season for *Hypomyces lactiflourum*, a bright orange, parasitic earth tongue that grows over the gills and caps of several species of milk mushrooms and that tastes like a cross between almonds and sea scallops. There were other tasty varieties of boletes and chanterelles growing in the woods, but the *Hypomyces* were the real prize. At first I was useless. I couldn't find a single mushroom. But after I'd eaten the *Hypomyces* (sautéed in butter and onions), I began to find them with nearly the same skill as my friend. "Once you taste them," she said, "it's strange, but you seem to develop an affinity of some kind. You begin to see them everywhere."

As I was writing this book, I began to see the idea of sex everywhere when it came to rape. I worried about myself as I clipped items from the newspaper or jotted down remarks that came my way. Still, I recorded what I thought I was finding.

For example, on April 21, 1995, a headline in the *San Francisco Chronicle* caught my eye: "Lawmaker's Odd Theory on Rape." The article reported "implausible" remarks made by Republican Rep. Henry Aldridge to the North Carolina House Appropriations Committee as it debated a proposal to eliminate a state abortion fund for poor women. Aldridge had the floor because he was trying to apologize for earlier remarks he'd made that implied that victims of rape or incest were sexually promiscuous. In a case of trying to get one foot out of your mouth by shoving in the other, Aldridge said, presumably after his apology: "The facts show that people who are raped—who are *truly raped* [italics mine]—the juices don't flow, the body functions don't work and they don't get pregnant. Medical authorities agree that this is a rarity, if ever." Margaret Henderson, president of the North Carolina Coalition Against Sexual Assault, and "some of [Aldridge's] fellow legislators" were outraged. "It's really common for rape victims to be blamed for being raped. But this is the first time I've heard of rape victims being blamed for becoming pregnant," Henderson said.

The word *odd* in the headline is interesting. One meaning of *odd* is "left over as a remainder." It also means strange or peculiar. The reporter also used the word *implausible* to characterize Aldridge's remarks. The implication of the language is clear: Aldridge's ideas are both old-fashioned and idiosyncratic.

The Republican House Speaker Harold Brubaker was quick to distance himself, saying Aldridge's comments "are not the opinion of the leadership of the House." Yet only some of his fellow legislators were outraged. One suspects that others may have listened respectfully, what with "medical authorities" backing Aldridge up.

I enjoyed playing around with Aldridge's sophistry. *True rape* never results in pregnancy. If a woman gets pregnant after a rape, she must have cooperated by letting her "juices" flow, so she wasn't *really* raped. Providing state funds for poor women to have abortions for pregnancies resulting from a rape is, therefore, illogical. They weren't really raped. If they had been, they wouldn't be pregnant. What could be more obvious?

I couldn't help but see Aldridge's comment as a fascinating case of male projection. The idea that the female withholds something (her "juices") if she is overpowered, that the female still has "control," seems to reflect the male experience of the sexual act. By projecting male sexuality onto females, Aldridge is able to ignore the fact that the penis is sometimes used as a weapon.

It's absurd, of course, and would be hardly worth commenting upon were it not an indication of how deeply the idea that women are responsible for their rapes is buried in our culture. This idea would deflate like a soufflé jerked from the oven before its time were it not supported by a deeper idea—that rape is "sex." Aldridge's absurdity is a variation on the same old tune, all the more disagreeable in his case

204

because it was so self-serving. Victim advocates like Margaret Henderson didn't exist prior to the feminist movement of the 1970s. If Aldridge had made the same remarks implicating the victim when Victoria was raped, he would not have been challenged. This article is encouraging because his views are discredited all around. But it is also troubling because he is, after all, a lawmaker who was elected to his office by the good citizens of North Carolina.

Somewhere out there in the backlash is a Jurassic Park keeping alive things we'd rather not think about.

I read accounts of cases such as this one from 1996 with further confusion: A Wisconsin judge sentenced a Southeast Asian immigrant found guilty of four counts of sexual assault for repeatedly molesting two young girls to twenty-four years' probation (as opposed to the eighty-year prison sentence he could have gotten) so he would have the opportunity to continue English lessons to help him assimilate better into American culture. And what was I to think of the case of the Tennessee judge who in 1995 released a rape suspect who claimed he heard voices telling him to rape? "The suspect doesn't need a guardian," said the judge, "he needs a girlfriend."

And while I'm on the subject of girlfriends, what about Admiral Richard Macke, who was forced to resign from the navy in 1995 for telling reporters that the three American servicemen who raped a twelve-year-old Japanese girl in Okinawa (seriously straining U.S.-Japanese relations) could have avoided the problem by hiring a prostitute? "I've said several times, for the price they paid to rent the car, they could have had a girl." But this "gaffe" (as it was referred to in both the *New York Times* and *Washington Post*) was just the latest in a series of incidents that suggest that the navy has made little headway in changing its attitudes and behavior toward women since the Tailhook scandal in 1991, when scores of women were assaulted at a convention of naval aviators.

In the month that Macke was forced to resign, the movie *Seven,* with a rape-torture scene one *Entertainment Weekly* film reviewer remarked was "too horrible to describe," was number one at the box office. *Showgirls, Leaving Las Vegas,* and *Strange Days,* three films also released in 1995, have brutal rape scenes that only partially hide good old-fashioned sexploitation behind the aesthetic of new cinematic realism. (According to statistics compiled by New York–based Women's Action Alliance in 1993, one out of eight Hollywood movies depicts "a rape theme.")

And last but not least there are the implications of the remark made by the San Diego detective that some officers in the department thought of rape as "assault with a friendly weapon." They got half of it right at least. If two adult males had been raped instead of two females, I doubt these police officers would have employed this expression to describe the crime. Rape is "friendly," it would seem, only when female sex organs are involved, the same reason rape is "so very personal."

Watching a movie rape scene does not, in my case, induce flashbacks or send me gagging to the theater bathroom. None I have seen come close to the horror of the real thing, and at least you can always cover your eyes in a movie. Rather, scenes suggesting that rape is a "sexual act" remind me that, as a rape survivor, I may always have to carry a portion of blame for another's crime. Even if it is generally accepted that a woman who is raped wasn't "asking for it," how do others know that she didn't really like what she got?

■ ■ ■

My dinner companion was right that rape is "so very personal" and that writing about it is personal, too, but not in the way she thought. The most personal part of being raped had less to do with what happened to my body for three hours on October 11, 1985, than with what happened to my spirit. The loss of faith that there is order and continuity in life—that life is meaningful—is the most personal of all losses. What is more personal than the answers to the ultimate questions of human existence that each of us over a lifetime struggles to ask—or not? To lose faith in life was, for me, the loss of a connection with the intangible world—with soul, spirit, anima, essence, vital force, or whatever one chooses to call it. How could I have explained to this embarrassed woman my most intimate and personal beliefs about life and how the rape shattered them?

If I accepted the idea that talking about rape was in some way *like* talking about one's sex life—very personal in that way—I had another dilemma. Sex and violence are *everywhere*—movies, television, rap music—and often at the same time. American movie audiences have become sexual voyeurs. Sex (often violent sex) is an industry—pornography—that makes millions of dollars a year. Whatever else I could say about sex in American culture, a glance at the supermarket magazine rack tells me that sex is anything but so very personal.

I was irritated with this woman because I resented the fact that talking about rape (as a personal experience rather than a social phenomenon) produces a cringe in the people around me. This cringe feels silencing, although that is not always its intent. It confuses me when I feel it. I'm attempting to define my experience in terms of a violent assault and the residual trauma. But other people seem to be defining me in terms of a shameful sexual encounter. Words, no matter how precise, seem only to get me deeper into the briar patch. Where are the words? I need to find them so I don't have to feel that I am talking about something "embarrassing" when I talk about rape.

Language seems to be against me. The word *sexual,* or *sex,* seems to have become a kind of universal modifier for violent acts or persons. Rapists are now often called "sexual predators." We speak of a "sex crime" registry for "sex offenders." Although the term *sexual assault* is not in my 1995 edition of the *Random House Webster's* dictionary, it is in common usage and is sometimes used as a synonym for *rape,* although it is a more encompassing term that includes molestation, sodomy, oral penetration, and other abuses. The word *rape* (in English usage since around 1400), which is defined as "the unlawful act of forcing a female to have sexual intercourse," means technically that there has been penetration of the vagina by a penis. The term *sexual harass-*

ment is in my 1995 *Random House Webster's,* where it is defined as "unwelcome sexual advances, esp. when made by an employer or superior, usu. with compliance as a condition of continued employment or promotion."

The dictionary definition of *rape* is much broader in actual use. In order to increase the degree of detail in its reporting of criminal offenses, the Justice Department has in recent years, for example, devised new definitions for rape offenses such as "forcible sodomy," "sexual assault with an object," and "forcible fondling," and acknowledging same-sex rape, has defined rape as "the carnal knowledge of a *person,* forcibly and/or against that person's will...."

There is a good reason why the term *sexual assault* has come into vogue. *Sexual assault* puts the concept of violence into the word *rape.* It reflects a historically recent clinical, political, and social analysis of the phenomenon of rape that attempts to drain off the toxins of blame-the-victim, and to shift the criterion of rape from the behavior of the victim to that of the criminal. It is an attempt to take any ambiguity out of the word *rape.* But if sexual assault is still being described as "assault with a friendly weapon" by some law-enforcement officers, changes in language aren't getting us very far. There appears to be a current deeper than language.

■ ■ ■

The first definition of the word *sexual* is "of or pertaining to sex." That's more complicated than it seems because there are eight definitions of *sex* in my dictionary, ranging from the "sum of the structural and functional differences" between male and female to engaging in "sexual intercourse." It is its second definition that may cause some of the confusion: "occurring between or involving the sexes: sexual relations." Thirdly, it means "having sexual organs."

To refer to violent and/or nonconsensual intercourse as a "sexual act" is to run the risk of blurring the second and third definitions. There is no "sexual relation" in rape. The only relation is one that has to do with power—one side having it, the other side not. It is "sexual" only in the sense that sex organs are involved and both the rapist and his victim have them.

True, sex organs are complicated. In our culture, they are generally considered private. Anything connected with them is, in this sense, "so very personal." You can be arrested if you display your sexual organs in public. Then again, you can go to a nudists' gathering where not displaying them in public will probably get you booted out the door. I read somewhere that men in one Amazonian tribe are terribly embarrassed if the string that holds their penis up against their bodies—their only "clothing"—comes undone. Privacy is relative when it comes to sex organs, but it seems all humans possess a notion of it.

The fact that changes in language have been required to drain the swamp of victim-blame suggests that it is deeper and wider than it seemed thirty years ago. Ambiguity remains, despite valiant attempts such as this one from a student handbook written by a community college in upstate New York:

> If a person engages in non-consensual sexual intercourse due to physical force, coercion or threat—actual or implied—the act is considered rape in New York State. Sexual intercourse is defined as vaginal penetration. A person who is mentally incapacitated, asleep, or physically helpless due to drug or alcohol consumption, or unconscious, is considered unable to consent. If intercourse takes place without consent, it is considered rape.

And this in boldface type:

> If a woman says, "No," regardless of the circumstances, it is not a matter for interpretation. "No" means no. Sexual intercourse following a spoken "No," or any other expression of refusal, or demurral, even without further resistance of any kind by the woman, is rape, a felony in New York State.

This appears to cover the bases. The burden is on the male to recognize conditions that indicate lack of consent. If he does not, he is a rapist.

The language in the handbook is precise, but a 1992 rape case in Texas illustrates that no matter how precise the language, the blur between sex and rape can still be sighted, like the Loch Ness monster. The Texas case involved a woman who was awakened in her bedroom by a knife-wielding intruder "demanding sex," as the newspaper account put it. The victim apparently grabbed a portable phone, locked herself in her bathroom, and called 911. However, after the "intruder" (was he not by this time a "rapist"?) broke down the door, "knocked the phone out of her hand, assaulted her with the knife, and ordered her to take his pants off," the victim, facing the inevitable, tried to talk him into wearing a condom to protect herself from the possibility of being infected with the virus that causes AIDS.

A grand jury refused to indict the attacker because some jurors believed "that the woman's act of self-protection might have implied consent." Their action set off a storm of protests and "baffled lawyers on both sides of the case." The assistant district attorney called the grand jury's action "very strange, bizarre even....Something about this case just worried and upset them. I am genuinely puzzled." The director of the Washington-based National Coalition Against Sexual Assault, Cassandra Thomas, was less puzzled. "We say to victims, 'Do whatever you can to protect yourselves.' Now we have to say, 'Be careful of how you protect yourself because it could be construed as consent or complicity.' This woman is having her own ingenuity used against her."

Although the jury's decision was later overturned, it reveals deep societal beliefs about rape that are still beyond the reach of words. In regard to the question of whether rape is sex, society still seems disbelieving in much the same manner that people must have been hundreds of years ago when they said, "Are you trying to tell me the earth is round? That's ridiculous, it's obviously flat."

The difference between sex and rape is consent. What "worried and upset" the grand jury is what has worried, upset, and, more important, silenced rape victims for centuries. Rape is so very personal because if you live to speak of it, there's always the possibility you consented to a sexual act, as the woman in Texas sadly discovered.

When I started this book, I assumed that the stereotyped images of the rapist as an oversexed male who is the victim of a provocative female, or a sexually frustrated man who rapes to release pent-up needs, or a sex fiend with insatiable and perverse desires had gone the way of the flat-earth theory. A. Nicholaus Groth and H. Jean Birnbaum, to cite just one example, described rape as a "pseudo-sexual act" in *Men Who Rape,* an extensive clinical study published in 1980. Rape is not motivated by sexual desire, they conclude. "Quite the contrary, careful clinical study...reveals that rape is in fact serving primarily nonsexual needs. It is the expression of power and anger....[Rape is an act] addressing issues of hostility (anger) and control (power) more than passion (sexuality). To regard rape as an expression of sexual desire is not only an inaccurate notion but also an insidious assumption, for *it results in the shifting of the responsibility for the offense in large part from the offender to the victim*" (italics mine).

But as I wrote, I began to feel that the subject of rape was like a black hole. Every word written or spoken about it seemed to be drawn into this gravitational collapse, leaving every victim, myself included, speechless. What could I say to someone who feels that writing about rape is "so very personal," especially when I know that the discomfort is largely the result of embarrassment?

Although changes in language—reflections of changes in our understanding of the difference between sex and rape—have helped, it seems that the distinction between these two very different acts is not yet clear. The definition of rape has been unpacked, examined, and repacked in a way that attempts to clarify what "without consent" means. But the lack of clarity about consent is problematic enough that in Pennsylvania and several other states rape victims are forced to sub-mit to polygraph tests. A 1993 report by the U.S. Senate Judiciary Committee found that rape victims are far more often subjected to polygraph exams than victims of other crimes. In a robbery case, it is the suspect who is most likely to be polygraphed; in rape cases, the chances are much greater that both the accused and the woman making the accusation will be polygraphed.

I'm glad I wasn't living in Pennsylvania in 1985 for another reason. In Pennsylvania "No" is not good enough. According to Pennsylvania law in 1994, if a rape victim does not *physically* resist her attacker, she is not being raped. She is engaging in sex. This is like saying that if you do not physically resist a mugger, you are engaging in a consensual robbery.

The woman who wondered how I could write about something so very personal seems to be right—rape *is* different. Is it different because sex and rape are fused not only by language created to divide them but by something beyond language? Something deeper, darker? This confusion is always lurking in the background if you have been raped. You drag victim-blame behind you like a dead snake. I think if only I can understand this confusion I will feel connected to other people, instead of feeling cut off from them. I can do that thing everyone keeps saying I need to do—"come to terms," "integrate" the rape into my life. Can I come to terms if the terms are not shared?

I was trying to make the case that night in New York that some people have been arguing (and to judge from the student handbook cited earlier, with some success) for years—that rape is a crime of violence. Who accuses a man (or a woman, for that matter) mugged at gunpoint of "asking for it" because he happens to be walking down the street with a wallet full of credit cards? Who faults him for nonresistance when he hands over his wallet? Who, because of his ready compliance, questions whether, in fact, he was *really* mugged? The victim of a mugging is not held responsible for the crime and therefore has no reason to feel ashamed. He, or she, can tell the story at a dinner party and there's bound to be someone at the table with a better one. I have heard people conclude an account of having their home robbed while they were away with "We felt like we'd been raped." No cringe. No discomfort. It was *personal*, but not *so very personal*. If rape really is in the same category as being mugged or having your home broken into, why don't people respond the same way?

Other people's embarrassment or discomfort makes me feel as if I were the rapist's cocriminal, an accomplice who is "confessing" something. If a woman is raped by a stranger who attacks her in her home, she will be blamed less than if she were raped by a man she invited in for a drink (although as the Texas case demonstrates, not necessarily). The last twenty-five years have, it is true, brought changes in attitudes about rape, and new laws (such as rape shield laws that limit the admissibility in a court of law of a victim's prior sexual history) reflect those changes. But there remains an ambiguous center of shifting blame that flows *between* the rapist and his victim. Law professor Susan Estrich, herself the victim of an aggravated rape, devotes her 1987 book *Real Rape* to an analysis of how rape-reform legislation has yet to change how judges look at the most common type of rape, and the most underreported—rapes that are committed by someone known to the victim. If the rapist is not a knife-wielding stranger, but a boyfriend, neighbor, or coworker, the law, Estrich writes, still "binds us to the past," where the victim is implicated in the crime.

Camille Paglia, the feminists' Antichrist, has argued that the women's movement has put young women in danger by hiding the truth about sex from them. The truth according to Paglia is that "sexual violence is rooted in men's sense of psychological weakness toward women," and sexual differences are based in biology. "Men must struggle for identity against the overwhelming power of their mothers.... Feminism, with its solemn Carrie Nation repressiveness, does not see what is for men the eroticism or fun element in rape." Aside from the fact that young women are in danger not *from women* "hiding the truth about sex" from them but *from men* who behave violently toward them, Paglia's view of men is grim. Most men don't rape. Are they "abnormal" males, biological freaks? I think not. Men I told about my rape were generally less embarrassed than women, but no less appalled.

Paglia, a writer, ironically seems to have no faith in words. The feminist attempt to refashion the world through language, she says, is a dangerous fantasy that "keeps young women from seeing life as it is." I agree with her that young women must be wary, but as a rape survivor, I find that these words sting because, although she states that rape is an "outrage that cannot be tolerated in civilized society," she is reinforcing the notion that rape is normal, part of our human biology, even, God forbid, fun for men. The rapist's "passionate sexual desire" is the motivation for his behavior in this scenario. Rape is, in some mysterious way, a kind of sex *between* males and females because the other side of the male's "passionate sexual desire" is the female's resistance and ultimate submission to it. I believe this view of sex silences, disconnects, and isolates millions of rape survivors, who, if they live to tell their stories, "confess" at their peril.

■ ■ ■

This book itself, as it came into being, seemed to lead me deeper into the heart of the confusion. Generous friends who read my manuscript as it went through several drafts showed me sides of the problem that made me feel I could never finish the book because the writing of it itself seemed to reveal more and more layers of meaning, each of which I needed to understand to go on. Two of my male readers raised problems with the manuscript that my women readers did not. In each case, the problems had to do with sex. My friend Paul, a novelist, had a problem with the description of the rape that baffled me. "Something is missing," he said after he had read the first chapter. "You've left out the sexual part. I think you chickened out."

I stowed his comment away in the back of my mind for nearly a year. Was it, I wondered, that a woman could imagine what it meant to say, "Over the next three hours he raped me," and that a man could not? Was it impossible for Paul to imagine that a penis might "in the scheme of things" be an incidental? Rape is every woman's worst nightmare, all too imaginable. Forced sexual contact (which in its most general form is a woman saying no and a man not taking her at her word) is something every woman who read my manuscript had experienced to some degree, although my experience is probably the outermost point on the continuum of consent. With the area of consent as murky as it seems to be, perhaps some men have a different nightmare about rape: that they will be accused of it.

Paul was right. I hadn't described the feeling of the rapist's penis in my vagina, the state of my vagina at the time, the feeling of the rapist's penis in my mouth, his orgasm (which I hadn't noticed), or his manipulations of my breasts. I didn't think it was necessary. It seemed to me that I had described "what it felt like" to be raped from my own perspective. Was Paul thinking that rape was a sexual act—that the rapist was motivated by sexual desire and that, although I was unwilling, like Scarlett O'Hara, in some sense my unwillingness was part of the erotic content? Or was I overreacting?

How many images had my generation absorbed from movies and books of a woman, usually an angry one, turning her back on a man in a gesture of rejection and the man roughly pulling her back, kissing her passionately? She struggles only briefly, then puts her arms around his neck and kisses him back with equal passion. A woman's unwillingness, these images suggest, is an essential ingredient of her pleasure, which can only be released by the man's aggression. Only then will she realize how much she wants him. This view of sex makes lack of consent by the female a part of normal sex.

This has been the image of sex between men and women in Western culture for centuries, and well before Freud. Ovid, the great collector of ancient mythology (a treasure trove of rape stories, by the way), had a word or two on the subject in *The Art of Love:* "Women often wish to give unwillingly what they really like to give."

It would seem from the number of articles about date rape in recent years that Ovid would feel right at home in our high schools, colleges, and universities. According to one survey of 6,159 college students enrolled at thirty-two institutions in the United States, more than one in four college-age women had been the victim of rape or attempted rape. Fifty-seven percent of the assaults occurred on dates and 42 percent of the victims told no one. One college survey found that 43 percent of college-age men admitted to using coercive behavior to "have sex," including ignoring a woman's protest and using physical aggression to force intercourse. Another survey of younger adolescents (eleven- to fourteen-year-olds) found that 65 percent of the boys and 47 percent of the girls said it was acceptable for a boy to rape a girl if they had been dating for more than six months.

Sexual assault is often a girl's first "sexual" experience. When a friend's daughter was fifteen, for example, she was sexually molested by a male "friend," who afterward began spreading rumors about her among her classmates that she was a "slut" and "whore." Sadly, her classmates were only too willing to believe him. He was not just covering his tracks. He may, in fact, have believed that her unwillingness was an ingredient in her pleasure, which he released through force. "No" means "Yes." Why would the student manual my friend sent me go to such lengths to define what "No" means unless there is some prevalent misunderstanding about it?

The student manual is attempting to change behavior through language, but the attitudes that support this behavior are not going away. In November of 1995, to cite only one example, an E-mail listing seventy-five reasons "why women (bitches) should not have freedom of speech" was sent by four Cornell University freshmen to twenty friends, who passed it along to countless other Internet addresses. The flood of forwarding crashed at least three campus E-mail systems, and the incident prompted angry responses from campuses across the country. Here are a few items from the list:

11. If my dick's in her mouth, she can't talk anyway.
20. This is my dick. I'm gonna fuck you. No more stupid questions.
35. Female drunks are annoying unless they put out (for which they don't need to talk).
38. If she can't speak, she can't cry rape.
39. Of course, if she can't speak, she can't say no.
47. Nothing should come out of a woman's mouth, SWALLOW BITCH!

49. Whores get paid by the hour not the word.
53. If it hurts, I don't wanna hear it.

Cornell administrators investigated the incident and were criticized on two sides—by women's rights activists for deciding not to punish the students and by free-speech advocates for conducting an investigation at all. The students (referred to as "pranksters" in one newspaper account) apologized in a letter to the Cornell student newspaper for what was intended as "a joke" among friends. "We had no idea," they wrote, "that we were really being taken seriously and seriously offending people until we received a letter from a young woman who had been sexually assaulted. At that point we realized exactly how far this has gone....We truly realized that no matter how bad we could feel, this could not compare, to any degree, to the physical and mental torture this young lady was forced to endure." They go on to explain that the list is "full of stereotypes taken from our society today. *We have seen almost everything on that list in some kind of TV show, rap song, Internet list, comedian's act or t-shirt*" (italics mine). Regrettably, true.

A year before this incident a college student was arrested for posting computer messages on the Internet describing his fantasy of the binding, rape, torture, and murder of a woman in one of his classes. "Torture is foreplay, rape is romance, snuff [murder] is climax." Again, freedom-of-speech issues were raised in his defense.

These are terrible words. I read them with particular horror. They go further than confusing sex and rape. They make them the same thing.

If the prevalent view of sex between men and women is still something Ovid would recognize, rape is not different in kind from "normal" sex. It is different only in degree. Are rapists like other men, only more so? And if they are, does that imply that rape victims are like other women, only more so?

In a 1992 television interview with news anchor Peter Jennings, Dr. Barry Buckhart of Auburn University, a leading expert on men who rape, suggested that rapists are only one extreme of normal male sexuality as it expresses itself in contemporary culture. Buckhart made the point that flashing someone the finger in a "Fuck you" gesture is more than a terrible insult. Viewed symbolically it represents the fusion of sex and aggression in American culture. "This culture," he told Jennings, "teaches men it is okay to inhibit their empathic connection to women," and this is what permits them to rape. "Forced sex originates in the minds of men." Jennings concluded the program by stating that we are living in a "rape culture." Power and anger expressed through pseudo-sexual acts—rape itself—is a cultural norm.

The most forgotten victims of rape are men themselves. Statistics are hard to come by on the number of men who are subjected to the rage and power of other men. I keep a little notebook to record the times I hear a joke about prison rape on television or at the movies. The list is very long. By making these jokes we diminish the idea that rape is about power. Consequently, sex is not associated with men raping men as readily as it is with men raping women. But men rape men to assert power—the same reason they rape women. Men who are raped (in prison or otherwise) suffer its aftermath just as I and millions of other women have. By preserving the idea that rape is a kind of sexual act, we can ignore its male victims and what their numbers tell us about violence in American society.

Recently I heard a politician say, "Weakness is provocation." He was talking about his opponent's foreign policy, but I couldn't help thinking of its broader cultural implications. Men do not view women and children as potential physical threats, as women do men. Women and children sometimes see men as threatening because statistically they are. This is not a victim mentality. It's a victim reality. Men do not think of themselves as prey to the anger and power of women or children. They do not see themselves as weak. To be weak is to be provocative. If you are attacked, according to this logic, it is because you were asking for it. The words of this politician are easily understood by his audience. In fact, they make perfect sense.

The actor Ned Beatty wrote a short essay for the *New York Times* a few years ago that described his experiences as a rape survivor, although his "rape" was only a fine piece of acting. In 1972 he appeared in the movie version of James Dickey's novel *Deliverance*. His character, Bobby, is forced to squeal like a pig as he is being raped by a backwoods villain. No viewer will ever forget that chilling and horrifying sound. "Most men," Beatty wrote, "don't have to live with the fear of being raped. My experience tells me we couldn't do it very well." He goes on to say that as a result of this role, he has been subjected to innumerable instances of men shouting at him, "Squeal like a pig." His response is anger because he is proud of his work in the film. "Somewhere between their shouts and my threats lies a kernel of truth about how men feel about rape," he concludes. "My guess is, we want to be distanced from it. Our last choice would be to identify with the victim. If we felt we could truly be victims of rape, that fear would be a better deterrent than the death penalty." Judging from the swelling ranks of prison inmates and the common knowledge that rape in prison is routine, he seems to be right that some men are incapable of identifying with the victim.

No wonder I can't get away from these confusions when I talk about my own experience. I cannot step outside of the system of beliefs that are the social context for my narrative. Being able to talk about my rape with the same ease I might talk about being mugged is impossible as long as I am living in a "rape culture."

Another reader of my manuscript commented that it was difficult for him to understand how I was able to marry Steve after going through the rape. "There's the whole question," he said, "of how you could have sex with Steve after being raped. You're going to have to explain that." I was surprised by this remark, and mentioned it to my mother several days later on the telephone. "How could he have wondered how I could make love with Steve?" I asked. "Is it because he's a man?"

"It isn't just men who don't get it," my mother said. "After your article came out, I got a call from Betty, who was in Hawaii on vacation." Betty was a close family friend who had known me since birth, a woman I loved dearly. "She was shocked, and wasn't even sure you

219

were the author. She thought there might be somebody else with your name. Then she wanted to know if the article was true, and I told her yes. That you had been raped. I guess she thought you were writing fiction. She said, first thing off, that she just didn't understand how you could have gotten married after being raped."

"What did you say?"

With her usual skill at cutting to the chase, my mother answered, "I told her it never crossed your mind *not* to marry Steve."

I had been surprised by these remarks, although perhaps I shouldn't have been. Troubling feelings did intrude during sex with Steve early in our marriage, especially in my most vulnerable moments. Sometimes when we embraced late at night while I was in a semiconscious state I would become startled and would struggle to get away until I realized where I was and with whom. I worried at first about these occasional "emotional hijackings" in my marriage bed, but my concern about such intrusions in our love-making evaporated over time. In my case, they were infrequent and, like intrusions from the past in other contexts (such as sitting with my back to a door), I learned how to manage them.

I was surprised by these remarks because I felt they denied the complex impact of rape on the whole of a victim's emotional and spiritual life by confining the damage to one part of her life. They also implied that consensual sex and rape were closely related—so much so that for some people the idea that a rape survivor could enjoy making love with her husband was difficult to imagine, if not impossible to believe.

■ ■ ■

I ran across a definition of rape in *Demonic Males* that intrigued me. Here is how Craig Palmer, a researcher who surveyed the literature in 1989 for cases of rape among nonhuman species of mammals, defined rape: as a copulation where the victim resists to the best of her (or his) ability, or where a likely result of such resistance would be death or bodily harm to the victim, or to those whom she or he commonly protects. (Palmer found rape to be routine among only two species of nonhuman mammals: orangutans and elephant seals; he found reports of occasional rape from studies of chimpanzees, captive gorillas, and wild howler monkeys.) The term *forced copulation* is often used to describe rape in nonhuman mammal species.

The issue of "consent" is not central to this definition. It is impossible for a scientist to observe "consent" directly, since it is an interior state. John Mitani, who studied orangutans in southeastern Borneo, described the forced copulations he observed as involving "protracted struggles between females and males" during which "females whimper, cry, squeal and grunt" while males would "grab, bite or slap females before they could copulate. While thrusting, males continued to restrain struggling females by grasping their arms, legs and bodies." The orangutan females Mitani observed cannot report that the copulation was "against their will." Furthermore, will, the faculty of conscious and deliberate action, is viewed as a human characteristic. What looms large in this definition is the fact that resistance would be "likely" to result in death or injury. An animal's "consent" is framed in objective terms.

Rape in humans is not so simple. As the student handbook makes clear, consent or the lack of it is the sole criterion. The definition of rape used by the Justice Department in its National Incident-Based Reporting System (NIBRS) in 1991 was "the carnal knowledge of a person, forcibly and/or against that person's will; or, not forcibly or against the person's will where the victim is incapable of giving consent because of his/her temporary or permanent mental or physical incapacity." The "appearance" of consent, as in the case of the Texas rape victim who had the presence of mind to talk her rapist into using a condom, is a central problem for adult female rape victims. It would seem it is less so for adult same-sex rape victims—unless, perhaps, the victim is a homosexual.

Human beings "have sex"; animals "copulate." Although they denote the same thing—sexual intercourse—they have different connotations. The term *forced copulation* seems to describe my experience better than *sexual assault*. When the woman in New York told me that she wondered how I could be writing about my rape, "a sexual thing ...such an intimate act," I felt angry because she seemed to think that I was writing about a "personal" sexual experience. For Paul to tell me I had left something out of my description of the rape, the "sexual part," disturbed me for a similar reason. And for friends to wonder how I could have sexual relations with my husband after being raped implied that I had had "sex" when I was raped.

I began to wonder: Had I had a "sexual experience" with the rapist? In only one sense is the answer yes. His penis did enter my vagina—at least three times. Apparently he was having trouble ejaculating and, lacking the stimulus of my fear, he needed moans of "pleasure" to complete "copulation." These I "faked," but it would seem to his "satisfaction," judging from the semen the doctor found in my vagina. Although it did not hurt at the time because I was numb to all pain, my lack of consent, as evidenced by the fact that my vagina was as tight and dry as a drum, did result in injury to vaginal tissues. It is common knowledge that some rapists who are unable to sustain an erection or to ejaculate kill their victims, blaming them for their sexual dysfunction. In these circumstances, a victim might well find herself actively trying to "sexually" stimulate her attacker in order to save her life. Whatever "pseudo-sexual" behavior on my part was required to ensure my survival would have been forthcoming if I had been faced with this circumstance. (Humans, like other animals, have an "instinct" to avoid bodily injury and death. For me, the instinct to live was not a decision. It was a response.)

Was this sex for me? If human sex—including sadomasochistic sex—is sex that is desired and willed, and where pleasure, however oddly configured, is the result, the answer is no. However, although I had no desire and experienced no pleasure, I did have what appears to be "consent." I instinctively "decided" to live—unlike any number of female saints half-remembered from my childhood who chose death over the loss of their "virtue." I did make "a deal with the devil." Would he have actually murdered me if, rather than lapsing into a detached state of what Livingstone called "a sort of dreaminess," I had had some other, more violent, reaction? Was it a case where "a likely result of such resistance would be death or bodily harm"? Judging from my objective behavior, the answer can only be yes.

Women do "make deals" with men in bed. Faking orgasm, having sex when they don't really feel like it. They do it for all kinds of reasons, including love. Women can "have sex" without having "sexual desire." And sometimes their motive might be to gain power. Was the deal I made with the rapist on the extreme end of a continuum of "normal" female sexual behavior? Is this why the victim is tainted with the vague stain of having participated in a sexual act when she is raped and lives to speak of it?

But there is a difference: A pretending woman has both the will and the desire to pretend, whatever her motive may be.

Still, I did, after all, "consent" in some way, didn't I? This fact, as evidenced by my survival, cast a long and terrible shadow over me for many years, and even now it has not entirely lifted. Perhaps it is at the root of what made me angry with the woman who found that I was writing about something "so very personal." The shadow cast by my "compliance" could only be completely lifted if I had "resisted" to my death. The fact is, I did not.

Attitudes about sex are highly charged and profoundly complex. Before the rape my basic attitude was that it was a pleasurable act—with the right partner. I wasn't "uptight" about it, wasn't particularly experimental. I had friends who made love in unusual places, including in the car while they were driving on a freeway. I admired their inventiveness, but I wasn't like that. I suppose you could call me a sexual moderate. Orgasms were not a problem but I didn't need three a day to be happy.

My basic attitudes toward sex and my own sexuality would be touched by the rape, but not in the obvious way. The rape did not create an aversion to sex, although I did not feel like having sex until I met Steve. I didn't feel I'd "had sex" with the rapist. I simply felt my body, including my sex organs, had been attacked. Yet my failure to die—

223

proof of some kind of "consent"—seemed to slowly and inexorably poison me. When someone implied that my rape was a "sexual thing," I could taste, but not identify, the bitterness of this poison.

I was comforted by the doctor's discovery during the pelvic exam at the hospital that there was proof of my "lack of consent" in the torn tissues in my vagina. But what if there was no vaginal "damage"? What if my body had "responded" to "pseudo-sex" by "pseudo-arousal" in vaginal secretions, as sometimes does occur—a purely biological response? Suddenly something that is hideous becomes linked to sexual functioning, something that is pleasurable. The perversity becomes not the rapist's perversity but the victim's. In my case, the fact that I staggered away from the rape alive made me feel perverse. This subtle aspect of the "sexual" part of my rape did not express itself "sexually." Without being conscious of it, for many years I simply blamed myself for living.

The strange feeling that I was "sexually" perverse because I had, although only "instinctively," made a "sexual" deal with the rapist deepened my self-hatred. My sexual functioning had been "sacrificed" on the altar of life itself. A psychiatrist once pointed out to me that it is terribly confusing for a person to be "forced by someone to do something." It raises deeply disturbing questions of how much choice a person actually had in the situation. To be "forced" to engage in "sexual" behavior—to "moan" with "pleasure," for example, as I was forced to do—is, she observed, "one of the ways that the rapist makes the victim feel profoundly ashamed. It is taking over, coopting, and twisting the sexual functions of the victim."

Yes, rape is violence, as feminists have argued for decades. And I must credit the woman in New York with naming what most horrified and disturbed her: the thought of being forced to "participate" in such a horrible "sexual" act. In acknowledging this dimension we must, however, be careful because "old" attitudes thrive. The inertia of centuries of social organization is an awesome force.

In 1988 a Rhode Island Rape Crisis Center surveyed seventeen hundred sixth- to ninth-grade students and found that a substantial percentage of these children believed that a man has the right to kiss or have sexual intercourse with a woman against her will, particularly if he has "spent money on her." Half of the students said that a woman who walks alone at night and dresses "seductively" is "asking to be raped." These children are now college students. Perhaps a few of them ended up at Cornell. It is easy to slip out of the quotation marks, to slide back into the belief that rape is "normal" and inevitable "sexual" behavior for both men (as Paglia sadly suggests) *and women*. Attitudes we long to believe have changed elude our attention, like the blackberry shoots in my garden, if we cease to be vigilant. We can call them "gaffes," "pranks," and "odd theories," but they are far more dangerous and silencing than these terms suggest.

Rape *is* different from all other crimes, and it is one of the most insidious. It is the only crime of violence that masquerades as sex. Rape is the wolf lying in Grandmother's bed, wearing her nightgown. Like Little Red Riding Hood, we are aware that something is different about Grandmother but are fooled nevertheless by appearances. Rape is a death force that can disguise itself as the life force to which all human beings are inexorably drawn. Rapists are sexual impostors. Many benefit from the confusion created by their disguise, just as many victims suffer from the consequences of that confusion. Rape mimics what it aims to devour—the mysterious life-affirming force that renews us and fulfills our most profound longings for union. Rape devours erotic love, the communion of body and being, the mysterious affirmation of existence beyond power and all its metaphors, the channel into and out of the center of creation where words and body disappear into the void of pleasure, the all-encompassing journey of two as one, and one as many and all.

FOURTEEN

Turning Point

and turn, and again find
the disorder in the mind.

ROBERT CREELEY, "The Hero"

December of 1990, the month after Steve and I stopped seeing Dr. Blanchard, was my final month in solitary, although I believed I would be there for the rest of my life. The rape specialist to whom Dr. Blanchard had referred me, Dr. Deborah Rose, was booked solid until early January. I had to survive until then. I felt like an astronaut on a space walk whose tether had come undone. There was just me and the void. And whatever oxygen was left in my tank.

During these weeks I felt as close to insanity as I imagine I could get and still come back. I was close enough to taste the bitterness of its isolation, and I felt the added shame of enduring this banishment as someone who had done her best to prevent it. Someone who had fought—and lost. This defeat seemed more bitter than the rape itself. In a sense I could understand how I had been physically defeated by the rapist that afternoon in Boston. He had the element of surprise in his favor, and he meant me harm. But I could not understand why his ghost, now a part of myself, was winning again.

My nightmares were frequent and more literal—I dreamed repeatedly that I opened the front door of my house to take out the trash and the rapist is there, materializing from nothing. All my strength goes into trying to close the door, but he seems to have superhuman strength and my efforts to lock him out are in vain. He forces his way inside. I feel I am wrestling with a dark, metaphysical force and wake up in a state of terror. This terror is not fear in overdrive, as I once thought, but another state altogether. In *All Quiet on the Western Front,* Erich Maria Remarque wrote, "Fear we do not know much about—terror of death, yes; but that is a different matter, that is physical." This is an observation the truth of which I came to know well that month. Occasions for making the distinction struck like lightning in the same place many times.

I recall an incident over the Christmas holidays with my seventeen-year-old niece, who was visiting from Pittsburgh. We were strolling arm in arm along a path in Muir Woods, a popular redwood grove in Marin County. I was glad we'd come on an overcast, chilly day. There were few tourists, and we had the place to ourselves. The tops of the ancient trees were lost in a mist that had crept in from the sea, and the creek we followed was lively with runoff from a recent storm. The trunks of fallen giants were thick with ferns and moss. In the subdued light, they seemed to blaze green.

Suddenly and without warning I felt a rush from behind that conveyed the same supernatural feeling as the recurring dream. I jumped like a startled animal. My niece seemed to absorb the charge and force of my terror. "What is it?" she said, spinning around on the path. There wasn't a soul in sight. There had been no sudden or strange sound, no external stimulus at all. It was an involuntary physical reaction to the ghost inside, although I couldn't have told her that at the time. I was as baffled as she.

I was also painfully embarrassed in front of my only niece, the child I had devoted myself to since her father's death long ago, when she was less than a year old. She didn't know about my rape and I had no intention of telling her. My reasons for not telling her or my stepdaughter (who was then fourteen) were complicated. I loved them, and I wanted to protect them from the pain of imagining what had happened to me. It would hurt them, as it had hurt my parents, my brothers, my friends. And I did not want to fill their minds with a fear of men by telling them what some were capable of, or use the rape to make my lessons in caution more effective. My knowledge of the truth made my worries about their increasing freedom agonizing. I did not have to imagine what could happen to the children I loved.

"It's nothing," I said, trying to think of some reasonable explanation. I didn't want my niece to know that her aunt was riddled with paranoid delusions. "It's a nerve chill—you know, like the kind you get when someone 'walks on your grave.' You've heard that expression?" She looked dubious but seemed willing to let my smile, false as it was, reassure her. "Phew! You scared the daylights out of me," she said.

The physical sensations of terror, including, most horribly, the sense of separating from myself, returned on this occasion in the form in which I had experienced it that afternoon so long ago. It lasted for several days. I felt as if I had been attacked again because my body was responding the same way. Once the terror faded, I returned to a state of chronic fear. But in addition to the fear, I felt something worse—self-contempt. I seemed to be a person who was grossly overreacting—not to something, but to nothing.

The attacks caused me to cut myself off from everyone to whom I should have been close. I pretended to be "normal," acting from cue cards that flashed in some part of my mind. I could not share my terror because I did have a remnant of sanity—I knew it was crazy.

While disconnecting me from others, it simultaneously linked me to the rapist. I was obsessed with the possibility that he might strike again and at any moment, and "he" did strike, again and again, when I least expected it. I would feel the sudden rush that rendered me panicked and helpless at various times of the day and in different places—in my office or driving my car, where I sometimes was convinced he was hiding in the backseat. He was there, charging at me out of nowhere, and when he was not attacking, he was threatening to attack. No place was safe, not even my home with Steve sitting next to me. Despite my best efforts, I was back in my attic in Concord, standing at the top of the stairs with a knife in my hand.

In the five years that had passed since that afternoon, I had moved. And yet I was in the same place. Only this time there was a Christmas tree in the corner.

■ ■ ■

I sought comfort from the one person in my life who I expected to understand my feelings—my friend Helen.

Helen and I went back a lot further than Boston. We met in Europe when we were both still wearing anklets and patent-leather shoes. We called ourselves Mutt and Mutt and were inseparable for three years. We shared the intensities, confusions, and vanities of early adolescence—or so I thought.

After we both moved back to the States, however, we'd lost touch—she moved to Oregon with her family, I returned to Virginia. We wrote a few times. Sent each other high-school graduation pictures: "Love ya! Helen," "Love ya! Nancy," in ballpoint across the bottom.

About a year before I was raped, Helen located me in New England through my parents. She was living in Santa Cruz, California, and was calling me for a reason. She told me that during the years of our friendship she was being sexually molested by her father, a high-ranking diplomat. She wanted me to help her remember the girl she had been because those years were a blank. "I was numb the whole time," she said.

She explained that as her marriage was failing, she'd begun to recall more and more about the abuse she had endured and that, after several years of therapy, she had sued her father for money to pay for her treatment. "He admitted he'd molested me and settled out of court," she told me, "but on the condition that I sign a legal document promising I would never go public with the truth. I was broke, so I signed it."

I was stunned, and felt guilty that I'd never suspected anything was wrong in her life.

"How many years did this go on?"

"It started when I was twelve—just after we met. I ran away when I was seventeen."

It didn't seem possible that I could not have known—that Helen hadn't told me or that I hadn't sensed something.

I told her what I could, remembering for her the innocence I'd thought we'd shared—how we set our hair with beer so it would hold our towering bouffants, how we danced to Ricky Nelson records, how we dressed up in my mother's evening gowns. I remembered the names of the boys we had crushes on and how we wrote them on my dressing table mirror in red lipstick.

"Do you remember how we used to rent a paddle boat in the botanical gardens downtown—that little lake with the swans, the one that had an island in the middle? You always brought a sketch pad. I loved watching you draw. Remember when we saw the cygnets riding on their mother's back? That wonderful picture you painted?"

No, she said, she didn't remember.

She told me she was an artist—a painter. I had saved a couple of her pictures and promised to unearth them from my files and send them to her. She was surprised I had saved them.

"I could never bring myself to toss them," I told her.

"I'm so glad you saved them. You know, I don't even remember that I was drawing then. It's as if I was walking around in a coma. But you have proof I had someplace safe to go inside, even then. It's the part of me that I use every day now."

When I told my mother about Helen's call, she, too, was shocked. "What I remember about Helen," my mother said, "was her beautiful smile. She was always smiling. Your father and I used to comment on what a cheerful girl she was."

When I moved to California, Helen and I saw each other often. The bond between us was still strong, perhaps even stronger because I was her link to a part of her past that seemed to exist for her only because I carried it.

Turning Point

. . .

A few days after Christmas, my niece returned to Pittsburgh. I was exhausted from the effort of trying to appear "normal" during a season that can deplete even the most normal of people. As soon as she was gone, I took down the Christmas tree; its bright lights and ornaments had only added to my misery. Then I packed an overnight bag and drove to Santa Cruz to spend a few days with Helen, who was renting an apartment a block from the ocean. At night, after the traffic died down, we could hear the sound of the waves if we sat on her back porch, although the price for this pleasure was a heavy coat and gloves.

We were sitting just so when I told her that I was about to start psychotherapy. I didn't tell her about the attacks of terror that were tormenting me. I felt if I articulated my delusions I would somehow take the final turn into absolute insanity. What felt safer was to tell her how furious I was that the rapist had driven me to a shrink. It was his fault I was falling apart. I told Helen that my rape was "worse than death," and that I felt the rapist had destroyed my life, that I could never rebuild it. "Never, never," I said. I hated him with my entire being. I wanted to see him dead. I wanted to kill him myself. I had never expressed my rage to another human being this directly. It was no longer deflected onto someone or something else in my life. It was the rapist I hated that night.

She listened and after a long silence said, very quietly, "Don't you think it's time you got past that?"

I was stung. I got up without a word and went to bed. I felt the oxygen had finally run out.

Helen, albeit with a certain impatience, had uttered a wish for me. She wanted me to live as she did, in relative peace with herself, unburdened of shadows thrown into relief by the glare of the past. But I didn't hear a wish. I took her remark as a reprimand. It would be a long time before I could hear it as anything else.

231

Starting Through

The best way out is always through

ROBERT FROST, "A Servant to Servants"

It's January 1991. I'm on the freeway in a driving rain, late for my third appointment with Dr. Rose. My windshield wipers slap back and forth. I hit eighty-five miles per hour—screw the highway patrol. Last night, like most nights, I could not sleep. It was close to five A.M., when I should have been getting up and out, before exhaustion felled me. Already I hate this drive to Dr. Rose's office in Palo Alto. The three-hour round trip feels like five. The whole way there and back I feel as if the steering wheel is about to fly out of my hands.

I consider myself both lucky and unlucky to have the eight A.M. appointment, the only time Dr. Rose can fit me into her schedule. I'm lucky that she can see me at all, but the early hour adds to the misery of having to plunge backwards into the rape and what it has spawned.

If the good news is that I have pressed on and am showing up at Dr. Rose's office once a week, the bad news is that despite Elavil, the antidepressant she has prescribed, I am still depressed. Reproaching myself for needing a pharmaceutical crutch, I am doubly upset that it isn't helping. I have told Steve that Dr. Rose has prescribed this medication for three months; I reassure him—and myself—that it will just "get me over the hump." He notices that it isn't working, but during this period of truce he doesn't say so. At least I am making an effort—and what an effort. I feel as if I am trying to run through waist-deep wet cement to get away from something invisible that is breathing down my neck. The distance, the traffic, the weather, my exhaustion, my fear are all part of the wet cement, dragging me down as I try to run for my life. And the financial cost—$115 a session, $460 a month—is a rapist's ransom.

By the time I get on the main street through Palo Alto, I am twenty-five minutes late. The rain has stopped, but the avenue is congested and I can only poke along. I wait for pedestrians, stop lights, cars backing out of parking places. I weave my way through town, turn right, wait at the light. I hunt for a parking place in the crowded lot behind Dr. Rose's office building. I circle, waiting for someone to vacate a space. I count the minutes—three, then five. An eternity.

Finally I see a woman sauntering toward her car, keys in hand. I back up, put on my turn signal to claim her space. She acknowledges me with a nod and slips into her car. She pulls down the vizor and applies lip liner, then lipstick. She brushes her hair. She stares at herself for a moment, then pulls down her seat belt, adjusts it. She starts the car, pumps the brakes. She leans over then, looking for something on the seat. I want to drag her out of her car and hit her in the face. Finally she backs out, slowly, carefully, as if she were driving a bus instead of a red Mercedes coupe. She waves, smiles. "Christ almighty!" I snarl under my breath, roaring into her space.

Inside the building, I dash down the hall to the stairway, taking the stairs two at a time, then hurry into Dr. Rose's waiting room, which is deserted. The door between her private office and the waiting room is open. It was closed when I arrived for the first two sessions. I hesitate for a moment. Should I walk in or knock? I approach the door. She is not sitting at her desk, which is directly in front of me. It is neat, with stacks of papers in orderly piles presided over by a vase of yellow tulips. "Hello?" I say, thinking she has stepped out. I'm thirty minutes late.

"Come in," she says from inside the room. I enter then, walk directly to my place, a comfortable black leather chair in front of the window. Dr. Rose is sitting in her chair, with her hands folded in her lap. She isn't reading, or making notes, or talking on the phone. She is simply sitting in her chair, waiting. She says, "Hello." It is a professional "Hello," unreadable.

Her office is tasteful and warm—an Oriental rug, a wall of bookshelves, a thriving ficus tree in the corner, paintings on the wall. She is wearing a tailored dress, a simple silver necklace, small silver earrings, black heels. She is a trim, attractive woman with short dark hair, around my age—mid-forties.

I get settled, feeling self-conscious. "I overslept."

Is she angry with me for keeping her waiting? Will she interpret my tardiness as an indication that I do not want to feel better?

Before she can respond to my first excuse, I add a second. "And the roads are ghastly." I don't tell her about the woman in the parking lot, or how I reacted to her. What I want is for Dr. Rose to tell me it is not my fault.

"I know it is hard for you to get here," she says.

I start to cry. "I thought you'd gone out..."

"This is your time," she says. "We're here to find out why you feel so bad—so we can help you."

Her words open the sluice. "I hope you have a good supply of these," I say between sobs, pulling a Kleenex out of the box on the table beside me. "I have the feeling I'm going to be using a lot of them." I try to smile, but I don't think either of us is fooled.

After the thirty-minute session, I sit in my car in the parking lot behind her office, chain-smoking, working up the will to drive home. When I do finally get home, I crawl into bed. I have gone back to consulting, and there are urgent messages from clients on my voice mail. But I cannot face them. All I want to do is sleep.

SIXTEEN

Ancient Anniversaries

For in this strange, this iris-region wild
I dream that dreadful things
Forever hold thy child.

DOROTHY WELLESLEY, "Demeter in Sicily"

One night in the winter of 1991 I heard a rape survivor on television explain in two sentences what rape was: "The rape is just the beginning. Then it's one long drop into hell."

As a child I was taught that hell was separation from God. The agony of hell was the agony of that separation. The rapist taught me something else about hell—that it was a place of division. It was a place in the heart where Before-and-After never make a story. Between the rage and the despair of these two sundered parts was the stage where what must pass for normal life unfolded.

In the months after I began therapy, I constructed a third being who could act *as if* she felt neither rage, grief, nor despair. She consulted with business clients (who, on the whole, seemed pleased with her performance), dusted furniture, planted bulbs, made soup. The as-if woman struggled to be a wife, a friend, and a mother to her husband's daughter, a girl of fourteen swept up in her years. What I experienced of life now seemed like a hologram of myself, a glowing, insubstantial fixture that somehow held in place for more than a year.

Although I was alive, I did not feel like living. And the living I experienced did not feel like life. For more than a year that life hung in the balance between a Before I could not reclaim and an After I could not yet understand. I managed for the most part to confine the woman who raged, grieved, and despaired over her plight to my weekly sessions with Dr. Rose.

Steve was not entirely happy with the wife he now had, but she was an improvement over the woman who seemed to hate him. She did not confide in him, as I once had. She rarely spoke to him about her meetings with Dr. Rose. Instead she retreated to her office at night, where she wrote in her journals for many hours, or, on the weekends, to her studio at the beach, where he was not welcome. Sometimes his experience of living with a woman who did not feel real provoked him to anger. When he stormed, the as-if woman turned into the woman who raged and grieved for the self she had lost and her fury overwhelmed his. The as-if woman was easier to live with, so he settled for her.

■ ■ ■

I know of no word in common usage to describe the actual condition of individuals who have experienced profound loss as they undergo the complicated, introspective process of self-redemption—my condition when I began seeing Dr. Rose. Perhaps there was a word once—when passages of the spirit had rites and rites had communities. When I found myself in this condition, I wanted a word.

I forget who said that the universe is made up of stories, not atoms. Obviously, it was a writer. I'd believed it ever since I'd nearly failed high-school physics. So when I couldn't find a word, I looked for a story because I needed to link my experience to the human story that bears witness to it. Other human beings had made the long descent into division that was my condition, one I hoped Dr. Rose could help me either accept or change. Surely there was a story for me.

There was one story that came immediately to mind when I began thinking along these lines. It was a Greek story about a rape and "a drop into hell"—the myth of Persephone and Demeter. I was familiar with its basic outline from having read Ovid's version in college. I discovered after a few days' research that the earliest extant version of the story was a Greek poem, *The Hymn to Demeter*, composed by an unknown Greek bard sometime between 650 and 550 B.C. I located two translations of this poem in a secondhand bookshop tucked away under a freeway overpass in San Francisco, and one overcast afternoon that winter sat down in my reading chair to see what the Greeks had to say.

The story begins with Persephone gathering flowers in a meadow. It was not a bird's song that caught her attention, but a flower—a narcissus with a hundred blooms "which Earth grew as a snare." The moment she reached for the breathtaking flower, the earth gaped open and Hades, lord of the underworld, thundered into the light, driving a chariot drawn by immortal horses. In an instant, Persephone is snatched up and dragged below. She screams for help, but no one hears her—only the echo of her voice is left, "throbbing through the barren air."

How strange it seemed to me that the Greek poet had framed the prelude to Persephone's season in hell with a moment of connection with nature—the narcissus with a hundred blossoms, a flower with mythical significance for the ancient Greeks, who believed it to have soporific qualities. Mine had started in a similar fashion—the "snare" of the unknown bird's haunting melody.

Because of the conjunction of the bird's song and the rapist's strike that afternoon in Boston, I suffered from a disturbing association between beauty and horror. Every rape victim lives with a set of complex and infinitely evolving associations, and no two sets are the same. Whatever is fixed in terror's beam assumes a startling significance in the landscape of an individual's feeling that time modulates but never completely erases. Associations can be created even by constructed moments of terror—swimming in the ocean at night has a certain charge for some moviegoers, I suspect, because of a grisly scene in the

1975 movie *Jaws*, where a swimmer is devoured by a shark. Or a scent may be laden with such profound associations that it seems to produce long-vanished rooms or faces.

These resonating chords are sometimes baffling for those unfamiliar with the heightened awareness that often accompanies traumatic experiences. I was struck, for example, by a detail in one newspaper account of the rape trial of Kerry Kotler, mentioned in an earlier chapter. In an attempt to discredit the victim, she was asked by Kotler's defense lawyers how she could recall that the handle of the knife held against her throat was blue and that the nozzle on the water bottle Kotler used to wash away his semen was red, yet not recall whether or not Kotler had a mustache. My experience suggests that she remembered such trivial and, under normal circumstances, immaterial details because her attention was focused on those elements of the assault that were the cause of her terror and humiliation—the knife and the water bottle. I would not be surprised if she were troubled by water bottles, especially those with red nozzles, for some time to come, nor do I find it odd that Kotler's mustache escaped her attention. Packing boxes still trigger an unpleasant association for me, although I use them when I need to. I am aware of a dissonant note within when I hear someone use the phrase "shut up," and find that even my teenage stepdaughter's disorderly room evokes a mild uneasiness I recognize as an echo of the particular circumstances of that day long ago. A lover's words or touch, or even something as seemingly insignificant as the color of his socks, might also evoke these associations. Victims of traumatic injury learn to read this subtext. Spouses and lovers, if they are attentive, learn to read it as well.

The association between natural beauty and horror was especially painful for me. It was more than recognizing that a solitary walk in the woods or along a deserted seashore might not be as safe as I had once imagined and that it was wise to find a companion—if you could find a quiet one. It was deeper than the empirical knowledge I now had that being a woman alone was to be at risk. It was the loss of the solace of wild, natural places or wild corners of tame ones. The rapist had damaged my capacity for what I felt was a form of prayer. I withheld the devout attention I had once given to the gifts bestowed on my senses by nature in order to protect myself from the evil that seemed to lurk just beyond the visible world. It was a deprivation that impoverished my mind and spirit for many years.

I knew there was no design to this unfortunate accident and that its cruelty was merely random. Yet I sometimes allowed myself to wonder whether I could find some metaphysical purpose to it. Was this the challenge to faith that comes to each of us eventually? God, however conceived or wherever worshipped, asks for faith where none is warranted. Could I ever pray again now that my faith had been tested?

I felt comforted by the poetic detail of the narcissus, the warning unheeded, although I cannot explain why the companionship of Persephone, a creature of legend, made me feel less alone.

The poet has little to say about Persephone's experience in the underworld—a place of murky gloom that is completely cut off from the upper world of gods and humans. Her rape is implied, the translator's notes tell me, by the language, especially the use of a Greek word—*biazomenes*—that has connotations of overpowering force, as in "suffering violence," and by Persephone's unwillingness, her cries of protest, and the suddenness and violence of her transition to the world below.

It interested me greatly that the poet described Persephone's rape as a brutal transition from the world of light to the world of darkness. He had gone to the essence of the matter—the wound to the soul. I thought about the rape scenes I had seen in movies, how literal the medium required them to be, drawing our eyes to bodies.

Perhaps if I had read the poem before I was raped I might have considered the poet's silence about Persephone's physical experience a strange omission. But reading the poem as a woman who had been raped, I was moved by the truth of these ancient words. It was the separation from the world of light—from meaning, memory, nature, mother, from earth and fecundity itself—that constituted the violation. It seemed that an unknown poet who had been dead for more than two and a half thousand years had, in a few elegant lines, summed up what the experience of rape really was—the sudden tearing open of solid earth that produces the unimaginable nightmare of death.

It was also a metaphor for the moment when Before turns to After—the moment that cannot be undone and that changes life forever.

The image of the sudden yawning of the earth came to mind recently when I heard a doctor describe the moment he knew he had been infected with HIV—his hand slipped while he was performing an autopsy on a man who had died of AIDS. In an instant, one he cannot forget, he lost the life he had had and began to live another—the life of a man living with AIDS.

The poet devotes only 40 lines (out of 495) to Persephone. The rest of the hymn concentrates on her mother's grief and fury. Demeter, goddess of the grain, rushes around the world with torches in her hands, searching in vain for her daughter. After several frustrated attempts to pry the truth from her fellow immortals, Demeter learns of her daughter's fate from Helios, the god of the sun, "observer of gods and mortals." She is so grief-stricken that she leaves the realm of the gods to wander the earth as an old woman. At the town of Eleusis she finally settles down in the king's household and eventually reveals her identity, ordering the people to build her a temple. Here in her sanctuary she retreats, "sitting apart from all the immortals, wasting with desire for her daughter."

I saw myself in Demeter's wanderings and grief. I thought of my longing for my lost self as I read of her desperate search—my fierce but ultimately futile attempts to reclaim the part of myself that the rapist had stolen. I thought of my attic near Concord, how I had struggled to make it a sanctuary. I thought of my studio at the beach, where I had gone to grieve. It seemed I, too, had rushed around the world searching for my own innocent daughter, the woman who felt safe.

I thought, too, of my own mother, who had never spoken of her feelings about what had happened to me. My rape had separated us. After those weeks in Virginia, I felt her gradually slipping away from me. I wanted to protect her from the pain that I felt in Concord. I longed for her, yet I spared her the sadness that was mine and that I knew would be hers if I spoke of it. There was nothing she could do to help me. She knew this, and that knowledge must have seared her, as it did me.

When I married and the rape submerged to undergo its strange metamorphosis, I could not tell her what I myself was incapable of understanding. My silence protected her, and was my own design. She had not requested this protection, nor, looking back now, do I think she needed it.

But in time it began to seem to me that she had abandoned me. I imagined Persephone, curled up in a corner of hell, seeing shadows of the dead that were only shifts of darkness, like a wind through the gloom, remembering Demeter and wondering why she did not come to her rescue. But not even a powerful goddess could enter the realm of the dead. There was nothing my mother could do. Although I had been blessed with a closeness to her that few of my friends seemed to enjoy with their mothers, I had lost it in the descent I had made.

I sensed that both my mother and I were cut off from aspects of ourselves. She had lost the connection with the daughter who had been raped. My mother had known me for thirty-nine years. But she did not know the woman I had become, the one who was divided from herself, the one who lived as-if. This fragmented woman was a stranger. I had lost contact with my real mother and, increasingly, with the part of myself that had once provided comfort—my own maternal aspect.

Demeter's grief turns to a terrible rage that she vents on the world of humans, causing a devastating famine that is so severe, mortals can no longer make sacrifices of grain to the gods. Zeus, ruler of heaven and earth, becomes concerned and sends messengers to Demeter, urging her to relent. But she refuses. She will only restore the earth when she is reunited with her daughter. Could I, I wondered, use my rage to re-create a whole and authentic woman?

Zeus finally orders Hades to release Persephone, but Hades compels her to eat a pomegranate seed before he carries her back in his chariot to her mother at Eleusis. Having tasted food in the underworld, Persephone must return to the gloom a third part of each year, Demeter tells her when they are at last reunited. "When the earth blooms in spring with all kinds of sweet flowers, then from the misty dark you will rise again."

At the end of the poem order is restored—fertility returns to the earth, the people of Eleusis are taught Demeter's sacred rites, which "are not to be transgressed, nor pried into, nor divulged," and mother and daughter rejoin the assembly of the gods on Olympus. But the order that is established after Persephone's rape is a different order, one that includes new mysteries.

Autumn is Persephone's anniversary, too, I thought as I read the last lines. When she descends again, the world withers, but only for a season. For the Greek poet, the union of mother and daughter is one that will forever include a new cycle of separation and reunion. Perhaps I did not have to forget hell. Perhaps I had to remember it. That afternoon in 1991 I did not have any idea of how I would construct my remembering, but I began to think of my weekly trips to Palo Alto as a way to rescue my lost self. My grief had turned to rage, the rage I had shared with Helen. Was it a rage that might, as Demeter's had, be used to make a deal with the devil?

■ ■ ■

I put the poem aside for a long time—several years. Then I read a few scholarly articles about it. I discovered that this poem, set to music, was once the central text of a religious rite, the Eleusinian Mysteries, that dominated the Greco-Roman world for nearly a thousand years or longer. Cicero called them Athens's greatest gift to humanity, although, unlike democracy, this gift did not get passed down to us. Whatever the mysteries were, they are safely locked away for eternity, as the ancients apparently wanted them to be. The nature of the rites held at Eleusis was a closely guarded secret. The hall where they were conducted held several thousand men and women, and the mysteries, which lasted a week, took place every autumn for a thousand years. But no one ever described them. Most scholars agree that worshippers seem to have experienced in some form the sufferings and reunion of Persephone and Demeter.

For the people of the ancient world this myth provided the central drama of a ritual that revealed a secret so profound that no one to whom it was revealed ever spoke of it directly. Aristotle said that the participants did not learn something but were made to experience something; Plutarch said that terror, anxiety, and bewilderment turned to wonder and clarification. The rhetorician Sopatros described his experience at Eleusis this way: "I came out of the mystery hall feeling like a stranger to myself." Even if these endorsements are examples of Hellenic hyperbole, I would still like to have had a firsthand look at one of these gatherings.

I was struck by the fact that for these ancient people a story that made rape a metaphor for the process of descent and rebirth had such power. Men, too, apparently found meaning in it. These rites provided a structure for making sense of their world. But in the world I inhabited, one that owed much to the ancient Greeks, there was no ritual that could help me turn my terror and bewilderment into clarification. Indeed, there seemed only to be silence.

Yet as I contemplated the myth of Persephone and Demeter, whispers from that vanished past did seem to reach me. Although Persephone's redemption was not the ultimate triumph of good over evil through freely chosen heroic action, it was, nevertheless, redemption. She seemed to be the classic victim. Like me, she had no training for her ordeal and was given no choice in the matter. She was forced against her will to make the descent into Hades, forced again to eat the food of the dead. In this myth, and perhaps in the mysterious rites that had so impressed Plutarch, the way back from victimization is not triumph over adversity. It is transformation through grief, rage, and loss.

There are few models for this process, although I found what I could in an old pagan story. In a culture that has lost the feeling that the language of the transcendent has a referent in reality, it becomes increasingly difficult to imagine what the *process* of transformation might be like. How can I transform the "victim" into someone who can bridge the darkness and the light, as Persephone does at the end of the tale? I am surely not the first to experience the difficulties of making this nonrational, raw journey in the context of a secular worldview that regards the phenomenal universe as essentially mechanistic, a cosmos that can be understood through the medium of human cognition. As the ancient people who gathered at Eleusis each year seemed to know, you cannot think or fight your way out of hell. You must feel your way out.

The story of Persephone and Demeter is one of the few Greek myths that focuses on female protagonists, and the fact that rape is central to their lives did not surprise me. Probably because the myth of Persephone and Demeter puts female experience at the center of its narrative, it has been a staple of women's studies courses for some years and has been analyzed from many theoretical perspectives, including Freudian and Jungian psychoanalysis. It has been of great interest to a wide range of feminists, such as sociologists Nancy Chadorow and Carol Gilligan. It embodies what some writers view as an archetypal woman's journey, a female rite of passage. The little I read on these interpretations of the meaning of the myth and its relevance to contemporary life—all interesting and provocative—seemed not to address my particular, and I felt peculiar, needs. My interest in it was not scholarly or theoretical. I was reading it on a literal level as a story about a real experience. From my limited perspective, it seemed to me that whatever else the story was about—the psychological relationship between mothers and daughters in Western society, for example—it was also about real rape. I wondered if other rape survivors would read this story as I did—with the eyes of a modern-day Persephone who was looking for a way to get out of hell.

■ ■ ■

Contemplating this myth more than twenty-eight centuries after it was first recorded, the writer Karl Kerenyi remarked that it contains "the universal principle of life—which is to be pursued, to be robbed, raped, to fail to understand, to rage and to grieve but then...to be born again." People who have not been raped find profound meaning in this pagan story of death and rebirth. If you have been raped, however, the fact that rape is more than a "metaphor," that it is an experience you have had, gives urgency to your search for meaning.

When I thought about the power this story once held for both men and women alike, I wondered what we have lost in the sieve of time. The redemption in the ordeals of Persephone and Demeter is a relation between the darkness and the light. It is not an ultimate vanquishing of the dark forces, but a reconciliation with them.

I took comfort in the fact that Persephone must return to Hades each year—she was not "putting her rape behind her." She was not "forgetting about it." She moved forever between the worlds—the world of light, the world of darkness—she had come to know.

According to Tanya Wilkinson, a psychotherapist and teacher whose excellent study *Persephone Returns* examines the individual and cultural dynamics contributing to the schism between victims and heroes in contemporary Western culture, the rape of Persephone "shows us, in no uncertain terms, that there are tears in the fabric of life that cannot be completely repaired, directions taken that, even if unchosen and unfair, can never be fully reversed because the self is changed by them." Innocence cannot be re-created. Once it is betrayed, it must be transformed. The problem with the victim's experience, it seems to me, is that we are losing the language of transformation and perhaps as the words fall away, we are losing a sense of them having a referent in human experience. While heroic myths continue to shape our culture as they are retold in mass media, the myth of Persephone and Demeter may become increasingly inaccessible to future generations.

When Helen told me that it was time I got past believing the rapist had destroyed my life, she was telling me that there was more to Persephone's story than her descent into hell. If it still sang, as it once did, perhaps she would have put it in those words—and I would have understood what she meant. But neither of us knew the secret story told so long ago in a temple in Eleusis. Helen may have sensed that in my dark rage I was ready to rush, as Demeter had, "like a bird over the dry land and sea, searching." And she may have known that I would need to find the will of a furious Demeter to get my lost daughter out of Hades.

Perhaps the wisdom of words that are brittle with age survived the centuries. I'd like to think so.

SEVENTEEN

In the House of Gathering

The room shall speak, it must catch me up
and hold me, I want to feel that I belong here.

ERICH MARIA REMARQUE,
All Quiet on the Western Front

"I think it would help you." Helen is on the telephone. I am still hurt, still hiding it. We haven't spoken for almost three weeks, since my visit after Christmas. "It's a new, experimental treatment called Eye Movement Desensitization and Reprocessing—EMDR. It's short term, something like four sessions. It wouldn't interfere with your therapy."

"That's a mouthful," I said. But I wrote it down, and the name she offered: "Francine Shapiro."

"I know you're mad at me," she said. "I hope you know I wasn't blaming you."

I was silent.

"You there?" she said.

"It sounded like it to me," I finally said.

"I'm sorry you heard it that way."

"I'm ruining my marriage. I can't write anymore. I can't sleep. I'm depressed all the time. I hate myself."

What I didn't say was that I hated Helen, too. My rage, incoherent and frightening, instantly turned into crushing and silencing shame. After all, I thought, she was trying to help me. Still, I felt she was heartless and insensitive.

After I hung up the telephone, I sat staring at the name and phone number I had scribbled down. Then I grabbed my coffee mug and hurled it with all my might against the wall, shattering it to pieces.

■ ■ ■

Soon I was again on the freeway to Palo Alto, for what would be the first of four two-hour sessions with Francine Shapiro, a clinical psychologist who was a senior research fellow at the Mental Research Institute there. In 1991 Shapiro's "discovery"—EMDR—was on the clinical fringe in the treatment of post-traumatic stress disorder. Although in 1995 she published a weighty tome for clinicians about EMDR, which is now used by more than eighteen thousand clinical psychologists in the United States, and *Sixty Minutes* devoted a segment to her treatment method, EMDR is still somewhat of a mystery: There are theories as to how, or why, it works, but there is still no definitive explanation.

EMDR is based on what Shapiro describes in her book as a "chance observation" she made one day in 1987 while walking in a park. "I noticed that some disturbing thoughts I was having suddenly disappeared. I also noticed that when I brought these thoughts back to mind, they were not as upsetting or as valid as before." Curious about what had changed the nature of the thoughts, she discovered that when these disturbing thoughts had first appeared, her eyes "spontaneously started moving very rapidly back and forth in an upward diagonal." She then started moving her eyes deliberately, while concentrating on disturbing thoughts and memories, and "found that these thoughts also disappeared and lost their charge."

Over the next several months Shapiro worked out a procedure, using her fingers to guide patients' eye movements, and in 1988 conducted a controlled study with twenty-two victims of rape, molestation, or Vietnam combat who were suffering from traumatic memories. Shapiro found that patients treated with EMDR, as opposed to those in the control group, who were asked only to describe the traumatic memory in detail, showed "substantial desensitization and pronounced cognitive restructuring of perceptions regarding the traumatic event." In other words, the memories "lost their charge."

In our first session Shapiro explained that the purpose of the procedure was to "unlock" information from my nervous system, and that we were attempting to produce eye movements similar to those found in the rapid eye movement (REM) stage of sleep, the stage when dreams occur. The eye movements, she said, would help me bring this "unconscious material up to be processed."

The sessions were devastating for several reasons, not the least of which was that my eye muscles are the weakest muscles in my body. I had to work hard physically to follow her fingers as she asked me to focus on particularly disturbing images from the rape. The physical strain itself was disturbing for another reason—the rapist had controlled me in the first minutes of his attack by jabbing his fingers into my eyes. After a few minutes of trying to follow her hand, my eyes ached, as they had ached that day. Perhaps this re-creation of one of the physical sensations of the rape intensified my images. Whatever the reason, they came back with sickening vividness.

The most disturbing image was the image of myself blindfolded and bound. I started with this. I visualized myself lying on Pamela's bed with my hands taped up behind me, my eyes covered with duct tape, my body naked from the waist down, my bra unhooked, my shirt torn open. I saw myself as the rapist had seen me, as I had seen myself as I had fled my body to "watch" from above. What I saw was the image of the "trussed chicken" that had come spontaneously to the policewoman. To me, the image of a powerless, ugly, worthless object.

It is not surprising that this image was the image that I could not "process," or that the policewoman's metaphor of being tied up like a chicken about to go in the oven was itself another disgusting image of insult that I had to assimilate. She had gone to the heart of the matter, although I doubt that she knew it. The shame of my naked helplessness, my raw, utterly passive exposure to the will of another human being, set this image inside a transparent stone that could never be broken open and never be dissolved. The stone was cold. And it was lodged in the center of my soul.

It would take EMDR and two and a half years of intensive psychotherapy to get to the point where I felt I could live *with* this image in the stone, because living with it was what I was going to have to do for the rest of my life.

I saw the icy stone and held it before me as I followed her fingers back and forth. When she stopped, I was in a state of collapse, unable to stand, unable to control my tears. After a long struggle to get control of myself, I was able to repeat the procedure. The second time I felt pain in my arms, as if the rapist were in the act of yanking them up behind me. Then I ached all over. My legs seemed to shrivel up until they felt like stubs. But I did not cry.

Systematically over the course of a month, while I continued my weekly visits with Dr. Rose, I worked with Francine Shapiro, visualizing the rape itself and its immediate aftermath. It was excruciatingly painful. It was not a "cure," but I believe it did change the nature of my awareness of the experience. I'm glad that I had the sense to pursue psychotherapy for the long haul. Still, I believe that EMDR did play a role in my being able eventually to "process" the same information in yet another way—in written language. The writer Julian Jaynes once remarked that language is "an organ of perception, not simply a means of communication." I think he is right. This book itself is another phase of regeneration, another translation. Perhaps excavating these images "from my nervous system" that winter in 1991 has helped me construct this narrative. Perhaps someday neurobiology will be able to explain the links between neurons and the soul. Scientists may in time discover a fast, easy way to heal the past. The path I took was neither.

■ ■ ■

Undergoing psychotherapy—exploring and interpreting unconscious conflicts—is an unnatural act. For me it took the severest anguish, and the hope that the anguish could be relieved, to keep me struggling to get through it, week after week. Year after year. Carl Jung spoke of the man who lives in the "House of Gathering"—the patient in psychoanalysis. He is brave enough, Jung wrote, "to withdraw all his projections," and when he does he becomes aware of how thick his own shadow is. "Such a man has saddled himself with new problems and conflicts. He has become a serious problem to himself as he is now unable to say that they do this or that, they are wrong...." Before it gets better, it gets worse.

For two and a half years I was "a problem to myself" as I confronted my shadow in Dr. Rose's office. Perhaps if I had undergone psychotherapy before the rape, it might have been a different story. But I had felt no pressing need before. I lived a middling happy life that sometimes confused me and that seemed not always to be authentically mine. I felt I worked too hard at pleasing other people and was vaguely aware of an inner struggle with guilt when I acted from my own needs. But my condition seemed no better or worse than that of most people who occasionally feel confused by their feelings or behavior.

The unconscious exerts a pull that profoundly shapes us. Becoming aware of this hidden domain was the work that lay ahead of me as I began psychotherapy with Dr. Rose. Sequence is an illusion required by the rules of narrative. But in writing about my experience with Dr. Rose I impose a sequence where there was none in order to render coherent in language mysteries I do not understand. What transpired in Dr. Rose's office was chaos, the chaos of creation. I did not know it at the time, but what I had to do there was create a new consciousness—in a sense, a new self. One that could live with the icy stone, the image of the rape frozen in its center.

When I began psychotherapy I did not have any understanding of the way the feelings spawned by the rape had submerged in the darkness beyond my awareness, nor would I understand for some time to come the way these new feelings, descending into the invisible depths, had awakened dormant conflicts from early childhood. Old patterns of feeling that had been banished by the woman who had listened to the bird's song that October afternoon—the woman who was happy enough—would slither from the mud of the remote and incomprehensible past to torment me. I have only a little more understanding now, but a deeper appreciation for the predicament that consciousness presents—it is a work in process, its limits unknown. There will always be a shadow, despite the occasional flicker of light I can cast upon it. What has changed, I suppose, is that I now accept that it is there.

I did not record what Dr. Rose said to me in our first two sessions or on the telephone beforehand, although I began to keep detailed notes afterward. The only thing I do remember from our first meeting was that I told her I felt I was going crazy. I believed I was a breath away from institutionalization, and I expected her to recommend it.

Instead she was able to convey the idea that my feeling of insanity was a common response to rape. She acknowledged the true horror of my experience and the misery of my present condition. She assured me that feeling insane in the aftermath of rape was normal. She made me feel that although I felt crazy, I was not. But our third session in early January when I found her waiting quietly in her place, I wrote in my journal: "For the first time since the rape I feel that there is someone who has no reason for *not* wanting me to feel what I feel."

Now I realize that the someone who did not want me "to feel what I feel" was myself.

■ ■ ■

In an article she published in the *American Journal of Psychiatry* in 1986 entitled "'Worse Than Death': Psychodynamics of Rape Victims and the Need for Psychotherapy," Dr. Rose makes the point that the loss experienced by rape victims is both "profound and devastating." It touches on "every stage of psychosexual development, self-concept, and object relations" (i.e., our unconscious images of ourselves and others and of our relationship between ourselves and others), "as well as affecting sexuality and relationships with others." In other words, the loss is global. Rape trauma cannot be "compartmentalized" in some part of the self because no part is safe from its searing devastation.

The source of this loss is the threat of annihilation that Dr. Rose believes every rape victim experiences. "Although this is readily recognized when the victim has been physically damaged by the assailant in ways other than those occurring from forced sexual intercourse," she writes, "it is experienced as an ever-present danger by all rape victims."

Obvious sources of the threat are the use of either a weapon, life-threatening physical force, or verbal threats of death. My rapist was of the most obvious sort, brandishing death in constant verbal threats. Also contributing to a victim's sense of loss is the knowledge that many rapists do murder their victims. This common knowledge was a torment for me and made the rapist's threats all the more believable.

But even if no death threats are made, Dr. Rose notes that "the victim is aware of the rapist's murderous rage. Sudden unconscious movements by the victim, such as a sound made involuntarily on awakening, can lead to a frightening, forceful, angry act on the part of the assailant," who needs to have total control over his victim.

Even in cases of "acquaintance rape" that Dr. Rose has encountered in her work, where no weapon, explicit threat of death, or murderous rage was used by the rapist, her patients nevertheless experienced their rapes as traumatic. The "life-threat" in these cases involved the victim's "whole social network, her job, how she experienced herself in the world, whether she could trust the people she knew."

But the threat of annihilation has another source as well. "A sense of death and loss also occurs," she writes, "through the destruction of important aspects of the self. Attitudes needed for psychological survival often are destroyed." Most victims, she notes, lose "basic trust" and "primitive omnipotence." Although I did not know it when I began psychotherapy (I did not read her article until 1994), I had to start over—from the beginning. I could not trust myself and therefore could not trust anyone else—Steve, Helen, my mother, and at times Dr. Rose herself.

My experience of being out of my body and "watching" myself and the rapist was not unique. Dr. Rose writes that many victims describe "leaving their bodies, floating, and looking down from above at their bodies being raped." Psychiatrists consider this a defense employed by the ego to protect itself from being completely overwhelmed. "The overwhelming of the ego is experienced," Dr. Rose states, "as the death of the old self, a self that will not return.... Unfortunately, this defense persists, and the old self is replaced by a numbed, wooden, deadened, distant self." Trying to function with this "wooden" self—the as-if woman—was itself a source of grief for me. Living seemed only to remind me of my departed loved one—the awake, flexible, feeling, and connected self that I had lost.

The loss of the capacity to trust or to feel any sense of autonomous existence was part of the reason I felt that my rape was "worse than death." I was surprised to find this expression in the title of Dr. Rose's article in 1994 and to discover that my bizarre experience of having died was not uncommon. Several women who wrote me after my essay was published expressed a similar feeling of having died the day they were raped.

The fact that those closest to me found this characterization self-pitying, melodramatic, or metaphoric infuriated me. It was not an exaggeration but a precise description of my condition. I prayed for and fantasized about physical death constantly during the first months of psychotherapy. I came to think of my literal death as the metaphor that would complete the act of murder that had already taken place. I still do not know why I did not kill myself. Perhaps it is because I was very good at imagining it. Dr. Rose kept me suspended between these two deaths—the one I had already experienced and the one I longed for. For a time this suspension was all I knew of life.

• • •

Although rape trauma shares many of the psychological aspects of other traumas, the way that it differs from them is central to the nature of the internal devastation it wreaks. As in torture, the source of the injury is *another human being acting intentionally,* not an inanimate object or an accident of nature or man. This factor casts a long shadow in the victim's unconscious mind—the shadow of the torturer himself.

This occurs because of a phenomenon psychiatrists refer to as "projective identification." The classic story that therapists tell to illustrate how projective identification works is about a man who needs to borrow a rake from his neighbor. The man is certain that his neighbor is not going to lend it to him. He walks to his neighbor's house saying to himself, "He's not going to lend me the rake. I just know he's not going to lend it to me." At this point the man is projecting—he's afraid his neighbor won't lend him the rake. He gets to his neighbor's and knocks on the door. The neighbor opens the door and says "Hello." The first man shouts, "You can keep your goddamn rake!" Of course, the neighbor slams the door in his face.

The man who needed the rake has created the very thing he was dreading and the neighbor has become a player in his drama. Projective identification is common with people who fear rejection; they are often aggressive, which causes other people to back away from them, just as they fear. And projective identification and reenactment are linked—the schoolyard bully is probably the kid who is being beaten up at home.

According to Dr. Rose and other experts, most rapists are engaging in projective identification and reenactment. Sexual abuse in some form is often lurking in a rapist's past. His victim becomes the recipient of feelings that he cannot "process," as Francine Shapiro puts it, and that make him what he is—a human being monstrously out of control.

The rapist projects his unbearable feelings of helplessness, humiliation, pain, rage, guilt, and terror onto his victim, who then becomes the container for them, just as he has been made a container by his own abuser. Although rapists act like animals, they are, sadly and horribly, human beings. Unlike the orangutan who raped the cook in Biruté Galdikas's research camp, a human rapist has linked a biological, sexual urge to an uncontrollable human need to rid himself of overwhelming feeling that has shattered him. "Tremendous aggression and overstimulation by feeling occur when a person feels shattered in this way," Dr.

Rose states. A rapist leaves his helplessness and shame, his rage and self-hatred behind with his victim. "He's not feeling helpless anymore," Dr. Rose once told me. "He's powerful; he's in control. You're helpless. You're out of control. You're disgusting, devalued, worthless, dirty. He isn't anymore."

A rape victim absorbs these projections and is forced to become a participant in her own injury, to play the central role in the rapist's reenactment of his own "worse than death" experience. She internalizes the projections of the rapist, and they become a part of her unconscious life. "Getting in touch with your anger," an expression that many people use casually, means for a rape victim getting in touch with the rapist now living inside of you.

This identification with the rapist through participation in his reenactment may explain why many victims appear to lack conscious anger toward their rapists. I have long been aware of my limited ability to focus my anger at the man who raped me, and friends have remarked on this over the years. Indeed, when I think about him I am conscious of feeling something closer to pity. Dr. Rose cites the case of one victim she treated who "yearned to face her assailant and tell him what she felt. Yet when he pleaded guilty...she balked at speaking at the sentencing hearing. At the last minute, she did manage to write a speech but decided not to give it after the judge stated sentiments similar to her own." This patient's unconscious conflict over her feelings of rage and hatred silenced her so completely that during her first year of therapy she expressed no anger toward the rapist at all.

Except for that night on Helen's back porch, I could not express my rage at the rapist—even with Dr. Rose. The rage was there, of course, but I either turned it against myself as debilitating self-blame or, like the man in need of the rake, attacked those whose support I needed most. Like him, I suffered the predictable consequences.

My relationship with Steve became a wallow of hostility and rejection. Each rejection hurled me into a horrifying maelstrom of rage. Although I often projected my rage onto Steve, who frequently behaved like the neighbor in the rake story, the guilt I felt afterward was worse than the momentary satisfaction I received from having someone else to blame. Without basic trust or a sense of autonomy, I was incapable of supporting myself or feeling support from others. I concluded that this impoverishment was because I was worthless—a "nothing." The rapist had treated me as a worthless "nothing." Now I was treating myself that way.

For reasons I would not discover until my second year of psychotherapy, I believed that what made me worthless was the impulse to express my needs, to be an "authentic" human being. Steve wanted to be supportive, but I wouldn't let him. I blamed him for what I saw as his lack of support and felt he was heartless, cold, brutal. Then he blamed me for turning him into a monster. We had nowhere to go but around again, or to divorce court.

This possibility so frightened and pained me that more often than not I turned my tremendous aggression inward. Fortunately, after I started psychotherapy I had Dr. Rose to keep me from drowning in a flood of self-hatred and self-blame. I blamed and hated the parts of myself that had failed to protect me from overwhelming loss—those maternal aspects of myself that had once been capable of providing comfort and coherence but that had abandoned me. Although the Greek poet did not tell us what Persephone felt in the underworld after her abduction, I sometimes feel I know. She felt her mother had failed her. Her mother did not love her and had never loved her. She was so "bad" that even her own mother abandoned her. When she opened her eyes and saw the abhorrent figure of the Lord of Death reclining on his throne, it was like looking in a mirror.

Before I began therapy, the only "self" I possessed was an infantile self. I was helpless before the unrelenting assault of my own unconscious feelings, especially rage. To feel it was to become "like" the rapist, to dwell in his hateful, dark world. Fantasies of revenge were impossible for me after that dark ritual in the garden at Concord when I had "burned him alive." I was incapable of any form of self-comfort. I had regressed to a state of mistrust and fear that could only be endured by constant projection—the source of my misery with Steve—

or by the numbing denial of a "wooden" life. Like the rapist himself, I was a human being hopelessly out of control.

Dr. Rose speculates that the failure of victims to report rape may stem from unconscious conflicts over rage and hatred that are, she writes, "central" to rape victims. If left untreated, these hidden conflicts create debilitating guilt—the source of both depression and self-destructive behavior. Suicide and suicidal thoughts, abuse of alcohol, cigarettes, and drugs, the ending of relationships and the loss of employment are frequent among rape victims who do not receive effective treatment. Turning to prostitution or subsequent involvement in abusive relationships is not uncommon.

"Failure to seek therapy," Dr. Rose writes, "is another form of self-destructive behavior." She cites the case of a victim of a rape and robbery seeking therapy on an emergency basis. The victim "repeatedly told the therapist...that she had filed a claim with the Victims of Crime Program." But then she suddenly discontinued therapy, "leaving the therapist to discover that the victim had lied about filing the claim. The therapist was not reimbursed for the treatment and thus was robbed as the victim had been."

Although an encounter with a force of nature—a hurricane, an earthquake, or perhaps even an orangutan coming into sexual maturity—may be traumatic, acts of God do not leave the awful shadows of the human tormentor's massive rage, shame, and helplessness in a survivor's unconscious mind.

The presence of this human shadow is what links rape and torture, and what may distinguish them from other trauma, rendering them "too terrible for words." The human need to pass on unbearable suffering through actions that re-create it is a story we sense may never end. The telling of it makes us all feel helpless and ashamed.

It seems to me now, looking back on the astonishing complexity of my own reenactments, that I was telling the rapist's story over and over again. My life had become his narrative, although only now, as I write, can I catch a fleeting glimpse of this terrible truth.

It has not been easy to grant the status of "human being" to the man who raped me, and yet I must. I find strange the comfort it brings. Perhaps this comfort comes from the thought that it is only by seeing him as a human being that I can hope that the conditions that created him might be otherwise—not for him, and because of him, not for me. But someday. For someone else. I cannot forget the suffering he brought me. Nor does my intimate knowledge of the nature of his suffering, knowledge that causes me to pity him, lessen my longing to see him locked behind bars forever. The only forgiveness I can muster is to call him human.

■ ■ ■

In 1991, my first year of treatment, I did not know that Dr. Rose was refining a model for "psychodynamic psychotherapy" with rape victims that she set forth in the professional journal *Psychotherapy* that spring. In the article, which I read after I started this book, she describes how rape victims, who feel internal devastation from an experience that is "outside that which is expectable in human experience," surround themselves with a "trauma membrane" that replaces the damaged self—that dynamic bundle of conscious and unconscious forces that determine human behavior and attitudes. It is an exoskeleton, a self on the outside.

I would not have understood this concept had I read her article in 1991 because I was still inside my own trauma membrane. Even now it is difficult for me to translate my feeling of being inside this membrane into language, and the technical language of psychotherapy seems especially removed from the actual experience. I now think of this membrane as almost impermeable and nearly, but not quite, opaque. The outside world is a shadow cast on the surface. Words are heard on the inside, but their meanings are deformed and twisted when they come into contact with the membrane. Inside this membrane, you interpret the indistinct mutterings from beliefs and feelings that you are not even aware you have. They make your interaction with others a constant drama of insult.

Without basic trust or a feeling of autonomy, it is impossible to experience empathy from others. But empathy is what you want, what you desperately need to make that very connection. It seems an impossible dilemma when you are facing it. You feel, as I did with Helen or Steve, that others are intentionally hurting you just as the rapist did, and you feel this all the time.

A therapist has to work with someone who is inside this trauma membrane. This work is exacting and dangerous. It must be exhausting, although Dr. Rose never seemed to find it so. The fact that Dr. Blanchard had described Dr. Rose as a "specialist" was reassuring to me, and I was more inclined to trust her because she was. I was luckier than I knew to be referred to a psychiatrist with Dr. Rose's experience and knowledge. Ironically, I have Dr. Blanchard to thank for my good fortune. As I was to learn, psychotherapy with a rape victim can be as complicated and specialized as spinal surgery.

Dr. Rose knew what to avoid in the early stages of our relationship—silence, the appearance of judgment, or discomfort with my story, for instance. I would have experienced any of these behaviors as excruciating rejections. My initial experience of Dr. Rose sitting in her chair, waiting, was therefore a powerful image of support that would, over the years, become a symbol for my own relationship to myself. As strange as it may seem, had I found her otherwise occupied that day I was late—or, as I feared, out of the office—or had she responded to my reasons for being late without taking into account the validity of my condition, the difficulties we later encountered in the process of exposing my defenses might well have driven me out of therapy forever.

■ ■ ■

In the 1970s the treatment for rape trauma was predicated on the assumption that the psychological crisis was relatively short-lived. Crisis-intervention counseling, which included talking about the experience, reassurance, and support of behavioral adjustments, was considered sufficient. It was assumed that the experience could be integrated after several weeks. Psychotherapy was not the treatment of choice unless the victim had a history of psychiatric difficulties. Since a history of psychiatric problems is no more common in rape victims than in the general population, it is likely that the majority of victims—emotionally healthy individuals—did not end up on a psychiatrist's couch.

But studies of rape victims and of survivors of massive disasters done in the late 1970s and early 1980s found something quite different. In a 1986 article in the *American Journal of Psychiatry,* Dr. Rose reviews findings (she cites ten studies) that concluded that the majority of rape victims "remained symptomatic and reorganized their personalities around the symptoms, conflicts and defenses activated by the trauma."

Because psychotherapy has not been viewed as a primary treatment for rape trauma (unless the victim had preexisting psychiatric disorders), a victim seeking help from a psychiatrist may find herself more alone than ever. The model for psychotherapy based on the unique psychodynamics of trauma is still being formulated.

In her writings Dr. Rose discusses the complex technical problems psychiatrists face in dealing with rape victims. One example is what can occur during "countertransference." Broadly defined, countertransference is the unconscious response of others to the victim, the assault, and the rapist. Family, friends, therapists—all bring unconscious feelings to their interactions with rape victims. Fear of helplessness, the central insult of rape, is universal. Reactions to victims are grounded therefore in defenses against the fear of helplessness, as well as against other fears. My father's expressing desire to castrate the rapist that day in his workshop, for example, may well have been not only a way for him to seek revenge on my behalf, but also a way for him to defend himself against his own feelings of helplessness. At the time his rage was unwelcome and terrifying to me because my own rage was murderous and I dared not feel it.

Blaming the victim in all of its variations is another unconscious defense against feelings that are universally traumatic. It seems to me likely that the woman in the amber necklace was trying to protect herself—which is understandable. So was the woman at the dinner party who found rape "so very personal." So was the relative who criticized me for going into therapy the first year after the rape.

Therapists also defend themselves—by minimizing the impact of the rape or by blaming the victim. When the patient transfers her feelings of helplessness or rage onto the therapist—as indeed the patient will do if treatment is working—it can arouse unconscious feelings in the therapist that sometimes result in a complete breakdown of treatment. "The therapist," Dr. Rose explains, "may become passive and hesitant to explore the victim's experience of the rape.... In the extreme form, the rape may never be discussed or may be considered to be unimportant in the patient's therapy. It is not rare for a victim to have a psychiatric hospitalization following a rape and *yet have the staff never bring up the assault* [italics mine], even when the victim openly talks about the importance of the rape to her." The unconscious responses of others—including therapists—as they defend themselves against their own unconscious fears can reinforce the conflicts and defenses of victims. Silence can turn a rape victim's experience in psychotherapy into another experience of insult.

When I consider the larger number of rape victims in relation to the few psychiatrists trained to treat them, I worry. Dr. Rose was not on my health insurance company's list of preferred providers for psychotherapy. None of the other psychiatrists on the company's list had special expertise in the treatment of rape trauma. Although I argued that my condition required a specialist, the company refused to pay for my visits with Dr. Rose because she was not in their network of providers.

She kindly applied for inclusion in their network in order to lighten my financial burden, but her request was met with silence. The company did not even return her phone calls. We both eventually gave up. The bill for my treatment—well worth the cost to me—was nearly $15,000. I was fortunate that Steve and I had the financial resources to choose a specialist who was not covered by our health insurance. After my third meeting with Dr. Rose I intuitively felt that at last, and through sheer luck, I had stumbled upon someone who knew how to treat my condition. I sensed that my rape had, somehow, "reorganized my entire personality" and that I needed massive restructuring. In my case, psychotherapy with a specialist in rape trauma was to prove to be the right choice.

The cost of my treatment—$15,000—is more than six and a half times larger than the average mental-health care cost of $2,200 for rape victims as calculated by the Justice Department in its first comprehensive survey on the price of violence, published in 1996. Because no known estimates on the costs of mental-health care for rape victims were available, the Justice Department surveyed 168 mental-health care professionals, asking respondents to detail the number of visits "by clients being served *primarily* [italics mine] as a result of crime victimization." This modest figure suggests that most victims who seek treatment (according to the survey, only 25 to 50 percent do) are being treated with short-term counseling following the models for treatment considered effective in the 1970s when rape trauma was viewed as a short-lived crisis.

It took me five years to get into treatment, and many rape victims delay much longer. By the time I did, my primary problem was depression. I spent the first nine months with Dr. Rose focusing on the many problems that stemmed from the consequences of my reenactments of the rape in my marriage and close relationships. The rape was essentially invisible. It exerted a massive gravitational pull on my behavior and on my beliefs about myself and others, but its influence could only be traced by the perturbations it created in my overt behavior. As far as psychiatrists go, it is possible that only a specialist such as Dr. Rose would have included me in her list of clients being treated *primarily* "as a result of crime victimization" if the Justice Department had contacted her for its survey. I'm fairly certain Dr. Blanchard would not have.

■ ■ ■

Every rape intersects with an individual victim's preexisting character traits—those of nature, those of nurture, and those formed by their interaction. Our unconscious defenses and conflicts, the matrix of beliefs about ourselves (and hence the world) formed in early child-hood, are our deepest mysteries. Our shadow has a beginning, although we may not remember how it came to take on the shape it has, one that is not replicated in any other human being. It seems to me now that my rape acted like a chemical injected into my psyche that intensified whatever unconscious defenses, conflicts, self-concepts, and beliefs were already within. It was a psychic steroid—what might once have been merely disquieting, what might have brought me to feel unloved or abandoned, confused and unappreciated, all the secret and hidden self-loathings and self-doubts that I carried for thirty-nine years, could no longer be ignored.

The upswelling of conflicts from early childhood was a baffling aspect of my treatment with Dr. Rose. I believe that had I not been raped, the small, frightened person who had long since been banished from awareness would be there still. This small child from my own past had crept away from me long ago—so long ago that I had forgotten she existed. The rape's devastation pulled her from the shadows and gave her a voice. I might have continued to live a middling happy life without her. I cannot say now that I am grateful for the rape because it brought her back. If I'd had a choice, I would have settled for the middling happy life. But now that she has returned, I welcome her.

I discovered her in a dream in late March of 1992. I had spent fifteen months with Dr. Rose "withdrawing my projections" from the world outside myself. Reaping this harvest increased my pain rather than relieving it. I cried through many of the sessions but found myself feeling better for a few days afterward. I was beginning to sense that the pain was an antidote, albeit a bitter one, to the feeling of death that haunted me. Still, I didn't like it. My desire to spare myself often resulted in my missing appointments by oversleeping, a costly "remedy" that made me feel wretchedly ashamed.

As time went on, however, this gathering of projected feeling began to change the way I experienced my intimate relationships. I no longer felt completely "overwhelmed" by the needs of my family and friends because I was learning how to trust myself more, to protect myself bet-

ter. I felt less helpless and therefore less angry. Steve and I were spend-
ing more time in a "blame-free" zone, which seemed to be expanding
imperceptibly in the center of our domestic battlefield. I felt that my
life was more "in control." I no longer felt I was drowning in chores
and paperwork, social obligations and the demands of my consulting
work. I was writing again, although I still felt hobbled creatively. And
Dr. Rose and I had survived a phase of my "transference."

I was furious at her for charging me for sessions that had to be
skipped because of vacations with Steve and the children at Lake Tahoe
or trips to Virginia to see my parents that were planned months in
advance. I felt "trapped" by a policy I had previously accepted and
twice threatened to stop seeing her. Therapy was "suffocating" me, I
told her. She was "insensitive to my needs." This rough patch did not
seem to surprise her. She knew it was coming. I wasn't ready to leave
and she skillfully convinced me to continue, although I do not remember how. The place that Dr. Rose had carefully constructed held. It did
not now feel safe, but it was sturdy—and sturdy was what I needed.

That March I had a vivid dream. In the dream I am standing alone
in a barren landscape when suddenly a young child appears beside me.
"I am your daughter," she says. At first I don't believe her. We talk. She
says that she has been "in exile." She explains why I am her mother and
finally convinces me. I weep—first from sadness that I have lived so
long without her and then from joy at our reunion. When I wake up,
her words and the joy evaporate. I feel only sorrow and loss.

Dr. Rose and I discussed this dream a few days later. I knew it was
significant, but I didn't have a clue why. Dr. Rose observed that this
child represented a "banished" part of myself. She pointed out that in
the Garden of Eden story the idea of punishment is associated with
"banishment" and with terrible shame. "She has been punished with
exile," Dr. Rose said. "She is trying to return, but you are having a hard
time claiming her."

Although this dream represented an impulse toward self-union, this
impulse itself created conflicts. I was afraid to explore what had driven
her away in the first place. It would take me another year of work to

discover who this child was and why I had exiled her. This shadow child represented complicated beliefs and feelings about my own needs that I had formed very early in my life. I had exiled the part of myself that had needs of her own.

Before the rape, this neglect of myself had not troubled me enough to merit investigation. After the rape, it was crippling. The rape had been an experience of another human being demanding—on pain of physical death—that I put his needs first. My needs did not matter to him in the slightest. All my feelings had to be suppressed and my compliance in my own abuse—my choosing to live—produced a profound sense of shame. This encounter with a selfishness so pure and deadly seemed to lock into a primitive shame that I had never permitted myself to feel.

I was not neglected or abused as a child. My parents' behavior in the weeks after the rape was emblematic of the way they had nurtured me all my life. There was no traumatic experience lurking in my past. My brothers had never hit me. I had been spanked twice by my mother, never by my father. There was no creepy uncle, no stranger with candy. I hunted for memories that might "explain" this exiled part of myself, aware that I was now "selecting" from the phantom realm of childhood elements that were being altered through the selection process itself. "Truth" was impossible. What was possible was a reconstruction of how I imperfectly understood the condition of being a child.

I was raised in an era when children were considered "good" when they were "seen but not heard"—a prescription that I find myself wishing were used more often when I am seated next to children in a pricey restaurant. Perhaps this expectation was part of my belief that expressing an "authentic" self was "bad" and my feeling ashamed when I did. I was the only female among three brothers and five male cousins and in many ways my family mirrored society's view of the female as "second class." Their natural aggressiveness had, on many occasions that I remembered during this period of work with Dr. Rose, required me to suppress authentic feeling. I must have wanted to express my "true self" more. I recalled with Dr. Rose, for example, that in elementary school

I longed to go to an all-girls school. My parents could not afford to send me to a private girls' school, and so nothing ever came of my need for the kind of "protection" from male competitiveness it might have provided. My Catholic upbringing was no doubt a factor in how I understood my darker impulses. Dr. Rose and I explored this territory for clues, coming up with the usual suspects. There were also the unknown contributions of biology itself—neurological circuits that shape how a stimulus is recorded in feeling and memory. Not every rape victim or combat veteran develops post-traumatic stress disorder. But I did. Perhaps I was physically "oversensitive."

Ultimately, it does not matter why I emerged from my childhood with the belief—unconscious for so many years—that the part of myself that had her "own" needs deserved exile. It was a way for a child to resolve the conflict her unmet needs presented. No parent is perfect, as I have learned in being a parent myself. We all emerge from our childhood with a shadow. To have one is to be human. But my unconscious belief that some part of myself deserved to be punished affected how I experienced the rape. In a sense, the rape was a "metaphor" for my own unempathetic response to myself. Until I could feel this ancient aspect of myself was a part of myself I wanted, I could not experience the reunion of "mother and daughter" that is so central to the Persephone and Demeter myth. Nor could I strike a deal with the devil, as Demeter had done, to bring about this joyful redemption.

I had many unconscious conflicts about this union with myself that once again were brought to consciousness in a dream. Only this time it was a nightmare. Three months after my banished daughter announced herself, I dreamed I was fleeing from a battle that was taking place in an ancient time. In my panic to escape I plunged into a dark, stagnant lake surrounded by sheer, forested cliffs. The scene is chaotic—other screaming warriors dressed, as I am, in torn furs and hides thrash about in water that is red with blood and thick with the carcasses of dead men and cows. It is difficult to swim because of the bloated corpses. The enemy is about to overtake us. Desperate to save myself, I find a tree clinging to the bank and hide behind it with my legs still deep in gore.

I then feel something floating in the water and, thinking it is a carcass, reach down to push it away. To my horror, I see that it is a "prehistoric" turtle with a long neck and jagged teeth, very much alive. It grabs my arm with its huge viselike mouth. I fight to escape from its hold and wake up screaming.

The dream was so distressing that when I reported it to Dr. Rose, I told her I thought I might be having a nervous breakdown. I felt therapy wasn't helping me. She was particularly interested in this dream and even seemed pleased that I had had it.

We spent months exploring my unconscious conflicts about reclaiming my "daughter," who was now symbolized by the "prehistoric" turtle. This dream told me that I was losing the battle against keeping this preverbal part of myself in exile, but also that it terrified me. We thrashed among the corpses of my child's past to try to find a pattern to the fear and self-blame that seemed to be keeping me from union with myself. This process, still mysterious to me, seemed to dissolve the last obstacle. We returned to the dream many times during this year, and each time its meaning seemed to change. Eventually, I came to see the turtle—this prehistoric survivor—as a strong and necessary part of myself. I came to value its protective shell, its strength and its ability to flourish in a "stagnant" place of death. I came to admire its habits and skills. I felt Dr. Rose did, too. Vitality returned to every part of my life—slowly, like a seep into desert rock.

Over the course of these years in therapy I internalized my relationship with Dr. Rose, just as I had originally done with my family as a child. Only this time I was an adult with an adult's capacity for understanding. I learned to trust her and thus to trust myself. This was how the shattered self had been constructed in the first place, how it had to be constructed again. My relationship with Dr. Rose became a model for my relationship to the various aspects of myself—for my consciousness itself.

■ ■ ■

There came a day in the early spring of 1993 when Dr. Rose and I were ready to part. I had moved back and forth between the child I had been, the raped woman, and the woman who came month after month to a room that caught her up and held her. I had come to realize that if remembering is to re-create, then the understanding of the past itself can be transformed by the present. And I had learned that some redemption can be found in even the deepest losses.

Over the months and years in that room with Dr. Rose, I had even learned to value the darkness of my terror, perhaps in some way similar to those kindred souls who gathered two thousand years before me at Eleusis.

Steve had reemerged, recognizable as the man I fell in love with upon first seeing him. Even my rage was transformed, as stones are smoothed by drops of water or centuries of footsteps.

I walked out of Dr. Rose's office for the last time realizing that although she knew me as well as anyone knew me at that moment, I knew nothing about her. I did not know whether she herself had been raped or if she was married or had children. She was in many ways a complete stranger, yet she had built a sacred place for me and had guarded its boundaries faithfully, at times fiercely. She had guided me to a new life.

"I don't know how to thank you," I said. And then, afraid for a moment of the woman I had become, I asked if I could come back if I needed to—for tune-ups.

"You have my number," she replied.

"Good-bye, then," I said. She wasn't a hugger, but I hugged her anyway.

Epilogue

In a dark time, the eye begins to see.

THEODORE ROETHKE, "In a Dark Time"

It is June 1993. Helen and I are posing for a photograph outside the modest clapboard building that serves as the gallery and office of the Santa Cruz Art League. Behind us is a camellia laden with pink blossoms. Holding the camera, Steve bends his knees just before he takes the picture, mimicking my father, who we wish could be with us.

"Bending my knees," Steve says for Helen's benefit, "unlocks my camera finger."

Helen and I are laughing when he snaps the shutter. Then he takes our arms—Helen on his left, me on his right—and escorts us inside. We pause in front of the sandwich board at the entrance: "Envisioning Women: Breaking the Taboos—An Art Exhibit of Women by Women."

Helen and I both have pictures in the show. The guest curator is a woman from a museum in Southern California. The only reason I have a painting in the show is because Helen insisted I submit something I'd done the previous winter and that she had seen tacked up in my studio at the beach. "I'm not a painter," I'd told her when she suggested it. "No, but I am, and I say it belongs in this show. Get it framed—with a big mat—and ship it down here as soon as you can."

At first I was excited when she called to tell me the curator had selected my picture, but a few days before the opening I began to wish I hadn't let her talk me into being in the show. I had painted the image of the chicken carcass that had come to the policewoman after she'd taken my report. Although the picture was small, only six inches by eight, it had taken me months to complete it. I'd spent hours in my studio sketching elements that eventually ended up in the painting—the chicken carcass, the bed on which it lay, and the green monster's head that protruded from beneath it. The more I worked on these elements, the less charge each seemed to have. When I finally started the picture—using watercolors and ink—the pain was manageable and seemed to become a source of energy.

What is bothering me as Steve, Helen, and I hesitate for a moment in the doorway of the gallery is the thought that this image of my helplessness is intersecting with the outside world. I am embarrassed—not because the painting is primitive, but because other people will be looking at my shame.

The crowd is evenly divided between men and women—friends and family of the artists whose work has been selected for the group show. The turnout is respectable. Steve leaves for a moment, returns with two plastic glasses of white wine.

We drift around the room looking at the pictures until we get to Helen's. It is an elegant pencil drawing—a young woman's bare torso. On each small breast is the imprint of a hand, drawn in red. The lines are minimal, the strikes of the pencil faint but skillful.

"The outline of the hands remind me of a brand," I say.

"I drew this quite a few years ago—it was hard for me to look at it for a long time. I kept it in that storage closet in my studio. I remembered it when I heard about the show and thought, Why not? I've only done one other painting about my abuse—an abstract."

We work our way around the room until we are two pictures away from mine. It seems only Helen and I have tackled the big taboos—incest and rape.

A young man in blue jeans and a black leather jacket is standing in front of my picture. He sips his wine, moves closer to the picture to see it better. I feel my face flush, watching this young man. I know he is trying to read the words that I have scribbled on the black bars that run vertically down the left side of the painting and that resemble the door of a prison cell. They are the terrible words that came out of the rapist's mouth. They are scribbled, as if the hand that wrote them were trembling.

The young man leans down, reads the title. *Raped and Trussed.*

Steve notices my face is flushed and puts his arm around my shoulders.

"It's so strange," I say, "to see people looking at my worst nightmare, but it's even stranger to realize that I'm standing here looking at other people looking at my worst nightmare. It changes the nightmare."

The young man walks away. The three of us take his place.

"You know, that little wedge of blue under the bars—I can't tell whether that door is opening or closing," Helen says. "I like that because really it should be both."

"I keep thinking there's this paradox—you go on with your life and you remember, and it's one motion."

"The dark side is part of who we are," Helen says. "It's dark, but standing here looking at all this art, it doesn't feel so dark."

"That reminds me of something I read the other day—about Balzac's death," Steve says. "It fascinated me. You know what his last words were?"

"What?" Helen asks.

"He said, 'I see a black light.' "

Helen thinks for a minute, smiles. "Strange. It's like he got to the answer and when he said it, it was a contradiction."

Then Steve asks me to stand in front of my picture—for a photograph. He bends his knees again, and I laugh.

272

Epilogue

■ ■ ■

Raped and Trussed is hanging on the wall in the room where I have written this book. It reminds me that it is the darkness that makes the light visible, and not the other way around. It reminds me to bless the light I have found.

But it also reminds me that rape is an evil. It is not an act of God but an act of man. Because it is a human evil, I have hope that human beings can, in time, do something about it.

■ ■ ■

I went back to see Dr. Rose while I was writing this book. This time I did not go as a patient, but for recommendations on books about trauma that might help me understand my own journey.

It had been a year since I'd made the trip to Palo Alto, and the familiar drive brought back the memory of the woman who felt she was running through wet cement. I was happy that she wasn't driving anymore. While landmarks disappeared in my rearview mirror, I measured another distance, the one inside.

After I got settled in Dr. Rose's office, I commented on the pleasure of this discovery. She, too, was pleased.

I told her about the response I had gotten to my *New York Times Magazine* essay from the woman in the amber necklace and how her remark had silenced me for weeks, but that I had decided to put it in the book. "I think she is right, and I think she deserves credit for being honest. At the same time, I don't want to believe that rape should be hidden."

"She was speaking for all of us really," Dr. Rose replied. "It is very difficult for people to face how unbearable rape, torture, and other atrocities are. Many people become physically ill—they vomit, for example—when they read or hear accounts of atrocities. People cover their eyes, even in movies. We can't face it. Even in my own profession, I've found that people have a hard time. There's resistance. At conferences you might get scheduled for the last session, when most people

273

have left town. Not long ago a colleague of mine invited me to make a presentation about rape trauma at a monthly professional seminar she held in her home. People came, but they were all hanging out in the kitchen and wouldn't come into the living room!"

We both burst into laughter.

"They were hanging out where the treats were, which is a good thing to have when you're teaching people about rape. You need some oral sustenance to help them feel better. The resistance is human, a reaction we all have when we imagine being a victim. It's horrifying to us. It's the same reaction the victim has, the one that makes a victim be silent and try to avoid it, to compartmentalize it. It leads to a kind of psychological coming apart. We can't understand these fragments of ourselves. We don't know how to help ourselves with the feelings we have when we see them. So we think we've become monsters. We do our best to wall it all off and avoid it. Remember the snapping turtle, the terrible prehistoric scene, the dead bodies in the water?"

"Yes," I said.

"We all try to avoid that nightmare—and finding out what it really means."

I told her then about my experience with the painting of the trussed chicken. "My worst nightmare is hanging on my wall. I look at it every day. It doesn't frighten me anymore."

"Remember back in the 1960s when we had a cancer education campaign—the seven warning signs?" Dr. Rose said. "It educated people about a disease that terrified them and that was once unspeakable. I'd like to see something like that for rape, for other trauma. Helplessness is traumatic, and ignorance makes us all feel helpless. That campaign not only saved lives. It made people feel less helpless, less afraid."

"I've been sending chapters of my book to my mother as I go along. Last week she told me that it has helped her—that for years she'd been frozen at the feeling that someone had hurt her child in the worst way imaginable."

"She wasn't sure who her daughter was after that unimaginable hurt. She didn't know. Earlier you said silence makes it harder for you and for others who have been raped, and I agree. But your mother is telling you that it also makes it harder for everyone else."

■ ■ ■

On the tenth anniversary of the rape I mailed the first chapters of this book to my agent in New York. As I stood in line at the post office, I knew that I would go on, whether or not my story ever made it into print. Speaking, even if only to myself, Steve, and my parents, was blessing enough.

For many nights I had slipped out of bed in the dark hours before dawn, leaving its warmth and the comfort of Steve's slow, even breathing, to find a woman waiting at the desk where I wrote. I turned on the lamp and sat down. I worked until I could just make out the branches of the elderberry outside my window as the blackness turned to gray. Then I slipped back into bed as the birds began to wake. Turning toward me in his sleep, but not waking, Steve gathered me back in his arms.

And then one dawn, more than two years later, when I had finally finished this book, I saw that the woman at the desk and the woman in his arms were the same woman again. And there was a gift I hadn't expected. The years of remembering with words had given me back my birthday.

I was born on July 26, 1946.

Acknowledgments

Although the seed for this book was planted when I wrote the essay "Returns of the Day," it would never have taken root and flowered if others—both friends and strangers—had not nurtured its growth at every stage: Melanie Beene, who read the essay the day after I wrote it and told me, with her tears, that my words had touched her; Lydia Fakundiny, who generously helped me edit the original draft; Cyra McFadden, a writer whose work has long inspired me, who fine-tuned the essay and passed it on to another gifted writer, Laura Palmer, who then guided it to Nora Kerr, my wonderful editor at the *New York Times Magazine;* Julie Metz, Marti Copleman, Erica Weinstein, Maureen McNeil, whose letters to the editor supported me, as did those from so many other survivors, whose names I am not at liberty to share, who wrote to me directly. These letters, and those I received from Gail Skoff, Barbara Jay, Carol Field, Sally Lilienthal, Leilani Duke, Larry Josephson, Maggie Brown, Nellie Hill, Juliana Grenzeback, Evelyn White, Jim Moore, Doris Cellarius, Patty Backlund, John Connolly,

276

Acknowledgments

Sands Hall, Judy Andry, Jerry Lutovich, Morrie Warshawski, Renee Golden, Tamara Traeder, and Heather Cohen gave me strength I did not know I had.

I am indebted to Kris Dahl, my agent, who provided the catalyst for this book and whose wisdom set me free. Without her advice, I would never have been able to find my way to the words on these pages. Thanks also to Holly Blake and the Headland Center for the Arts in Sausalito, California, for providing me with a quiet place to begin my work, and to Nancy Reid, Arden Jones, Gerald Stevick, Nancy Legge, and Christina Hoffman, who read and commented upon the early pages.

I cannot imagine that this book could have been written without my matchless, wise, talented, and patient editors at Crown Publishers— Elaine Pfefferblit, who edited the manuscript through many revisions with rare and stunning intelligence and sensitivity, and Ann Patty, whose commitment has been unwavering. I was sustained personally and creatively by their faith in the book; their thoughtful editing significantly improved its final shape.

I am indebted to Freida Chapman, my friend for thirty years and a poet of uncommon gifts, whose devotion to this book was a rare blessing. Her critical and sensitive readings of the manuscript improved its quality and focus. I also received invaluable assistance from Chloe Aaron, whose friendship, advice, and editorial comments were crucial. A special thanks to Perrin Ireland, whose writing inspired me and whose encouragement sustained me throughout, and to Miranda Kaiser, my dancing star.

For information, advice, inspiration, and friendship I am grateful to Simone Reagor, Suzanne Simpson, Fenton Johnson, Sara Livermore, Barbara Hall, Irving Wiesenfeld, Annis McCabe, Sue Yung Li, Maud Morgan, Susan Rice, David Aaron, Ellie Coppola, Shelby Van Meter, Anita Knight, Mary Grace Smith, Neva Goodwin, Lynn Freed, Linda Coe, Sam Fisk, Pamela Worden, Susan Bailey, Christopher Corkery, Jennifer Dowley, Susan Tixier, Chris Enos, Brian Dowley, Andrew Daland, and Kate Winter.

I am particularly grateful to Dr. Deborah S. Rose for providing research materials and for her sensitive review of several chapters. I also thank Gunilla Jainchill for her professional review of certain sections of this book and for her friendship.

Most of all, I am indebted to my family. My husband, Steve Stevick, supported my work in every way conceivable. He read and commented upon every draft, offering invaluable editorial assistance. His intellectual and emotional support, his unshakable faith in my writing, and his unfailing sense of humor carried me through. My mother, Frances Jamerson Raine, was an excellent reader and an inspiring critic. Her faith in me was big enough for both of us. My father, Thomas C. Raine, was my rock. I am grateful to my stepdaughter, Elizabeth Stevick, who lived through the long days of writing with me, a loving companion and tireless cheerleader, and to my stepson, Sayre Stevick, for his support and assistance with legal research. I thank my brothers, Edward and Thomas, and my niece and nephew, Aimee Carlesi and Christopher Raine, for their love and encouragement.

I owe a special debt of gratitude to Nancy Ziegenmeyer and Migael Scherer, rape survivors whose books gave me hope and inspiration. I stand on their shoulders.